SAMADHI
The Great Freedom

By the same author:

Ashtanga Yoga: Practice and Philosophy
Ashtanga Yoga: The Intermediate Series
Pranayama: The Breath of Yoga
Yoga Meditation: Through Mantra, Chakras and Kundalini to Spiritual Freedom

SAMADHI
The Great Freedom

Gregor Maehle

Kaivalya Publications

Published by Kaivalya Publications
PO Box 181
Crabbes Creek NSW 2483
Australia

First published 2015

Copy editing by Eryn Kirkwood
Layout by Bianca DiPietro and Ashley Souter

National Library of Australia
Cataloguing-in-Publication entry
Creator: Maehle, Gregor, author
Title: Samadhi : the great freedom /
                Gregor Maehle.
ISBN: 9780977512676 (paperback)
Notes: Includes index.
Subjects: Samadhi.
                Yoga, Raja.
Dewey Number: 181.45

Dedication

To our Divine Mother who ever holds us in Her tender embrace, even at times when we seem ignorant of Her. To this infinite intelligence, who simultaneously expresses Herself as a limitless number of universes and an even more unfathomed quantity of beings.

There is no force in the world that can divide You. You are fully contained within every one of us. None of us can ever rest until we have fully attained You with every part of our being.

In order to enter into You, oh vibrant heart of all phenomena, we completely surrender our identity. We then stand in the triumphant immediateness, totality, and nakedness of the mystical state. With mind arrested, past and future disappearing, abiding in eternity, we are ushered into Your presence. In Your eyes we see the infinity and omnipresence that is the wellspring of all sacred traditions of humanity and this entire cosmos. There is no limit to the ecstasy and glory that is You.

May we never lose sight of You.

To You I bow.

Acknowledgements

To the ancient sages of India who inspired this work and to each living being that crossed my path. For all of you who became my teachers, without whom this work could not have crystallized.

.

DEFINITION OF THE DIVINE

Can you remember a time when you were truly in love? Or when all that you felt was pure love? This could be the first moment you held your newborn child or your first experience of love. Perhaps it is the moment you married. It could be when you saw a parent on their deathbed and felt only gratitude for the service they had provided you. It might also have been during a spiritual experience. What each of these situations has in common is their capacity to invoke a feeling, an understanding, of pure love. In this book, I use the term *God* or the *Divine* to describe that which enables us to rise above the level of human instinct.

Contents

Preface

There is precious little literature on *samadhi*, although it is a vast subject. The few books that are available speak of *samadhi* in such a general way that they are more books on common sense than on the technicalities and contents of *samadhis*. By sharing my insights on this subject, I am in no way suggesting I am "enlightened" or a "guru." Instead, I wish to discard these categories altogether, as they divide us into castes of gurus and enlightened ones on one hand and followers and unenlightened ones on the other. Such categories—as with any categories that create hierarchy and division among people—must be a thing of the past if humanity is to flourish. I hope to replace these outdated beliefs in gurus and so-called enlightened ones with our combined efforts to move humanity forward on the path of spiritual evolution. Given the many predicaments in which humanity currently finds itself, it is obvious such evolution is urgently required.

That I have had spiritual experiences and am able to explain their structure is a predictable result of my 38 years of practicing all major aspects of yoga. It is with a sense of duty that I submit this material. It is time that democracy is manifested in the spiritual field and that the glaring inequality in this area is removed. To this end, all of my books have been written to place the technical tools in your own hands, thereby removing the need for a "guru." Much of this information was previously available only within more or less elitist organizations.

The message of this book is simple: If a flawed human being like me can experience a series of spiritual awakenings, then, using similar technology, so can you. For many reasons, mystics in the past have played their cards close to their chest, cautious in passing on their knowledge to others. There is no more time for such secrecy. At the root of the many global crises humanity faces today, I see foremost a spiritual crisis; that is, we do not know who we are. The method I describe in my books is certainly not the only one, but it is one that will enable you to discover your true identity.

In writing this book I hope to help you avoid the dead-end streets and obstacles (of which there are many) that I experienced and to assist you in succeeding more swiftly than I did.

Introduction

In this text I am humbly sharing my experiences with the set of states known to yogis as *samadhi*. I wish to awaken within you the desire to experience these states yourself and the confidence that you can do so. It is our birthright—and even more so, our divine duty—to seek out and experience these states. They are natural. I go as far as calling the eighth *samadhi*, the final one, the natural state. In describing the eight *samadhis,* I have tried to remain faithful to the *Yoga Sutra* whenever possible. However, Patanjali has described some of the *samadhis* with a single word. In these instances, I have filled in the gaps with personal experiences. Some of these experiences might be seen as interpreting the sutra and, from a scholarly perspective, could be criticized as subjective. However, this is a practical text on how to obtain an experience of *samadhi* for those who want instruction on the states of *samadhi* and how to perform them. *Samadhi* is the ultimate spiritual experience; to explore it only from a theoretical or philosophical perspective is nothing short of a missed opportunity.

To see Buddha, Lao-tzu, Jesus Christ, Aurobindo, or Ramakrishna in the mystical state, we'd be unable to distinguish any differences in their experience. Only when we define the mystical state through a theoretical framework will any differences among them appear. Thus rather than limiting these states to such frameworks, I use metaphors from all of humanity's spiritual cultures to describe the state of *samadhi* as accurately as possible. It is the mystical state that is of greatest interest—not so much the philosophy that follows. Philosophy has its place in preparing one for the spiritual state, but it's more important to know when to leave the philosophy behind in order to soar.

THE CORE CRISIS

Many yoga practitioners today are estranged from the experience of *samadhi* and do not even try to access it. It's not uncommon to believe this state of heightened spiritual awareness is something reserved for ancient sages with long beards, sitting around in nirvana, irrelevant to and disinterested in modern life. In fact, not only *can* we return to this pristine state of *samadhi*—but we must. It is our duty and our moral obligation to seek out and rediscover our inherent wisdom. Our very existence, and that of our modern society, depends on it.

Humanity is beset with a multitude of crises. Depression, autism, and other mental disorders are on the rise. The myth of the "war to end all wars" has succumbed to a state of permanent warfare, in which we stumble from one geopolitical crisis to the next. But wars are just the tip of the iceberg. All civil violence combined today causes nine times the number of deaths incurred in any warfare. Is violence an inherent part of human nature? I don't think so. It is the by-product of our total alienation from our true identity, which is the embodiment of divine love, freedom, creativity, and beauty.

At the same time, environmental destruction through human greed via looting and pillaging the planet has reached an all-time high. Our energy supply is in crisis and wars over water supplies that are becoming increasingly scarce are forecast. Overpopulation, unsustainable agriculture methods, and the inhumane exploitation of animals are the thrust behind a looming food crisis. At the core, at the very root of each of these, is a spiritual crisis. We are staggering towards the inevitable and unnatural abyss of self-annihilation and ecocide. We have spent hundreds of years in battle against the imminent threat of an "outer world" to the detriment of our inner worlds— we have become our own enemy and are strangers to our selves.

Yogic practice and its culmination, the eight *samadhis*, offer us a way to experience our spiritual core and to become deeply at peace within ourselves. This peace will then radiate out into the world; contentment will overcome greed and inner peace will trump outer conflict. The conflicts and crises we are manifesting globally are a reflection of the conflicts festering within us; as long as we have not come to a state of self-love, inner peace, self-worth, and

2

self-acceptance, society will continue to mirror these back to us.

DARWINISM AND THE POSSIBLE EVOLUTION OF HUMANITY

The evolutionists claim we have evolved from the apes through the process of natural selection; evidence for this claim is convincing. However, the more important question is "Where are we going from here?" and "Towards what are we evolving?" Given the current state of global crises, it seems we have a long way to go. The yogic *samadhis* (and similar states) have a great role to play in the coming evolution of humanity. In many ways, "humanity" remains more of a promise than a state we have actually achieved. Individuals like Gandhi, Martin Luther King, and Nelson Mandela have expanded our notion of what it means to be humane. The fact that we shot two of those three and incarcerated the third for a lifetime proves that our so-called "evolution" is still but a vision.

Yoga, with its eight *samadhis* and preparatory exercises, including *asana*, *pranayama*, and meditation, can be of assistance. But let me make clear from the start that yoga is not the only way to a better future. There are viable options in all of the great wisdom traditions of humanity. I happen to have devoted my life to yoga, but I continue to be enthralled by the insights of Sufis, Daoists, and others, and I will quote them, if necessary, to explain yogic states.

A GUIDE FOR INNER TRAVELERS

I have written this book as a narrative rather than just a technical manual, so that you can relate to it more easily and find yourself in these pages. I've been lucky to have had these experiences, which may be due more to circumstance than to skill. For this reason I am even more compelled to share these experiences with you, because you have the same right to them as I do.

Do not let anyone challenge you by saying, "Who are you to experience these states?" or "What makes you deserve ecstasy?" We are all children of the Divine and, as such, every single one of us deserves

3

to experience our origin. Nobody can take this right away from you, although they may try. Such attempts are often fueled by the assailant's belief in their own inadequacy or that they don't deserve to experience these states themselves. This sense of unworthiness is a primary obstacle to the experience of *samadhi*. In many ways, all other yogic methods aid in the removal of these two fundamental barriers.

RAJA YOGA: THE FINAL TIER OF ASHTANGA YOGA

In this book, I use the term Ashtanga Yoga to refer to the eight-limbed path of Patanjali, which constitutes in equal parts ethical rules, observances, postures, breathing exercises, independence from external stimuli, concentration exercises, meditation techniques, and *samadhis*. The term Raja Yoga describes the highest tier of this eight-limbed path, particularly the eight *samadhis*. *Raja* means "king"; as the highest and central part of Ashtanga Yoga, Raja is called "the king of yogas," or "the Kingly Yoga." This book is a progression of my previous four volumes, in which I have described Hatha Yoga (the ethics, observances, *asanas*, and *pranayamas*) and Kundalini Yoga (*pratyahara*, *dharana*, and *dhyana*). This volume on Raja Yoga completes the yoga of Patanjali, that is, Ashtanga Yoga.

If you happen to come across this volume before the others, don't put it aside to read the other volumes first. I succinctly summarize the findings of the previous books and it may be a good idea to start with this one. Many people practice yoga without knowing where they are going. There is much to be said for starting the journey by looking at the goal first and, from there, understanding how everything in the practice, all of its many techniques, will help you to reach that goal. This method of working from the goal back towards the start of the journey is often successfully used in technology, where it is called "reverse engineering." For example, NASA used this method when putting the first humans on the moon. In reverse engineering, we identify the goal first and then develop the steps that will get us there. The approach ensures you will arrive at your predetermined goal and not somewhere else.

Many modern practitioners only practice *asana* and believe it to be yoga. And because they don't understand the entire process, ultimately they achieve only health. Health is not to be dismissed as unimportant, but most animals in the wild are healthy. Even if you are healthy, you will still die a healthy animal, unless you make some additional efforts to develop your humanity and spirituality.

This book will help you understand the goal of yoga and to see each of the limbs in proper context. It presents a holistic view that will make practicing all of the limbs not only necessary but worthwhile and enjoyable. The approach is akin to building a house. When you build a house, you don't start constructing the foundation and decide where things will go as you move on to bricking the walls. You, or at least your architect and builder, will have figured out all of the details before construction begins. You need to have a plan. This book is the plan. From understanding how the foundation (*asana*), the walls (*pranayama*), and the plumbing and electrical (Kundalini meditation) will culminate in the roof (*samadhi*), you will understand the importance of each of the independent structures and will put them into place willingly. Due to this lack of understanding, many modern yogis practice only fragments of yoga and not the entire eight limbs. *Samadhi*, not just *asana*, is the quintessence of Patanjali's Yoga.

In his commentary on Patanjali's *Yoga Sutra* (Chapter One, Verse 1 [I.1]), one of the greatest of all Vedic sages, Vyasa, writes, "*yogah samadhih,*" meaning "yoga is *samadhi.*" He is saying that *samadhi* is the quintessence of yoga, its intrinsic and central constituent. But it is not the only part, just as a king is not the only part of society. If Raja Yoga (*samadhi*) is practiced without its support structures in place, it is unlikely to succeed. Raja Yoga is embedded within the other *yogas* that support it—and of which Kingly Yoga is its culmination.

Because Vyasa's statement is the crux of this book's subject, a few words should be said about the man himself. Vyasa divided the original one Veda into its four portions (for ease of passing it on).

5

He also authored the largest epic of humanity, the *Mahabharata*, which includes the *Bhagavad Gita.* But his achievements don't stop there. Vyasa authored an entire category of scriptures called the *Puranas*; in English these total 100 volumes. He went on to compile the most important Indian philosophical text, the *Brahma Sutras,* as well as the second most important text on yoga, which is called *Yoga Bhashya* and is his commentary on Patanjali's sutras. And yet the modern yoga movement pretty much ignores what Vyasa has to say about the practice, investing almost 100 percent of its effort into *asana* (postures)—to the extent that *asana* and yoga have become synonymous and practitioners often look to Buddhism for spiritual or meditation instruction!

Was Vyasa really serious about his statement that yoga is *samadhi*? As though to ensure our understanding, he goes on to say there are two types of yoga: objective (*samprajnata*) yoga and objectless (*asamprajnata*) yoga. These terms are nothing but two categories of *samadhi*. In other words, here he uses the term "yoga" instead of " *samadhi*" to emphasize his previous statement. According to Vyasa, *samadhi* is the central theme of yoga, and all other aspects, all of the limbs and techniques, including *asana*, *pranayama* (breath extension), and *dhyana* (meditation), are mere preparations for, tributaries to, the ultimate yoga.

So what is Patanjali's take on the subject? The ancient author who compiled the *Yoga Sutra* dedicates only three of 195 verses to *asana* and a mingy four to *pranayama.* This doesn't mean these techniques are not important; after all, they constitute two of the eight limbs. If they weren't essential, Patanjali would not have given them "limb status." However, 100 of Patanjali's sutras (over half) deal with one of the many types of *samadhi* that he lists. Thus both Patanjali and Vyasa believe *samadhi* is the core of yoga and gave most of their attention to this limb. It is time we let go of our preoccupation with postures and move forward on the path.

WHY DON'T WE TAKE THE ANCIENT TEACHINGS SERIOUSLY?

On one hand there is a belief that our ancestors were primitive, savage, and brainless brutes whose findings are outdated. The more I study humanity's spiritual history, the greater my belief that we moderners are wise, even advanced, in the realm of technology, but in matters of wisdom, spiritual maturity, and living in harmony with nature—it is they who are advanced. They have much to teach us. We need to be reminded to listen to the voice of the ancients, who have handed down an enormous heritage through the corridors of history. If we stop taking our modern achievements so seriously, we could learn a lot from the ancient teachings, on whose shoulders we stand today.

Conversely, we might believe the old teachers are superior to us, that modern life is too complex, or that we're unworthy of *samadhi*. A human being today is made up in the same way that it was 5000 years ago. Our structure is no different than that of the ancient teachers. If you read through the *Mahabharata* in its entirety, you will have to admit that life in those days was surprisingly complex, with society forming an almost inextricable maze. Yes, life may be fast now, but it is our choice whether to stay in the fast lane of ambition and competition or to slow down in the lane of introspection and insight. Yoga is a way of seeing everything that usually escapes our awareness, because life seems to fly by in the reflection of our rearview mirror. We forget that it's our choice in which lane we drive, and it is we who are in the driver's seat of our life.

GOD TRANSCENDENT, GOD IMMANENT, AND YOU

Another damaging attitude is "unworthiness" to attain *samadhi*. I wish to propose a radically different belief to those who feel unworthy: *samadhi* is your birthright and your divine duty! I will explain the rationale for this in more detail following a description of the eight *samadhis*. But here's a summary: The first piece of the puzzle is in the writings of Alfred North Whitehead, a British mathematician who, although he had never attended a single philosophy lecture, wound up teaching philosophy at Harvard. That's how significant his writings were. In his epic book *Process and Reality*, Whitehead concluded that God is a process. Yes, read that again: a mathematician teaches that God is an entity that undergoes change! From this teaching, a new branch of theology emerged called Process Theology. This only superficially contradicts the statement of the scriptures that God is unchangeable. The unchangeable, eternal, permanent aspect of God in philosophy is referred to as *God transcendent* (the God that is beyond reality or above the world). Most religions relate to this aspect of the Divine (i.e., the Father, the Brahman, the Dao). In India it is often called Shiva, but is also represented by many other names. The aspect of the Divine that Whitehead refers to in philosophy—and what Indian thought calls *Shakti* or *prakrti*—is called *God immanent* (the Divine here and now) and is the perceptible aspect of the Divine.

God transcendent is pure consciousness, but consciousness needs something to reflect itself in, in order to bring about its quality of awareness, thus leading automatically to immanent God. God immanent is the 14-billion-year-old history of this cosmos and the evolution of all life within it. Sri Aurobindo stated in *The Synthesis of Yoga* that nature (*prakrti*) is an act of yoga, a billion years long, to make all matter and all of life god-like.

Neither God transcendent nor God immanent has an ego (an ego means limitation in space and time), because both aspects of the Divine are infinite and eternal. Without ego, or "I," as Freud called it, God cannot individuate; that is, She cannot be limited to a particular point in space or a particular moment in time. This is where each of us enters into the equation: because neither the transcendental (pure consciousness) nor the immanent (material universe) aspects of God can individuate. The existence of the Divine will automatically, by law, bring forth an infinite number of beings like you and me, in which to individuate through. This third aspect of God, let's call it *God-all-beings* is you and I. Our very existence is the Divine individuating in time and space as an infinite number of beings. The most awe-inspiring effect of *samadhi* is to feel this omnipresent and omnipotent being of all beings. This "Ancient one of Israel" or "The Dao" breathes and experiences itself through you.

Experiencing She who is infinite love, intelligence, and consciousness within you has significant repercussions. Because there is no force in the world that can divide Her, she is fully contained within each one of us, which means none of us can ever rest until we have fully attained Her with every part of our being. This is what I mean when I say that *samadhi* is our birthright. Essentially nothing can separate us from Her, apart from our beliefs and our ignorance. Having this divine inheritance within us, it is our duty to overcome these limitations and experience our true state of being, which is *samadhi*.

VYASA'S FIVE STAGES OF MIND AND FOR WHOM IS SAMADHI SUITABLE?

As previously described, Raja Yoga constitutes the apex of Patanjali's yoga. Depending on your perspective, either the inner limbs (*dharana* to *samadhi*) or even just objective *samadhi* constitute Raja Yoga proper (with objectless *samadhi* often ascribed to Jnana Yoga). To whom the *Yoga Sutra* is applicable is beautifully described in Sage Vyasa's model of the five stages of mind. Remember, however, that this is only a model. In life you won't meet people with a stamp on their forehead saying "confused" or "materialist." Just as we know that light has either wave or particle characteristics, depending on the circumstances, people also express different characteristics under differing circumstances. We do not judge or determine that a person "is" or "has" a certain state of mind.

Vyasa calls the first state of mind *kshipta*, which means wild, out of control, or raving. In his commentary, Hariharananda Aranya says the only way the wild (*kshipta*) mind can concentrate is by thinking of the destruction of its enemies. Although we continue to hope that, as a global community, we've evolved beyond this mindset, judging from this morning's news headlines, there's still plenty of it around. This mindset is not ready to receive any teachings on yoga whatsoever, and if you would approach one who has this perspective with the yogic teaching, they would doubt your sanity.

Next in Vyasa's scheme is *mudha* mind. *Mudha* is often somewhat flatteringly translated as "infatuated," but "materialistic" is probably more accurate. The materialistic mind is first infatuated with the body— how it looks, its level of attraction, its sexuality and health. Those of a materialistic mindset tend to reduce themselves to the body; they don't believe in an immortal self or soul. That's why the body takes on such great importance. The materialistic mind is also obsessed with the hip pocket, as it looks at life from the vantage point of acquisition and accumulation of wealth. Not surprisingly, then, the materialistic mind makes an assessment of others based on whether they have an attractive body or an appealing bank account or impressive real estate portfolio. The materialistic mind also obsesses about its genetic progeny. Although it is important to love one's children and parents, the materialist cannot wrap their mind around the fact that humanity is a global family and that we have duties towards all beings.

A good example would be the characters portrayed in Mafia literature and movies. Mafiosi are usually depicted as committed family men, yet they won't hesitate for a moment to gun down the fathers of other children. Science now suggests the entire gene pool of humanity can be traced back to a single individual who lived several hundred thousand years ago in Africa. Opinions differ on whether that individual was male or female, but it appears its offspring were the first to communicate to each other through language. We are all relatives and family, after all, though our family tree dates back a few hundred thousand years. We need to move beyond this narrow view of defining our family as only those who are genetically closely related to us.

Due to its preoccupation with the body, of all the yogic techniques available, the materialistic mind can only relate to *asana*. *Asana* is acceptable (that is, it makes sense) because it enables us to feel the body, helps us to keep it healthy, and even makes the body look good. Since the materialist mind is identified with the body, it is interested in extending its lifespan and its capacity to derive pleasure; good health is recognized as one of those means. It would be more or less a waste of time to confront the materialist mind with the yoga philosophy or higher aspects of yoga. The end result would only be alienation.

Vyasa's third stage of mind, *vikshipta,* is usually translated as "confused" or "oscillating." This mind alternates back and forth between having glimpses of the eternal core of the human being or the divine beauty expressed in nature and being estranged from nature and the Divine. The oscillating mind can be stabilized with a continuous daily practice of all major aspects of yoga, including *asana, kriya, pranayama,* and Kundalini meditation. This process is usually referred to as the eight limbs of yoga, but really only the first seven are implied.

Although the *Yoga Sutra* refers to the eight limbs, they are not described in any particular detail. For more information, we must

"The work of the mind" includes all forms of work that life requires us to do. A living being is not created to be idle until it disappears into some elusive nirvana but is created to live and express itself. For example, an engineer with a mind tending to suspension (*nirodha*) may design a bridge and once that's done simply re-enter the natural state (objectless *samadhi*). He will not go on habitually thinking about idle subjects, as we do today. After it has achieved its objective and the problem at hand is fixed, the *nirodha* mind habitually ceases thinking and re-establishes itself in the heart of the Divine. For this type of mind, there is no conflict between being active in the world and experiencing the mystical state.

consult other texts, such as the *Yoga Yajnavalkya, Vasishta Samhita, Yoga Gorakshataka, Hatha Yoga Pradipika, Hatha Tatva Kaumudi,* and others. Devotional yoga, or Bhakti Yoga, can also stabi-

lize the oscillating mind; in this practice we look more towards the
Nirodha and the *Puranas*, such as the *Bhagavata Purana*. Ideally,
both sets of yoga—the technical and the devotional—are combined.

Imagine for a moment we have consolidated this stage of mind
and are now entering the next state, which Vyasa calls *ekagra*, the
single-pointed mind. Most of the *Yoga Sutra* and Raja Yoga are dedicated to obtaining this single-pointed state of mind. The essential
Raja Yoga is the objective *Samadhi and* most of the yoga sutras deal
with objective *samadhi*. This means that, apart from expressing the
metaphysics of yoga as a practical treatise, the sutras apply to the
small percentage of yogis who are of a single-pointed (*ekagra*) mind.
The single-pointed mind is traditionally defined as one that can focus on a single object for three hours without wavering. This capacity to stay with one object until its entire depth is fathomed is what
makes the mind so powerful and thus capable of objective *samadhi*.

But Vyasa's model does not end here. After the single-pointed
(*ekagra)* mind is the suspended (*nirodha*) mind. The suspended mind
is that which pauses after it has performed its task. Just as a muscle
would halt its effort once it has lifted a weight, the mind in *nirodha*
halts its thinking once it has completed its task. The *Upanishads* talk
of this mind being reabsorbed into the heart once its work is done.

If you have studied the modern mind, you will have noticed
that after our "work" is done, our minds are so agitated that we
either need to drink to relax or we need intense stimulation, like
watching television or a movie, to switch off. When bedtime arrives, our mind cannot calm down without a few more glasses of
alcoholic beverage or some sleeping pills. By the time we wake
up, the mind is so dull and heavy from the drugs we've consumed that we have to kick it back into gear with coffee or harder forms of speed, like crack cocaine or crystal meth. This may
seem like an exaggeration, but it is the current trajectory of our
civilization: take a drug to induce the state you wish to attain.

The suspended (*nirodha*) mind Vyasa refers to is the mind that tends toward objectless *samadhi*. Patanjali barely addresses object-less *samadhi*. He says that it comes after objective *samadhi* but lists only one category of it. He explains its fruit and says that it eventually leads to spiritual freedom (*kaivalya*). The simplistic approach to objective *samadhi* seems odd, when compared to the sophisti-cated approach generally lavished on the lower limbs (the yogic teachings on *asana*, *pranayama*, and Kundalini meditation are very complex). This is simply because objectless *samadhi* is not within the scope of the *Yoga Sutra* or Raja Yoga. Once the yogi has sur-passed the single-pointed (*ekagra*) stage of mind and gone on to the suspended (*nirodha*) mind, she is leaving Raja Yoga behind and entering into Jnana Yoga. Jnana Yoga is the domain of the *Brahma Sutra* and the *Upanishads*. I discuss Jnana Yoga briefly in Chapter 8.

YOGI OR HISTORIAN—WHAT IS YOGA REALLY ALL ABOUT?

Raja Yoga is not a one-size-fits-all system. It is in fact suitable for a narrow range of yogic practitioners—those who have completed the lower limbs but who are not yet ready for objectless *samadhi*. Although the metaphysical aspect of the *Yoga Sutra* generally ap-plies to yoga, its practices are intended mainly for yogis established in a single-pointed (*ekagra*) mind. Those with an oscillating or confused mind would find the methods too advanced, while those with a suspended mind would find them too introductory. I men-tion this because Western scholars often try to analyze the *Yoga Sutra* in isolation. They separate the yoga of Patanjali from all other forms of yoga and try to show the history of yoga as one of con-flicting schools. This may be of interest for the historian, but it is of no interest at all for the practitioner. For the practitioner and the yogi, there is but one tradition of yoga, and the *Yoga Sutra* must be taken in context together with all other yogic scriptures. The yoga described in the sutras could never succeed by itself, at least not from the meager technical details contained in Patanjali's text.

Our concern is which methods are suitable for an individual and at what point in their development are they appropriate. One person's method may be quite different from the techniques that are appropriate for another person who is at a different stage. For the practitioner, all yoga is one. It is one huge toolbox out of which we select suitable methods for a particular phase in our development, and it makes no difference in which *shastra* (sacred text) these techniques were described. There is no right or wrong, no Sutra Yoga versus Hatha Yoga, no yoga of the *Puranas* or of the *Gita* but only "does it work in this context, or does it not?"

Some very fine scholars are bringing new information to light about yoga's history, and I commend them for that. However, for the devout practitioner, fragmenting the yogic practices in this way is both confusing and counterproductive. I'm not concerned with exactly when the *Yoga Sutra* was written, how many chapters it originally had, whether there was one or many authors, whether it had an ongoing tradition, in which century it fell out of fashion, how it was rediscovered, or whether modern yoga is really based on it. What is important to me is the quality, intensity, and frequency of the mystical state that I may reach. How do I integrate these stages into my life, and how does that change me? How does it change my behavior, and how can I communicate and convey that change to others? Do you really think the mystical state cares whether you attained it by means of the *Yoga Sutra* or another tradition? No! Only the mind cares—and notably the mind that is not established in the mystical state!

The most important application of mystical states is for building society and civilization. Let's stop contemplating how yogis might have practiced in the past. Maybe there were large periods in history where they completely lost track. Does that change the work we have to do now? The question is how do we go forward from here. Do we continue on this technocratic trajectory, destroying the world and becoming extinct? Or do we manage through yogic techniques to establish ourselves in a state that shows the world and all beings as the infinite creativity and play of Divine

Love? This is what the world needs; this is what will heal society. This is the sum total of all yogic teachings. Looking at the sutras as isolated from the rest of yogic culture robs it of this capacity.

When asked by his students whether they should study the scriptures, Paramahansa Ramakrishna answered, "Don't be interested in the *shastras* (scriptures) for their own sake; be interested in the one truth underlying all *shastras*." The yogi seeks the one underlying truth, not just of all *shastras*, but also of all phenomena from the photon to the galaxy. In order to penetrate this vibrant heart of all phenomena that is the Divine, the yogi must surrender all objectivity. In order to enter the mystical state, we must surrender our identity and individuality completely—even if all of this will just reassemble once we leave the mystical state behind. This is the opposite attitude required of a scholar who is using the Western-scientific or text-historical method.

The text-historical method will analyze the history of a school of thought based only on its surviving texts. As yoga was based predominantly on personal and oral instruction, yogis reject conclusions grounded in this methodology, because it analyzes only a small part of the tradition and cannot therefore come to any valid conclusion. Another big setback of this method is that yogic texts purposely contain *sandhya*, that is, twilight language. This language was purposely constructed in such a way that a non-initiate (one who had not practiced the necessary methods) would not understand the texts and be led astray in their conclusions (this was done so that non-initiates could not corrupt the school). This is exactly what happens to modern Western scholars today.

The traditional method was that you learned from experts in the field, practiced the methods for a sufficient time, and then obtained the required experiences based on those methods. Only after that were you deemed fit to expound on the texts to students. Scholars who are using the text-historical method are expounding on the texts without having undertaken the first three steps. While they may act from noble intentions, their statements are confusing for practitioners.

15

During scholarly inquiry or academic research, objectivity is required; that is, you must be an uninvolved outside observer. Conversely, during objectless *samadhi* the observer becomes the very experience, because nothing but the naked observer (pure consciousness, or *purusha*) is left. Stripped of its impeding cladding, the observer reveals itself somewhere between volcanic or oceanic ecstasy (the Hindus would call it *sat-chit-ananda*). This is the most intimate, immediate, and subjective experience a human being can have.

In the words of the *bhakta* (yogi of devotion), once identity is discarded, the observer merges with and dissolves into the ocean of Divine Love. This may sound poetic or exuberant, but this state cannot be described in analytical, objective, and Western scientific language (which has its value in other contexts). My point is that there is more to yoga than what can be discerned from textbooks and historical analysis. If you want to experience this state, you cannot remain an objective observer, looking only at the experience from the outside and trying to classify or describe it. You must dive in and embody the experience yourself!

The yoga practitioner who wants to experience states of mystical union must ask the questions, "What do I need to do to get there?" "What practices do I need to apply?" After reading these objective and scholarly studies on yoga, are you clear about which practices to do and how to do them? Or are you even more confused? A yogi can learn more from her practice than from any accomplished mystic of any other denomination (including the Christian, Jewish, Taoist, and Sufi systems); she can learn more from her practice than from reading scholarly books on the *Yoga Sutra* which nominally deal with yoga, but have no experience in it. In that regard, you can learn yoga by reading the gospels, the ecstatic poems of the Sufi Hafiz, the Taoist master Chuang-Tzu, the Christian mystic Meister Eckhart, or the masters of the Kabbalah. These teachers have attained the mystical state, and yogis are well advised to study their accounts in order to understand how it feels to be there. I am not against historians or scholars or knowledge of any kind, for that matter. But it seems that novice yogis who are quite fragile in their devotion to various practices are easily confused by reading what is essentially of peripheral interest.

THE SUTRA'S PLACE IN YOGIC INSTRUCTION

The *Yoga Sutra* of Patanjali, although often the first text yogis look at, by itself constitutes only a small part of the yogic teachings. It must be studied in context with the *Upanishads*, the *Gita*, the *Yoga Yajnavalkya*, the *Puranas*, the *Tantras*, and the medieval *siddha* texts. The aggregate of these texts, and not the *Yoga Sutra* by itself, constitute authentic yogic teaching. From the practitioner's point of view, the differences between the *Yoga Sutras* and the *Gita* are inconsequential. What is important is their common goal and to what extent the practices support each other. At what times do I need to do this and when is another technique more suitable?

Different yogic texts (*shastras*) may describe different avenues to the same goal and even different sections of the same avenue. If you study the *Sutra* alone and consider it the authority on all aspects of yoga, you will find success hard to come by. The *Sutra* does not deal with all aspects of yoga. In fact, it deals only with very few. In this context the tendency to study each word of the *Sutra*, to take it for gospel, and to see how modern yoga stacks up against it, is a Philistine approach. It reminds me of the Dakini who asked Naropa whether he had studied the words of the *Tantras*. He answered *yes*, but then she asked him whether he had understood their meaning. When he replied that he had, she threatened to devour him. What is the moral of the story? Naropa was the dean of India's largest university; he was said to have had 30 PhDs (in ancient days these were probably easier to come by). The Dakini told Naropa to quit his job and go in search of her brother, Tilopa, who—although he appeared to be a beggar living on fish heads discarded by fishermen—embodied some powerful yogic states. The story goes on through many volumes, but the essence is that there is a vast difference between academic studies and direct realization. Which one are you interested in? There is no right or wrong answer.

What I'm suggesting is that if you want to have the direct experience of the mystic, you may have to invest most of your time and effort into having that experience; reading historical analyses of yogic texts might have to fade into the background as a hobby at best and may completely fall away as your questions are answered by direct experience. When that direct experience arrives, all questions (including those concerning the importance of the *Yoga Sutra* 500 years ago or whether postural yoga was connected with it at all) will become mere academics. All of these questions fall away when you stand in the triumphant immediateness, totality, and nakedness of the mystical state. Your mind is arrested, past and future disappear, and every hair on your body stands on end. Through your eyes you will see the infinite and omnipresent super-intelligence that is the wellspring of all sacred traditions of humanity.

THE DIFFERENCE BETWEEN YOGA/MYSTICISM AND RELIGION

Let me explain why I use spiritual expressions that border on the religious and why I say the essence of all religions is the same as that of yoga. Within each being there is an eternal, sacred core; once this core has been seen, the individual can place itself in the service of humanity and all of creation. The mystic is dedicated to searching for this core and its cultivation and, upon finding it, places themself in the service of all beings (yoga is a form of mysticism). A yogi is a person who practices a special set of techniques, collectively called yoga, to attain the mystical state. Once that state is attained, there is no difference between a yogic mystic and the mystic of another denomination.

All prophets, messiahs, *rishis*, buddhas, *siddhas*, and *tirthankaras* were initially mystics who had a so-called "peak experience." After that experience faded, they used metaphors particular to their culture and background to explain what had happened. Each person instinctively seeks the peak experience; that's why people have always been attracted to (and amazed by) the teachings of mystics. For this reason it was important to speak out once one had attained such a state. Without speaking out, you cannot convey your message to others nor can you contribute to their lives.

In order to enter the mystical state, one's mind needs to be suspended (*nirodha*); but once one leaves the mystical state behind, the mind is re-activated in order to describe the experience and to communicate it to others. The act of using one's inner word processor, seeking for terminologies and metaphors that describe the mystical state, will terminate the very state. That's why the description of the state will always fall short of the experience of the state itself; and the descriptions, while sounding similar, will always have a personal and cultural tinge to them. They may sound Jewish, Hindu, Muslim, or Christian in nature; but in the mystical state itself, this difference cannot exist because the mind is suspended.

If a mystic were very successful in their description of the experience, the surrounding culture would sometimes adopt that teaching as the only truth. Thus religion was borne. Religion simply means, "My mystic is right and yours is wrong." A religion is an organization that develops around the spiritual experiences of a particular mystic, such as Jesus, Krishna, or Buddha. This is how some of the most valuable descriptions of mystical states have come to be handed down within religions, such as Hinduism, Buddhism, Judaism, Christianity, and so on. The religion has crystallized as a dogma around the experience of a particular mystic. Although many people today are horrified by the excess and corruption of religion, the states that these mystics experienced and the descriptions they provided are still our pristine world heritage.

Although I cannot formally describe myself as a Christian, none of the crimes committed throughout history by the church can undermine the words that Jesus spoke. His example (and those of others) proves that two billion years of evolution on Earth is nothing but a giant act of yoga performed by nature to lift life from the amoeba to

19

an experience of the Divine. This is why I might quote from various religions and sacred traditions: all barriers break down in the mystical state, and all mystics describe only one state in ever-different ways.

Yoga was always more interested in the actual experience than in any theology or philosophy that arose from it, because the mystics believed it is the experience that will change the world and not its explanation. In his novel, *Siddhartha,* Hermann Hesse celebrates this view when his protagonist tells Gautama the Buddha that his teaching is the most perfect, most logical, and most consistent of all teachings; yet he will not follow it because there was one thing missing: the Buddha's own mystical experience. The missing part was what Buddha himself had encountered on that fateful night under the Bodhi tree that couldn't be expressed in his teaching. So Hesse's hero had to go and blaze his own path. Thus we have religion and dogma on one hand and spirituality and mysticism on the other. And this is exactly what yoga is all about. It is not what a particular religion says about the experience, but about having the experience *yourself* and knowing the tools and methods that will get you there.

THE ONE UNDERLYING TRUTH IN ALL SACRED TRADITIONS

While some unsuspecting mystics were morphed into founders of religions (usually post-mortem), others pointed out that the essential experience underlying all religions and schools of thought were the same. Only the sectarians and powerbrokers benefit by dividing humanity and driving us against each other. As the Machiavellian adage goes, "Divide and rule!" Ramakrishna, the 19th-century saint, is a notable example of the experiential current within Hinduism. Through various methods, Ramakrishna had attained what was called in his language, "realization of the Divine," in the Hindu Goddess Kali. Ramakrishna was a very curious person. He wondered what would happen if he applied the same method, concentration, and tenacity to other deities of the Hindu pantheon, a threshold that an orthodox Hindu would never cross. Within a few years he attained what he called "realization of the Divine through Lord Shiva and Lord Vishnu."

Shortly thereafter a new teacher emerged in Ramakrishna's life: the Advaita (non-dualist) Vedanta teacher Totapuri. Totapuri basically taught that the personal God and devotion are superstitious child's play and that only realization of the formless Absolute (*nirguna* Brahman) brought complete freedom. To his great surprise, Ramakrishna attained the *nirguna* Brahman in one straight sitting of only 24 hours. And to Totapuri's horror and disgust, he came out of this sitting to announce there was no essential difference between the non-dualist realization and the God-realizations he had previously attained. In fact, he thought worshipping a divine form better equipped you for an active life in society.

But it gets better (or worse, depending on your perspective): Ramakrishna did the unthinkable for a conservative Hindu and started to meditate on Muhammad and his teaching of Islam, even taking to Muslim food habits and dress code. After some time, he came forth and announced that the essential ecstasy and realization derived from Islam was no different than those gained in any school of Hinduism. Next, he meditated on Jesus and the Bible and, again, after some time announced that the same experience could be had from practicing Christianity. Then Ramakrishna developed his teaching (and what is the teaching of all mystics): there is one underlying truth among all sacred traditions of humanity; we must dedicate our practice to this one underlying truth. Though there may be cultural differences in metaphor, these are only superficial, and once the mystic enters the mystical state, these distinctions vanish (although they may surface again when we emerge from the mystical state).

INTEGRATION OF THE MYSTICAL STATE

At the beginning of our spiritual path we are thirsty for a spiritual experience. After we have a few of those, we may become frustrated to the extent that we regress to our prior materialistic and selfish behavior. Some of this is summarized in the term, "Dark

Night of the Soul." The night seems darker after having seen the blinding light of consciousness; expulsion from paradise (that is, the "peak experience") becomes obvious when we realize that we ourselves are the proverbial "emperor who wears no clothes."

The belief that a single spiritual experience will completely transform you is a pervading myth; the very definition of *experience* is that which has a beginning and an end. Each mystical state ends by us leaving it. A mystical state is one of concentrated and intense *sattva* (luminosity or wisdom). If held onto for long enough, all *sattva* turns into *tamas* (dullness, inertia), just as surely as day turns into night. This *tamas* can then express itself as the debauchery and decadence of cults and personality cults. Before the *tamasic* state sets in, we need to make a renewed effort of practice, which itself is *rajasic* (energetic). This effort is called *integration of the state*.

We may believe that all problems are solved once a mystical state is attained, but really we are only entering into a new phase, in which those states may become more frequent but far from permanent. Attaining spiritual freedom, or *"kaivalya,"* as Patanjali calls it, is not sudden or spontaneous enlightenment but a long sequence of spiritual awakenings called *samadhis*. In between these *samadhis*, the yogi must return to practicing an integrated compound of *asana*, *kriya*, *pranayama*, Kundalini meditation, and devotion.

In this book, we will explore what *samadhi* is, the obstacles to reaching it, how the obstacles may be removed, the roles of the Divine and the teacher, how *samadhi* is accessed, what exactly the *samadhis* are, and finally, what comes after *samadhi*.

Chapter 1
WHAT IS SAMADHI AND WHAT IS IT NOT?

SAMADHI, ENLIGHTENMENT, SITUATIONISM, AND DEVELOPING
THE CENTER

In this chapter I will clarify misconceptions about *samadhi* and show that there are varieties of *samadhis*, not just one type. Firstly, *samadhi* is not enlightenment. The term "enlightenment" was borrowed from the European Enlightenment movement of the 18th century and emphasized reason. Today it is often used to describe the spiritual state of completion that Gautama Buddha or other Buddhist luminaries had reached. The term is not used in yoga. Patanjali uses the term "*kaivalya*," which means freedom, liberation, independence, or even insulation. Let me explain the connotations here so that we know exactly what *samadhi* is not. In common parlance there is a mix-up of the state of spiritual liberation and *samadhi*, but the two must be differentiated.

Both the Buddhist "enlightenment" and the yogic or Hindu "liberation" imply finality, a completion. They imply that the practitioner has developed a center that is no longer shaken by outside circumstances. The psychological theory of situationism has it that our thoughts, actions, and choices are brought about by outside circumstances or situations. If you change a situation, then the person's choices and their behavior will also change. This is parallel to the postmodernist concept of a self that is fluid; for example, when I get up in the morning, I no longer have the same sense of self or personality that I had when I went to bed. This is something you can easily observe when studying your own mind. One day you may think you have solved all the problems of humanity, but a mere 12 hours later you may battle depression and self-loathing.

The Armenian mystic George Gurdjieff clarified this phenomenon when he said that we do not currently have a steady and developed center from which we act. Although he did not use the same concepts as modern psychologists, he basically agreed with situationism, in that there is no constant agent within us from whom decisions are made. Gurdjieff's work aimed to create such a center and, in this context, spiritual freedom is reached when the yogi is unshaken by circumstance or situation and confident in the knowledge of themselves as *purusha*, or consciousness.

At first, circumstance determines our choices. As yogic practice takes hold to a greater extent, we become insulated from situations and circumstances, and the quality of our decisions remains the same. This is what Krishna is talking about when he says,

> He who does not reject neither exultation, attachment, nor ignorance when they present themselves or desire them when they are absent, who is not wavering and disturbed through all these changes, remaining poised, who is established in the self and welcomes as the same happiness and distress, who looks upon a clod of earth and a piece of gold equally, who retains his equanimity whether presented with the desirable or undesirable, praise and blame, glory and shame, who treats even both friend and foe, and who has stopped identifying with outer activities, he is said to have transcended the modes of nature (*Bhagavad Gita* XIV: 22–25).

Krishna describes a person who is completely independent from circumstance and situation and asks that we find within us what is not cut by weapons, burned by fire, drowned by water, or blown away by wind (*Bhagavad Gita* II.23). It is this very essence from which great mystics, including Krishna, Buddha, and Jesus Christ, have acted. Because not even death can destroy this center, many mystics displayed otherworldly strength, such as showing no signs of concern when their life was under threat. Thus it is clear the mystics managed to escape the dilemma of situationism by developing this center that is entirely insulated from circumstance.

Yogis practice *samadhis* as the means to develop this center (apart from the preparatory exercises of *asana*, *pranayama*, and Kundalini meditation); and just as the *Yoga Sutra* lists eight limbs of yoga (i.e. *asana*, *pranayama*, and the other limbs), so, too, does it list eight separate states of *samadhi*. Right from the beginning we need to understand the *samadhis* are not the goal of yoga; the goal of yoga (to use Gurdjieff's language) is to develop a permanent center, and such a center develops from the practice of *samadhi*. It may be said that this center already exists in all people, but this is true only in a theoretical sense. If this center, which the *Yoga Sutra* calls *purusha*, or consciousness, were fully developed in everyone, it would be easy to sit in occasional meditation and spontaneously discover it. But for the vast majority of people, this is out of the question.

The lack of a center is also represented in Vyasa's model of the five stages of mind. While the out-of-control (*kshipta*) and materialistic (*mudha*) minds are swept away by circumstance and are entirely under the sway of situationism, the oscillating (*vikshipta*) mind is beginning to develop this center; however, as soon as external obstacles become strong, it is lost. This center has only become a reliable player once the single-pointed (*ekagra*) mind has arrived, at which point it finally experiences its culmination in the suspended (*nirodha*) mind. Only the *nirodha* type of mind acts naturally from this center.

SAMADHI ACCORDING TO THE YOGA SUTRA
The *Yoga Sutra* deals predominantly with *samadhi* and contains several definitions of it, but I simplify the term as referring to a set of states of raised awareness in which one can experience everything as it truly is. To enjoy this heightened awareness, we must withdraw our projection of what we believe to be reality and the world. This withdrawal of our projections takes place through suspending one's conditioning (*vasana*). Our conditioning, or robotic programming, is nothing

more than our past encrypted by subconscious imprints (*samskaras*). *Samadhi* can be called an altered state because normally our conditioning, the sum total of our thoughts, experiences, memories, and so on, will project itself into the future; during *samadhi* it does not.

The most powerful way in which conditioning manifests itself is through guilt, shame, and unworthiness. Because some of our choices in the past were not ideal (impossible to avoid), we attach them to our personality and feel unworthy of better outcomes. When asked about these feelings of shame, guilt, and unworthiness, many people will deny they play a role in their lives at all; yet these emotions are one of the most powerful obstacles to *samadhi*. If you feel unworthy to experience *samadhi,* or are resistant to it for whatever reason, then this subconscious tendency will intercept the experience. In later chapters we will discuss how to remove such obstacles.

One of the most important definitions of *samadhi* is given in sutra I.2: "Yoga is the stilling of the fluctuations of the mind." In this ensuing stillness, we can see our true nature, our true identity as pure and content-less consciousness. This is stated in sutra I.3: "Then the seer abides in its own nature." This statement can be understood through the metaphor of a pond. Imagine you are trying to see your face reflected in a pond, whose surface is ruffled by wind. You would see a distorted image of your face. If the pond were completely still, however, you could see yourself clearly. Similarly, our mind in its normal state is ruffled by "mind waves." These mind waves are, for example, superficial ideas we have about ourselves, such as attractiveness, success, power, satisfaction, intelligence, or lack thereof.

In yoga these are all seen as contents of consciousness, but not consciousness itself. Consciousness is like the container in which these contents are held. The function of consciousness is to be aware of how the varying concepts and identities through which you define yourself arise. If the waves of the mind are stilled, we can abide in the state that existed prior to any judgments. Before we had any idea about how to define and classify ourselves, there

26

was this awareness, this state of pure being. But then we thought, "Who am I"? And the answer was, "I am so and so. This is my name, my sex, my nationality, my wealth, my family, my fortune, my property, and so on." But in moments when all of that is taken away from us, pure awareness shines through and we realize there is an eternal core that is unchanged by birth, life, or death. It is unchanged in victory or defeat, in glory or shame. The question is, "To whom do victory and defeat, glory, and shame arise?" When we answer this question, we realize that this entity to which the phenomena arises is unchanged by whatever arises to it.

AN AFTERNOON IN THE FIELDS

In moments when everything is taken away from us, we may remember, in deep grief, that there is something within that cannot be lost or gained. Something that is forever and eternally uncreated and un-born and that will never die. I had such a moment in my childhood when I awakened to this entity. One late sunny afternoon, while walking through a cornfield, I was overcome by a sudden and intense urge to start running and running, faster and faster, until I collapsed. I was lying there looking into the sky and an intense happiness came over me. It was the pure joy of being alive, of having a body, and of living in this intensely beautiful world.

But then something strange happened. I noticed that somebody else was watching me. I had thought I was just a six-year-old body, not very gifted, not very smart, barely keeping up in sports and school. I could hardly understand my family and was unable to make myself understood. But as I lay in this cornfield, watching the endless expanse of the late afternoon sky, I saw an "other" me, looking out through my eyes. Having no preconceived idea what it was or what I should do, out of curiosity I let myself fall into it, as if letting my body fall into a pool. Submerging into this other being, I assumed its infinite expanse. This being had no beginning or end. It was timeless and eternal. It did not think. It noticed all of my limited thoughts, but did not produce thoughts itself. It witnessed my pains, joys, frustrations, and fears but stayed separate from these—pure and untouched. Whereas I could be submerged, almost drowned, in the drama of my life, this strange friend was the ocean itself. It was aware of the waves on the surface, but always remained the entirety of its unfathomable depths.

I stayed there with my newfound friend for an hour or so. In this hour, I learned I was eternal and infinite and that life was not what I had been told it was. I also learned to shut up. When I came home, my mother said, "Look at your shoes. Didn't I tell you to stay out of the fields? Wait until the farmer gets you. He'll give you a hiding!" I did not say, "Mum, I'm not afraid. Did you know that you, my personality, and the farmer are just images superimposed onto the screen of my consciousness?" I just said, "Yes, Mum."

Spontaneous experiences like these, though, are not easily integrated and often don't make life any simpler. Part of why yoga is so conservative in provoking such experiences is this difficulty of integration. In my example, what should a young person do with such an experience? Shortly after that I started to have run-ins with the village priest, who didn't take kindly to the new competition. This is why yoga emphasizes the preparation for such states more than their actual arising. Some people have provoked similar states through psychedelic drugs. But they are not truly yours unless you have done the groundwork, which in the case of yoga requires inquiry into yoga philosophy, devotion, *asana*, *pranayama*, *kriya*, and Kundalini meditation.

OBJECTLESS SAMADHI MUST BE AUGMENTED WITH OBJECTIVE SAMADHI

The above anecdote illustrates sutra 1.2: "Yoga is the stilling of the fluctuations of the mind." But this stanza only defines objectless *samadhi*, the higher of the two types. Taken out of context and without being supplemented by the other definitions of *samadhi*, one might think yoga was only about stillness—which it isn't! Stillness is important for a healthy mind and for spirituality, but it is not everything! If this were the case, yoga would just be an escape from the world and from our busy minds—not unlike taking a pill to treat depression. It would mean that yoga is only about bringing the entire world to a standstill. It's more than that.

Objectless *samadhi* is so overwhelming that the world seems (even if only briefly) a mirage, an illusion, or *maya,* and only consciousness looks as if it is real. Some mystics were so established in this state that they discounted the importance of the world, which, after all, is then just an illusion. Unfortunately, the philosophy arising out of this state can lend itself to abstaining from all social activism, even if it is sorely needed. This amongst other things led to the cementing of the caste system. It was made hereditary. Why change the social order if it's not real? Those permanently established in objectless *samadhi* rarely step up for the rights of women, racial minorities, or sexual minorities. They're more likely to say things are fine as they are and don't comment on difficult issues.

As mystics and yogis, we have social responsibilities, and if things need to be changed, we must stand up and change them. Labeling the world as unreal and an illusion seen from a yogic perspective reflects an overemphasis of objectless *samadhi*. This *samadhi* is the most powerful and most effective in regards to changing your psyche, but it must be augmented by the objective *samadhis*, which teach us about the reality and nature of objects, the world, and other people. They teach us that the world and others are not just a figment of our imagination, but that they are painfully (or joyfully) real and that we must interact with them.

When explaining the importance of objective *samadhis,* some people have replied along the lines of, "Meditation is not meditating on something. Meditation is our true nature. Focusing on an object keeps you prisoner of the known." These statements reflect Advaita Vedantic and Buddhist ideas about meditation, rather than yogic ones. Neither of them should be automatically accepted as right or

29

wrong; but my question is, "Why did the world arise in the first place if knowing it will imprison you? Does this mean God is some trickster? Somebody who gave you the world to enmesh you in it and who didn't supply you with the cognitive power to free yourself?" I want to question philosophies that consider the world an illusion, some mirage, or even an "untruth," as Gaudapada called it in his *Mandukya Karika*. This is also reflected in one of the Indian epithets for God, "*Mayin.*" To call God *Mayin*, which means "one who weaves the veil of illusion" is to believe that God is a trickster who imprisons you in an illusion from which it is almost impossible to escape.

In the same vein, some radical idealistic philosophies (which propose that the world is just an idea in your mind) treat the human body as "nothing," "mud," "a prison," "a grave in which we are entombed," "a deception," and "a valley of sorrows." These philosophies suggest the mind and body are obstacles to freedom, cages that keep us imprisoned and from which we must escape to bask in the sun of pure consciousness. The protagonists of these extreme philosophies are almost always men.

In India, the universe, either called *prakrti* (nature) or *Shakti* (energy), is considered to be female. Denial of the universe, then, removes all femininity from creation as being pure consciousness, which is considered male. These same philosophies espouse the male seeker to be celibate, so as not to be contaminated by femininity. The body, birthed and nurtured by our mothers, is discarded. Although the woman who conceived the only Son of God did so through Immaculate Conception, our mothers were sullied in the process. Is that not an insult to our mothers? And it's all conveniently sexist! That procreating is considered to be a karmic bond is evidenced in the fact that Buddha called his own son Rahula (the fetter), because he believed his son chained him to life. What's wrong with that? Oh, yes, right, the first of the four noble truths: "All life is suffering"! In this regard religions generally agree. They say the material universe, the body, and all that is worldly must be overcome and an otherworldly realm attained, whether we call it heaven or nirvana.

I do love the sun of pure consciousness, but it is only one side of the mystical experience. Taking both aspects of the mystical experience, the objectless and the objective, into consideration leads us to an entirely different worldview. A view in which the world is not a lie, a mirage, a cheat, or a valley of sorrows, and within which the body is not a tomb, mud, or a grave, and of which women are not obstacles or hindrances to spirituality. In this view the material universe and the human body within it are the crystallized body of the Divine. While the state of pure consciousness is personified in Shiva, the Indian God who sits absorbed in objectless *samadhi* on the icy and lifeless heights of the Himalayas, the universe is female in nature—and "woman" is its embodiment. She is not an obstacle to spirituality, but its carrier. If there was only objectless *samadhi*, we would all be thoughtless, motionless Shivas, and the world would be a lifeless place, a frozen image that contained nothing but . . . wait for it . . . nothingness, emptiness. What a male paradise! But what happened to fullness, overflowing joy, endless creativity, abundance, and blossoming?

This abundance only returned when the flowered arrow of Kama struck Lord Shiva. This opened him up to fall in love with Parvati, an embodiment of Shakti, the feminine divine creative force. The tales of the Shiva Purana following this incident present a subtle balance between solitary meditation on one hand and ecstatic participation in the world on the other. Notably, one of the eight *samadhis* is called *ananda*, the ecstasy *samadhi*.

WHY ECSTASY?

Through this particular objective *samadhi* (*ananda*) we experience this world, this universe, and its manifold creation as the crystallized body of the Divine. The Divine is not just consecrated in a handful of holy mountains and a few sacred shrines. No! There is no mountain and no location in this world that is *not* divine. There is no such thing as dead and dumb matter. Each site, each being in this world is sacred; each atom, each elementary particle is nothing less than the crystallized intelligence of God. The whole universe, the entirety of creation, is alive, en-spirited, and animated. To realize this, to understand that everything including us is an expression of—nay, is the very heartbeat and breath of—a higher intelligence; this is ecstasy.

Some modern teachers say that ecstasy is not spiritual, or that we should not be attached to it; or they say that awakening is nothing special, and just more of the usual. May they be blessed! Most religions discourage you from making personal contact with God, or they flat out claim that you can't. I believe they say so because ecstasy is truly revolutionary, in that it dissolves any control that external power structures have over you. There is an ancient Indian text called the *Vijnana Bhairava*, presumably revealed by Lord Shiva, who had a revolutionary tendency himself. In this text, Shiva says there is but one form of ecstasy, and that is the Divine one. He says it is a quality of consciousness, suggests that if you feel ecstasy, focus on its nature as arising from consciousness, not on the stimulus that seemed to cause the ecstasy. This industrialized and capitalist world knows we want ecstasy and they make us believe we can attain it if we buy enough drugs, sex, real estate, power, suits, dresses, food, or whatever it is they are currently selling. But Shiva says something entirely different. He says that ecstasy is our nature, and the only reason we can experience it is because it radiates from our very core.

No authority wants you to access that inner ecstasy, because once you do, your frame of reference shifts from external to internal. Whereas before you looked outside of yourself to determine who you are—to the government, religion, corporations, or ideologies—once you rediscover this inner ecstasy, alongside direct access to the Divine, these become your frame of reference and source of identification. And at this point, it is far more difficult for external spiritual authorities to "control our behavior." It is quite obvious how churches, gurus, and religious institutions for millennia have controlled our behavior to their own material advantage.

There is also a move of modern spiritual teachers who say you should not expect too much from spiritual awakening. They suggest that it's ordinary and normal, not much different from everything else; they try hard to reduce your expectations. This is certainly different from what I have experienced. I had experiences where I felt the entire universe burning with ecstasy. And I am in no way more precious, nor am I more deserving of that experience than you or anyone else. Ecstasy is the innermost nature of God, and because all of us are made in the image and likeness of God, each of us can feel it. It is your birthright; don't let anyone tell you otherwise.

IS IT POSSIBLE TO EXPERIENCE THE WORLD AS IT TRULY IS?
I've had students come to me with a somewhat sad look on their faces, saying they would like to learn objectless *samadhi*. That's the otherworldly, the more advanced, of the two types of *samadhis*. The dejected countenance tells me they actually want to commit a sophisticated form of suicide. Rather than committing some crime against the body, they hope to extinguish themselves into nirvana, a state that is free from pain (the term "nirvana" actually means extinguishing). When I tell them yoga places a whole raft of objective *samadhis* before the objectless state, they appear even more dejected, as if I have taken their toy away. But there are significant reasons why yoga builds you from the bottom up. Yoga says you can come to the wrong conclusions when you start with objectless *samadhis* (more on that in Chapter 6). Poetically described, objectless *samadhi* could be called "going beyond the world"; that is, not overcoming, but going beyond. But yoga first wants you to know exactly what you are going beyond. I met some meditators who said, "I don't need that. I know the world and it sucks. I want to get out of here." Think twice. Yoga says we do not know the world; we know only the interpretation, the map, and the shorthand we have made of it. How can that be?

This is exactly what Western science has been telling us for quite

33

some time, both the hard sciences and the humanities. Of the hard sciences, atom physicist and Nobel Prize laureate Niels Bohr said in 1908 that our scientific laws do not describe the world as such, but only what we know of the world (this statement is known as the Copenhagen Decision). In other words, our knowledge is just an internal dialogue that goes on in our head. Of the humanities, schools such as inter-subjectivism and post-structuralism have long asserted the view that our knowledge of the world cannot be isolated from our surroundings.

Our very language contains an incredible amount of built-in biases, heuristics, perceptions, and prejudices that make it impossible to even think without activating our conditioning. Thus, although both main branches of Western learning have made it clear that knowledge cannot exist independent from the observer, our society still goes about its Newtonian business and tries to ignore that fact. But the most mind-boggling aspect of it all is that, while Western academia has formulated these ideas in the 20th century, they were part of Indian thought (and yoga in particular) long before Jesus walked the earth. One of the most sublime and ancient yoga chants is dedicated to the king of the serpents (don't worry, it is an entirely different serpent than the one that passed the apple to Eve). The chant goes like this:

> om mani bhrajat phana
> sahasravidhrta vishvam
> bhara mandalaya anantaya
> nagarajaya namah

> OM, I bow to the king of the serpents,
> who embodies infinity, who carries the universe and simultaneously blazes forth all knowledge
> with one thousand, hooded, bejeweled heads.

The chant is addressed to the Nagaraj, the thousand-headed king of the serpents. One of his names is *Ananta,* which means "infinity." This is reflected in his common depiction as a snake biting into its own tail, thus forming a circle. He is also known by the name *Adishesha*, which means "residue." Adishesha is considered the combined residue of all universes that went before us. Patanjali, the author of the *Yoga Sutra*, is also considered a manifestation of this serpent of infinity.

The Nagaraj propounds a thousand versions, views, or interpretations of the one underlying truth, through his thousand bejeweled heads. These versions of the truth include all religions, all schools of philosophy, all sciences, all branches of knowledge, all schools of yoga, all cultures, and all languages. The thousand heads are a concession to the fact that, as soon as you use words, as soon as you attempt to filter the one underlying truth through a linguistic code, your words must necessarily be an interpretation of that truth—and not the truth itself.

The peculiar anatomy of the Nagaraj shows a thousand heads attached to a single tail. The tail is silent. It does not have a mouth to express itself, suggesting that no single mouth, no one view of the truth, can claim to be its sole representation. The tail represents the formless Absolute (*nirguna* Brahman), infinite consciousness, the unified field, *God transcendent*. The tail is the silent and inexpressible origin and base of the many heads. The law expressed in this metaphor is that "there are many ways in which the Truth can be expressed." The fact that it is impossible to reduce the tail to a single head means that no verbal truth, however elegant and eloquent it may be, has a monopoly on the tail. Although all religions, philosophies, schools of thought, and sciences may protest that they have exclusive access to the tail of Brahman, they all share joint access to the same truth and do not represent it exclusively.

The tail of the Nagaraj represents the experience of the deep reality obtained in *samadhi* that is beyond words and conditioning. In objectless *samadhi,* the word processor, our cultural biases and prejudices, and our map of the world are all suspended. While in *samadhi*, it is impossible to describe one's vision in words, which is why there is no *samadhi* religion, science, philosophy, or teaching. When mystics come down from these heights, they grapple for words to describe what they have seen in order to convey it to others. In doing so, they inevitably invoke conditioning, linguistic codes, moral values, and past experiences to cast into words that which is inexpressible. The words will necessarily remain poetic or mere metaphor. Thus, sages and mystics throughout the ages have had to exit *samadhi* in order to describe or teach it; it is their duty to do so. The experience is not for us to keep to ourselves, but to share. This paradox of being able to directly experience deep reality, the world as it truly is, yet unable to express or describe it is something many people in the spiritual realm fail to understand.

Of course this applies to my own words, as well. As beautiful as some of them may sound, they are my own conditioned scrambling to clothe the indescribable in a description, to cast the uncastable into form. Once I have found the words to describe my experience, I have interpreted them. Thus it may be said that my words are simply interpretations of yoga, and not yoga as such. This is true! However, whereas I began as one of those people wanting to escape this world as fast as I could (in many ways I found it unbearable), the practice of yoga has awoken me to realize this world is a most miraculous place full of beauty, wonder, love, and mystery. If I can open you to that realization, that the universe is not a cold and indifferent place, then it was worth it.

Although true reality can never be contained in words, it can be experienced directly by suspending the mind. The mind, which is conditioned, biased, and heuristic, can never wrap itself around infinity and eternity. Just visualize that for a moment—the mind wrapping itself around infinity. It doesn't work. But consciousness, which is infinite and eternal, contains the entire world.

MORE ON THE IMPORTANCE OF OBJECTIVE SAMADHIS

Thousands of years ago, India discovered the dilemma of the human mind, which took Westerners a few more millennia to discover. And it gave a solution to that dilemma, as well. Mind must be suspended in order to see reality. We can see our own true nature in objectless *samadhi* and the nature of the world in objective *samadhi*. Because no words spoken about these will ever adequately represent these states, we must have the experience ourselves. No assurance of any prophet, guru, Buddha, *thirthankara*, *siddha*, or *rishi*, will convince you, because words by nature are not convincing. No matter how great the person who speaks them, they are always just words. Therefore, reader, practice yoga and find out for yourself! My words may inspire you to do so, but no amount of talking or reading or thinking can show you reality as it is.

The reality of the world can be seen in objective *samadhis,* of which there are several types. Our mind is so clouded by our past that we see, hear, and feel only a fraction of what is to be perceived. Our normal perception passes through many cognitive filters, such as fear for survival, possibilities to exploit or gain from a certain situation, projection of past hurt and disappointment onto the present, and many more. By the time we are finished, only a tiny amount of what we actually perceive reaches our intelligence for interpretation. If everything passed through our filters at one time, we would be unable to function; the sheer amount of data could not be processed quickly enough. This explains the secret of consciousness: although it is aware of everything, it does not process, interpret, or modify sensory data.

Decades ago, in the middle of the night, I was riding my motorbike over an icy road, when I felt my front wheel starting to lose traction. Somehow I managed to break my rear wheel to exactly the right amount that my bike was sliding along like a sledge and eventually came to a halt, upright. When I stood with both feet on the ground, it was as if I heard a loud clonk in my head. Imagine if a computer had driven that bike, what enormous amount of mathematical simulation would have been necessary to land the bike upright. I was suddenly aware that what I had done—or what something had done through me—occurred without my even noticing. It just happened.

If I had tried it myself, I would never have managed, and I certainly wouldn't try such a stunt. I raised my hands in front of my eyes and looked at them in marvel. I became aware of these miracles of my body and mind, transporting me seemingly miraculously through this wonderland around me. I knew then that I had never really noticed anything at all and had lived most of my life in an unconscious daze. I was in awe of this strange and beautiful place called world, in which I, a semiconscious bio-robot, seemed able to get around on a fast-moving, fossil-fuel-powered, self-balancing appliance.

A police car pulled up next to me, and the officer asked if I had a problem. No doubt seeing some kid at the side of the road on a motorbike at midnight, arms raised toward heaven, would make me suspicious, too. My brain clonked back into 'normal' mode, and I said, "Everything is fine. Just feeling stiff and stretching a bit!" I started to do some awkward calisthenics. The cops were sufficiently convinced that I could resume driving like a responsible citizen, and they let me off the hook. Objective *samadhis* will show you exactly that. They will show you the true beauty and magnificence of the world beyond all conditioning, heuristics, and biases. They will show you the raw world, prior to us covering, molding, and mellowing it through our beliefs, fears, desires, pains, and expectations.

The great Advaita Vedantin Shankara stated, "The world should be looked at like the droppings of a crow" (*Aparokshanubhuti* stanza 4). This is exactly the attitude I wish to question, where spirituality is believed to be outside of the world, a different realm. Objective *samadhi* will show you the world is nothing but manifested spirit. Yoga and Advaita Vedanta differ in that regard, because Advaita Vedanta teaches that the world is an illusion; yoga teaches that the world is real. Yoga has revealed to me a world of majestic beauty that is the manifest body of God; and it is a world about which I deeply care. I cannot (nor do I want to) be indifferent towards it, as towards the "droppings of a crow." What yoga gave me and what I hope to offer is a complete re-enchantment of the world, not its dismissal. If we did, then, wish to go beyond the world as we know it, wouldn't we first want to know exactly what we were leaving behind? It was in this process of learning that I discovered a world that is intrinsically divine.

ENLIGHTENMENT VERSUS THE SPIRITUAL EVOLUTION OF HUMANITY

Before closing this chapter, let's return to the opening theme of enlightenment versus *samadhi*. There is a finality implied in the term enlightenment. You either are, or you are not. Once you have it, you are done once and for all—and you can pop off into nirvana, which reduces itself to nothingness and emptiness. Conversely, *samadhi* is an experience that has a beginning and an end. It is a process of various states through which you evolve, and even the last and most powerful of the eight *samadhis* is still an impermanent state. I want to challenge the notion that the spiritual evolution of an individual ever ends.

As religions evolved, it seems each needed to make the claim that its founder had reached the culmination of all possible spiritual evolution. Of course they had to do that, otherwise somebody would have come along to "top them." Ultimately there is little foundation for the claim that the spiritual evolution of humanity ends (unless we wipe ourselves off the face of the earth before we get anywhere).

If you propose an end point of evolution (such as enlightenment), as Buddhism does, you will always compare yourself against it and think, "Look! I'm still not enlightened!" We would benefit from looking at our spiritual evolution, both as individuals and as a species, as an open-ended process from which we look with curiosity about where it can take us.

Science has made great contributions in its concepts about the evolution of life. But there is not enough emphasis on where it is heading, only where it comes from. Having limited itself to empirical inquiry (that is, inquiry into sensory data, which rules out spirituality), by definition science cannot contribute to the spiritual evolution of humanity; and that's a great shame. We need a new form of science that will rectify that.

That being said, in ancient texts (the *Yoga Vashishta* being one of them), yoga has already taught that each individual evolves from primitive life forms, such as worms or viruses, through more evolved ones, such as birds and mammals, to eventually become human. Yoga's great contribution is to show how individuals, being human, continue to evolve towards a sage-like and semi-divine being. Aurobindo's great contribution was his claim that we need spiritual evolution for individuals, but also for the whole of humanity as one being. We are witnessing this now, albeit tentatively. We see it in Hindu yogis like Aurobindo and Buddhism's Thich Nhat Hanh, who said the next Buddha will be a *sangha* (a community of awakened ones). We see it in new Christian thought, which believes the second coming of Christ will comprise all of humanity receiving the Sonship. Everywhere is awakening to the fact that spirituality must become a collective effort, performed by all for all. To this end I hope this small work on the *samadhis* will be a humble contribution. I also hope we can move away from the idea that our spiritual leaders of the past have reached the summit of their evolution and that we can look forward, instead, to the next generation evolving beyond our current state and will support them in doing so.

Chapter 2
CONDITIONING, KARMA, AND THE OBSTACLES

This chapter deals with the obstacles to *samadhi* and the fact that there is no such thing as "spontaneous awakening." Even if it might seem as though you had a sudden awakening, in the years, decades, and lifetimes before this particular incident, you gradually removed the obstacles until a critical mass of spiritual innovation was reached and an avalanche of awakening was kicked loose. Ramana Maharshi confirms this by suggesting that all those who seemed to spontaneously awaken (as he had done) had performed the work required in previous embodiments. Here I discuss the obstacles to our quest. What do we need to change, and why? This can become a bit technical. I know that when I first started yoga, my eyes would sometimes glaze over when my teachers talked about these subjects.

CONDITIONING AND ITS HISTORICAL ASPECT

Yogis call the sum total of our past subconscious imprints *conditioning*. The problem with these imprints is that, as the word "subconscious" suggests, they fall outside our realm of awareness. You may think of yourself as having a certain personality, but your subconscious thinks in a completely different way. This is why we might see people behave in a way that is different from their proposed beliefs. The conscious mind may do the talking, but the action might be directed by the subconscious. The subconscious is an amalgamation of your past, often your early childhood, but yogis go much further. In sutra IV.9, Patanjali says, "The connection between memory and subconscious imprint exists, even if they are separated by birth, time, and space." What he means is that however long ago and however far away, even in different lifetimes and different worlds, the results of your actions will follow you around.

41

SAMADHI : THE GREAT FREEDOM

Here's an example. Were you ever in a romantic relationship with somebody who was not, in hindsight, a good match? Our conscious mind does not determine our mating behavior. You don't look at another person and rationally decide whether to court them or not. The decision is made according to past experiences and is often related to role models, like our parents. This is especially tragic when people repeatedly experience failed relationships because they continue to perpetuate the same sort of dysfunction over and over again.

The same might be said about financial success, friendships, professions, and so on. Most life decisions are not made through rational choice. Financial psychologists now say we are not equipped to make rational financial choices to our own best interests, but that our choices are formed by a variety of unconscious factors. If you look at the headlines that bombard us every day, you have to admit it is becoming increasingly difficult to believe that humans make rational choices.

Conditioning plays an important role in spirituality, too. If, for example, the messages received in your upbringing suggested you were sinful, unworthy of receiving love, incapable, not good enough, or any number of things, then you are unlikely to be comfortable with the amount and type of unexpected happiness that *samadhi* brings. Even if you do experience mini *samadhis* of a few seconds or a minute or two, your mind will simply blot them out and won't let you integrate them. This is important to note, because practitioners are often too impatient with the higher limbs of practice. It has taken a long time to accumulate your conditioning (according to some texts, trillions of lives), and the expectation of spontaneous awakening sounds suspiciously like the product of a society of instant gratification. It is certainly not a concept that was fostered in ancient cultures. In the *Bhagavad Gita* (IV: 1–3), Lord Krishna says to Arjuna, "This ancient yoga that I taught in days of yore to Abraham and Noah (I have substituted respective biblical names) was lost through the lapse of time. That's why I am now teaching it again to you." Arjuna replies, "That's strange! Abraham and Noah lived a long time ago, and you live now. How can you have taught them?" Krishna's reply is important. In fact, if we had to list ten of the most important sayings ever uttered on this planet, this one would make the list. He says, "Arjuna, you and I are ancient beings who have lived many lifetimes. The difference is I remember all of them, but thou dost not" (*Bhagavad Gita* IV.5).

There is another passage in the *Gita* where Arjuna mourns the fact that he may kill some of his relatives in battle (who have taken the other side). Krishna answers, "Never was there a time when we or any of these heroes did not exist. Nor shall there ever be a time when we or they will not exist" (*Bhagavad Gita* II.12). When I talk about conditioning, try to let go of the idea that you might have done some naughty things in the past. Let's open up the whole discussion. Have a look at your family—as far back as you can. Maybe on the mantelpiece there are some old pictures of your ancestors in the 19th or even 18th century. Can you imagine that some of their thoughts, hopes, feelings, or fears are perpetuated in you today? Look at the history of your class, caste, tribe, clan, or even nation. Can you see the collective conditioning that lives on in you? Do you remember a time when you watched a movie about a particular hero who stirred something within you? Do you recognize that archetype alive within you? Can you accept that this person is part of your make-up?

But I want to make the circle even wider. The Apollo moon mission entered our subconscious. When the Titanic hit the iceberg, it entered our collective conditioning. When Genghis Khan and his Mongols rode the steppe, a part of you and me was there. When the Romans put siege to Carthage, it entered our conditioning. When our remote ancestors in the African savannah started to use language, it formed our conditioning. But even further back, we can discern distinct primate, mammalian, reptilian, and even single-cell organism conditioning that permeates us. That very first protozoa was yours and my ancestor, and its memory lives on within us. A protozoa devours another by assimilating it. Can you see how much of our modern history is nations devouring and assimilating parts of each other, of our territory, population, resources, wealth, and history? To this very day modern nations are creeping over the maps like giant amoebas, devouring each other.

Remember, Patanjali said that however far back in time and far away in space we go, our subconscious imprints determine who we are today. This means the bulk of our conditioning is not personal and probably not even human. It is a collective that relates to the entire history of life on Earth. This is more evidence for the claim that spiritual evolution must be a whole-humanity effort, as conditioning was a collective effort, too. The big difference is that now we can think about this consciously and thus can move forward, consciously.

WHY DO CONDITIONING AND SUBCONSCIOUS IMPRINT EVEN EXIST?
Patanjali says "Subconscious imprints and memories are without beginning, since desire is beginning-less" (*Yoga Sutra* IV.10). Like you and me, this first amoeba had the desire to live and to experience. Let's call it "the divine spark of life." Because it is not feasible to make every decision anew, we and every other life form simply store each decision made, and when a similar situation arises, we quickly respond in a similar way—often in a way that ensures our survival. Although this process works well when dealing with survival, it does not work at all when moving towards spiritual awakening. Spiritual awakening means we suspend the subconscious patterns that made us successful survival robots.

This doesn't mean we delete our conditioning entirely. That wouldn't be feasible, either. Consider the following example: most people drive a car using their subconscious mind. If all conditioning were deleted, you would awkwardly and self-consciously struggle to make every turn, to learn every signal, to operate your car as though you had never done it before. The act of just driving means you have acquired subconscious competence. Thus, even the person interested in spiritual evolution can-

44

not dispense with their conditioning entirely. What we want is the *choice* to either act from conditioning or to enter a situation anew, to see it with fresh eyes. That's why Jesus said, "Let the children come, for the kingdom of heaven is theirs" (Matthew 19:14).

Children have the capacity to enter situations as though for the first time. Although we don't want to return to being childish, we want the choice to act with childlike purity and wisdom. The Kingdom of Heaven Jesus talked about is Judeo-Christian shorthand for

To tackle a situation with an adult mind essentially means to enter it loaded with the baggage of the ages. You and me (subconsciously) take into consideration almost every situation to ever occur on this planet to arrive at a decision. The ability to do so is the glory of the subconscious mind (its ability to compare vast swaths of data quickly), but is also its shortcoming (it cannot rest in the present and in its divine core).

what the Hindus call *atman*, the true self, our innermost core. This becomes clear when looking at another of the Nazarene's statements: "The kingdom of heaven cannot be found in this or that location, for the kingdom of heaven is within." In moments when we see the world from this center (the *atman* or *purusha*) we again become like children (in Zen, the beginner's mind) and look at the world in awe, as if seeing it for the first time. For this to be possible we must first understand that most of our choices are biased. Once we realize that, we can consciously override them if we choose.

Patanjali says that in (a particular) *samadhi*, memory becomes purified, as if emptied of its own form (sutra I.43). Everything tends to stick to memory (conditioning is subconscious memory); yogis call this stickiness *stainability* or *impurity*. Patanjali calls the capacity to go beyond that "purification." It refers to the fact that our entire past seems to stick to it and that we can't let it go.

THE PROCESS OF DECONDITIONING

Patanjali describes the process of yogic deconditioning (he calls it transformation, or *parinama*) in the third chapter of the *Yoga Sutra*. In III.12, he says, "If there is similarity of that idea that arises to the one that subsides, this is called a transformation towards one-pointedness (*ekagra*) of the mind." This principle is characteristic of yoga as a whole, which is to start with small steps, so that you can trace your progress, rather than trying to go all the way in one giant leap (which is most often unsuccessful). Conditioning tends to make the mind scattered and extraverted. Patanjali suggests slowly reigning in the mind, as we would slowly tame a wild elephant. Sutra III.11 goes a step further: "If the scattering of the mind is replaced by one-pointedness, this is called the *samadhi* transformation (*parinama*) of the mind." He names it "*samadhi* transformation," because focusing the mind is a prerequisite to objective *samadhi*. When Patanjali uses the term *samadhi* here, it is inferred in this context that he is referring to objective *samadhi*.

Sutra III.10 says, "The mind stays calm through repeatedly applying imprints (*samskaras*) of cessation of its activity." Here he clearly links deconditioning with the conscious placing of imprints (*samskaras*) as a way to achieve *samadhi*. That is, if you have a scattered and wild mind, you cannot just suddenly change it through meditation; you have to go through a slow process of getting rid of the imprints that lead to a scattered mind in the first place and then replace these with imprints of stillness. Sutra III.9 then describes the result, which is objective *samadhi*: "When the subconscious imprint (*samskara*) of mental activity is replaced with an imprint of the cessation of mental activity], then there is a moment of cessation of mental activity known as transformation (*parinama*) towards cessation (*nirodha*)."

It all sounds a bit technical but he is basically saying, "Your subconscious is what drives you mad. Slowly change the structure of your subconscious to that of peace, stillness, and clarity and that's what you will end up with. It took some time to acquire

Parinama is the process of transformation. It's important for modern Westerners who wish to reach their goal instantly to understand that there will be a process of transformation required to reprogram the subconscious. *Parinama* is the slow replacing of unconscious imprints with conscious ones. What is the quality of these imprints? Whereas before our imprints were dictated by subconscious conditioning (often fear, aversion, and pain), they will now be replaced by imprints of authenticity. It would be simplistic to translate transformation of *nirodha* as "stillness." During times when nothing is required of you, the suspended (*nirodha*) mind expresses itself as stillness. In such moments, stillness is authentic. However, when work or decisions are required of you, stillness would not be authentic, because action is then needed. In such moments the suspended (*nirodha*) mind will make us act for the greater good, or as Jesus said, "Not my will but thy will be done." *Nirodha* does not mean to escape the world and one's responsibilities. In the *Ashtavakra Gita* we find the story of the emperor *Janaka*, who retreats into the forest hermitage of a sage to find himself. After he reaches the stage of suspension (objectless *samadhi*) he wants to stay in the forest and simply meditate, but the sage sends him back to his court to fulfill his duties. "Never has there been one better equipped to fulfill the role of emperor than you in your newly acquired state." In modern language, we could say that such a person has overcome their personal hang-ups. Authenticity is the term that best describes this state.

your current conditioning, and the deconditioning process will require some time, as well." From a modern psychological perspective, this is obvious, so you might wonder, "what's the point?" The point is that the *Yoga Sutra* portrays an almost modern understanding of the human psyche that has nothing to do with superstition. It is thoroughly scientific, with "science" being a term that I have already suggested needs to be extended to include the non-empirical. Conversely, some modern spiritual teachers try to oversimplify the matter, and I wonder whether this is to fulfill a growing demand for simplicity within the spiritual market.

The process of deconditioning is also linked to balancing the lunar and solar *nadis* (related to synchronizing the left and right brain hemispheres and the parasympathetic and sympathetic nervous systems) and activating evolutionary brain circuitry (called *chakra* awakening in yoga). I cover these two subjects in Chapter 6 of this text but in much greater detail in my earlier books *Pranayama: The Breath of Yoga* and *Yoga Meditation: Through Mantra, Chakras, and Kundalini to Spiritual Freedom.*

CONVERTING MIND INTO INTELLIGENCE

Yoga calls the part of our thinking that is governed by conditioning *manas*, which is most easily translated as "mind." Whenever we make a quick decision, it is the *manas* at work. What we need to do is use a different part of our thinking for the process of spiritual awakening. Yoga calls this part *buddhi*. We usually translate that as "intelligence*"* or "intellect*"* but the term originates from the Sanskrit root *budh*, which means, "to awaken." The epithet "Buddha," the awakened one, is derived from the same root.

According to yogic science one way of looking at awakening is the conversion of mind (*manas*) into intelligence (*buddhi*). There is a straightforward explanation for this term, but to look at things in such a linear and temporal way only suits us because our minds are built on the operating system of time. Things don't really happen successively in this fashion, but our minds comprehend things this way, so we will use it as a reference point for the purpose of illustration.

Yoga explains the world as originating from pure consciousness. Pure consciousness is God transcendent, as noted in the introduction. Because pure consciousness (God transcendent) needs something to be aware of (creation) to bring about its quality of awareness, consciousness automatically leads to the manifestation of God immanent (the Divine creative force, the universes, and all creation). The one cannot exist without the other, so it is only metaphorical when we say that, in the beginning, there was only consciousness. What follows is

48

fascinating: Yoga says the first thing the divine creative force brings forth is intelligence, and after that is I-am-ness (sometimes called "ego"), and finally, as a distant third, is *manas*, or the mind. This means that intelligence is not limited to a particular person or a particular brain because it exists before the *I-am-ness*, or the notion of individuality. Intelligence is universal and ubiquitous. It is everywhere.

Yogic science would say that when Einstein discovered the formula for the speed of light, it was not his invention; it was divine intelligence using Einstein as a vehicle to express itself. The same is to be said for all great inventions, all art, all forms of matter and life. The problem with mind and conditioning appears only when you bring *I-am-ness* (the ego) or the *sense-of-I* into the equation. I-am-ness needs to be there because the Divine is by nature infinite and eternal and, thus, in order to express itself as a living being limited in space and time (us), infinity must take the form of ego/ I-am-ness. In other words, our ego is needed for the Divine to individuate through us.

Now, once you have those limited beings, such as the first protozoan, the first African ancestors to use language, and finally you and me, you also need to equip them with mind (*manas*) so that they can "fast-guess" and survive. Fast-forward, and now those beings have come of age and are spiritually mature. In moments of awakening they can suspend their mind and their I-am-ness and reconnect with the original divine qualities of consciousness and intelligence.

The purpose of this passage was to explain that we are not trying to eradicate conditioning, ego, or mind; these are tools the Divine uses to express itself as *us.* They are evolutionary necessities, and we will continue to use them. It is important to understand that the Divine, by definition, cannot have an ego, as *ego* means limitation in space and time. It is we who have localized egos and minds, so that the Divine can individuate through us and express itself as a myriad of beings. The ego- and mind-bashing of spiritual teachers such as Swami Vivekananda belittles the importance of humanity and its psychological make-up. The answer is not to eradicate or destroy our minds and egos, as Vivekananda and others suggest. To do so would mean turning us all into vegetables; I wonder what modern psychologists would say about that advice! We don't do the spiritual quest much good if we simplify things to this extent. The point is to evolve the entire human being, so that ego and mind can be used for the greater good of all living things.

What matters is that now we are introducing a moment of choice. When practicing higher yoga (*samadhi* especially) you gain the capacity to choose between using your mind and conditioning for quick survival tasks (where the subconscious is enough) and accessing deeper moments of pure intelligence, in which you suspend the mind and its conditioning.

TYPES OF KARMA

Let's have a look at where conditioning begins. In sutra IV.8 Patanjali says, "From the three types of *karma* result conditionings, which will produce corresponding actions." Conditioning derives from *karma*, and *karma* means "action." It is implied that we produce conditioning through our actions. The law of *karma* is the law of cause and effect. It means that something doesn't come out of nothing but is brought about by a cause, most of which we don't know because it is hidden.

In the above stanza, Patanjali mentions three types of *karma* called *sanchita, prarabdha,* and *kriyamana karma.* How are they connected to *samadhi*? We must concern ourselves with *prarabdha* first. Sutra II.13 says that *karma* results in one's type of birth, span of life, and type of experience. *Prarabdha* is the *karma* that has caused these things in relation to our present embodiment. Absolutely everything happening in your life is happening for a reason. We have caused everything in our life today through previous actions, thoughts, emotions, and speech. This is the most difficult aspect of *karma* for people to accept. We walk through life blaming others for everything that goes wrong. We default on our mortgage and the house forecloses, our relationships break down and our kids end up on drugs. We get slandered, convicted for fraud, incarcerated, and sick. We might end up in lawsuits and all sorts of conflicts; the entire world seems to be against us. We may curse God, the government, the establishment, the trade unions, the capitalists, the communists, the Jews, the Muslims, the Christians, the Buddhists, the whites, the blacks, the gays, the men, the women, our parents, our partners, our children, the media, or our genes for our miseries, failures, and shortcomings—or we just blame it on bad luck.

Q: But doesn't this lead back to "what's the point"? And to "why not eat tortured, factory-farmed meat? Those animals must have done something awful to "deserve" being in that situation?

A: That's a fallacy. We have to apply the concept of radical self-responsibility to ourselves but not others. In other words, I need to ask myself, "How did I get into this situation?" Then the answer is, "Through my own thoughts, words, and actions." The next question is, "How do I get out of this mess?" Answer: "By changing my thoughts, words, and actions." If you eat tortured factory-farmed meat, this will manifest itself as torture in your life, one way or another. In other words, use the science of *karma* to clean up your side of the street first and not to explain other people's behavior. That's God's business.

In the Old Testament we find these words: "Do not bless and do not curse. Revenge is mine sayeth the Lord." This sentence explicitly states that God is the law of *karma* and not us. We do not try to explain why somebody is in this or that situation, and we never use somebody else's situation to justify our own shortcomings. We need to think, speak, and act right to sort out our own *karma* independently of what we believe the *karma* of others to be. For example, we cannot entertain karmic transgressions towards others by justifying that it was their *karma* to be transgressed by us. How could we know what their *karma* is?

Here's a different approach: sit for a moment and imagine accepting absolutely everything that has happened in your life up to now as the consequence of your own actions. At first this is very painful, because it removes any scapegoat. If you accept this view, it means that if you lose your job, it's because you've caused it yourself. Of course, you could argue it was due to the poor economy and other variables. But whose choice was it to embark on a career in that particular industry? Maybe it was your parents, your genetics, or other necessities that pushed you into that direction, but you accepted it.

Then your relationship breaks down. You might say, "It's my partner's fault." But who chose to be with them? Who ended up in a relationship that was destined to hurt you in the first place?

Q: I don't see where predetermined destiny ends and free choice begins? Wouldn't *karma* have determined our "false assumption" that now we are free agents?

A: There is no destiny but the one you create. Because we are made in the image and likeness of the Divine, we are free. God is free and She cannot create anything conflicting within Herself; therefore, all of Her creations must be free. Freedom is our natural state; but destiny seems relevant because we are free to make substandard choices. Think for a moment: If we were not free to make wrong choices, then wouldn't God just be a heavenly dictator? Then how could God be free? Our substandard choices play themselves out according to the law of *karma*; we are free to make poor choices, but we must accept their results. By consciously accepting this (an act that Gurdjieff called "conscious suffering"), we can move forward and make better choices in the future, until the point when we realize our underlying freedom.

There was something within you that knew, but you didn't listen. Through our own conditioning we have drawn into our lives the

52

very people who hurt us and, through that, we are responsible for our own suffering. What I am suggesting is that you accept that you have caused whatever comes your way—and that includes so-called genetic and hereditary disorders, because according to yoga, we choose our parents and we choose our genes. Whereas a big part of modern biology suggests our genes determine our behavior, yoga says we have chosen our genes to manifest and bring about exactly that mix of pleasure and pain that will enable us to wake up.

There is absolutely no way to escape from this radical self-responsibility if you want to be in charge of your spiritual evolution. But the good news is that once you have worked through the initial and (as in my case) very humiliating inventory, then another realization dawns. If you have accepted that nobody but you created everything up to this point, then you can also accept responsibility for what will occur from here on.

You have accepted responsibility for creating your future life, your destiny! If you believe your life is determined by exterior factors such as God, the devil, genes, the government, the church, the

Q: How can we be sure it will be nothing like this life? Or might it be similar?
A: It will not be similar, because the karmic imprints pertaining to it would have already combined to form this life. Remember that all similar *karma* attached itself to this strongest impression in the karmic storehouse. If they were similar to this life, they would have already been consumed to manifest this present life.

gurus, the rich and powerful, the neoconservatives, the illuminati, the extraterrestrials, ad infinitum, are you going to succeed in your spiritual life? No, you will have sabotaged your capacity to succeed. The best way to fail is to give your power of choice to an external agency. But the only way to assume full power and responsibility

SAMADHI : THE GREAT FREEDOM

for the future is to accept responsibility for the past. And this means accepting that one's *prarabdha karma* (the *karma* that has formed this present body), is self-caused. It also means to be at peace with your past and accept that you cannot change it. For example, part of *prarabdha karma* is the body that you inhabit, the genes, the ancestry, the family, the community, and the nation you have been born into (or, better, that you chose to be born into). The past is something you cannot change; you can only accept it. But how you frame the past determines your ability to go forward from here.

The *karma* you create from here onwards is called *kriyama-na karma*. If we do not radically change our responsibility for our *karma*, our *prarabdha* (up to now) and *kriyamana* (from here on-wards) *karmas* will be largely the same, because your *prarabdha* will determine your *kriyamana karma*. Is that what you want? If your *prarabdha* (present) could be improved upon, then accept to-tal responsibility for all of your experiences, thoughts, and emo-tions, and create a different *kriyamana* (future) *karma*. Of course, taking full responsibility for all of our states implies effort. And so it is that the *rishi* Vasishta says in the *Yoga Vashishta*, "For one of true self-effort, there is no destiny." To understand *prarabdha* and *kriyamana* is to accept responsibility for creating your destiny.

Take a moment now and accept total responsibility for your fu-ture. Self-effort does not mean you wave a magic wand and suddenly change everything. It means that by reframing your perspective you can change its meaning and that, over time, you will be empowered to determine your own destiny. Remember that *karma* determines conditioning and conditioning is the unconscious robotic program-ming that determines how we live our lives. This programming does not change in an instant. How could it? It was not written and pro-grammed in an instant, so the reprogramming will also take time.

To intensify this resolve and call for radical change, let's look at the third type of *karma*, *sanchita karma*. *Sanchita karma* is similar to *prarabdha* in that it is *karma* you have created in the past. The

54

difference is that, when you chose your new embodiment, the strongest impression in your karmic storehouse drew you into the womb of your present mother. All other similar *karma* attached itself to this strongest impression in your karmic storehouse and contributed to who you are today—your body, your family, your background, your language and culture, your abilities and shortcomings, etcetera. All *karma* similar to the strongest impression was combined to form your present *prarabdha karma* and body. Everything that remains in the karmic storehouse is called *sanchita karma*. We don't know what remains there, but we do know one thing: It is very different from your *prarabdha karma*, because if it weren't, it would have turned into *prarabdha* and contributed to who you are now.

In other words, *sanchita karma* is pretty much like roulette, the luck of the draw. Not in the sense of what we contribute to the storehouse, but in terms of what will be drawn from it. The only thing we know is that it's different from who we are now. This is why yoga science tells us to make an effort now, in this lifetime, in order that we might go all the way and break free. *Sanchita karma* means you don't know what your next embodiment will be. You can only be sure it will be nothing like your present life.

How it will be different is impossible to determine; however, if you consider that you've been part of this initial creation of life from the amoeba all the way up to the human form, you must admit a lot has happened in the last few billion years. Many of these imprints would still be hanging around in your karmic storehouse. We can't rule out whether *karma* related to simple life forms may be present in our karmic storehouse. While that does not necessarily mean embodiment as such a life form, it could certainly mean a life in which you have much less choice than you have now. For this reason, the mechanism of *sanchita karma* means you should not postpone your spiritual evolution, but should wholeheartedly pursue it now.

We are now in the unusual position of having evolved to the extent that our choices are conscious. For most of the evolutionary process, our choices were unconscious, meaning they were based on fear, greed, retribution, ignorance, egotism, desire, etc. These are what Patanjali would call *klesha*-based choices. *Klesha* refers to forms of suffering that are unconscious. In sutra II.2, Patanjali says that in the beginning we must focus on moving away from those forms of suffering and towards *samadhi*, which means the journey goes from the unconscious towards conscious life.

ECOLOGICAL AND COLLECTIVE KARMA

The ecological crisis that currently engulfs our planet is a form of collective *karma*. We, as the collective human species, have chosen to exploit the planet with unsustainable practices for centuries. This exploitation was based on the belief that we live in a hostile, or at least indifferent, universe in which our survival relies on our capacity to subdue nature, to control it and make it our dominion. The consequences have led us to reduced and polluted drinking water, polluted air, mass species extinction, poisoned oceans, diminished topsoils, increased salinity, growing deserts, destroyed rainforest, melted icecaps and ruined tundra, rising ocean levels, increased mental disorders, including depression and autism, and the list goes on. If this trajectory continues for another one or two generations, it will become irreversible (some scientist say it already is). We are unconsciously destroying the very foundation of our life and this planet and are working towards making ourselves extinct, too. Robotic conditioning is the root cause of this behavior.

Although we have made incredible scientific and technological progress, our spirituality lags behind. Thus we find ourselves in this current situation, in which humanity wields the power to destroy itself at the push of a button; yet spiritually we are very much primates. Lacking the lucidity that would be necessary to responsibly wield such enormous power, we have in a childlike fashion exploited the earth and reduced the indigenous cultures of the world and many species; thus we have created a strong collective *karma* that is not easily escaped.

Many people are aware of this destructive trajectory but feel powerless to impact any change. We feel as if we are working against an unstoppable, unconscious, and monstrous mechanism. But in the same way this mechanism was once set in motion by just a handful of people, people who had a vision and who believed in what they did, so too can this mechanism be stopped and something else set in motion. In fact, all that is needed is a few people to radically liberate themselves from the collective *karma*. People like Lao-tzu, Socrates, Jesus, and Buddha have done this. If you look at their biographies, there is a distinct non-acceptance of all limitations that we as a species usually place on ourselves. What those four teachers had in common (along with many others who followed in their wake or who went before them) was they liberated themselves from superstition.

We are so used to bowing down to spiritual authorities that it feels near impossible to overcome our collective *karma* of superstition. Yes, I mean superstition; although we pride ourselves on being reasonable and logical regarding empirical science, when it comes to spirituality, we still hold on to stone-age superstitions, formed by our collective *karma*. Old beliefs—such as the belief that we are genetically pre-programmed robots encased in bodies and pursuing infinite selfish interests, such as survival, unlimited resources, and procreation—must be discarded in order for us to break free of the current trajectory of ecological destruction. Once we remember that we are all expressions of the same divine force, then we can accept a new form of living and interacting that is not based on self-destruction.

Spiritual evolution is not just an extravagant pastime that belongs to a handful of people. It must become a major human endeavor if humanity is to learn that we are an integral part of nature, of its very creation. It is erroneous to believe our survival depends on our turning against and controlling nature. We must work *with* nature, in support of the planet, and in harmony with each other and all other life forms. We are nature. We will come to understand this, if we can overcome our primate *karma* and conditioning. It is urgent and imperative that we do so.

WHICH KARMA IS THE RIGHT ONE?

You may ask yourself, what *karma* can we create that enables us to act selflessly? The answer is, "none." Let me explain. In sutra IV.7, Patanjali says, "The *karma* of the yogi is neither positive or negative; of the others, it is threefold." *Karma* that is based on negative conditioning inevitably leads to suffering down the road. On the other hand, *karma* that leads to pleasant experiences is "positive." In most of us concentration and choice are not adequately developed for us to stay in one category of *karma*. That's why *karma* will always produce a cocktail of future pleasure and pain for most people.

When Patanjali says the *karma* of a yogi is not positive, negative, or mixed, he means that all three types create more *karma* for the individual who takes action. If I perform bad actions, I will suffer in the future. If I perform good actions, I will experience pleasure in the future. But really it will be a mix. The yogi, however, experiences none of these three because her actions are not motivated by personal interest. She does not think, "How do I create a pleasant future for myself?" When faced with a decision, the yogi will enter a mystical state and then act out of consciousness, not willpower or reason. That is, the yogi surrenders to a force greater than herself and allows this force to make the decision: "Thy will be done." The way to explore this will is not through thinking and reasoning but through mystical union. The yogi places himself in the service of the Divine, and that force, creating and thus affirming life, does not produce actions from narrow, individual, or egoic interests.

Please note, however, that just because that force is life affirming does not mean it can't cause you to destroy anything or kill anyone. Any action derived from mystical union cannot be destructive, because that force in which you are united is life itself. Actions that are the product of such a union, versus the product of personal motivation, do not create *karma* for the individual. This has deep implications for the collective and ecological *karma*. We have collectively produced negative *karma* because of the very doctrine that tells us we need to make narrow, egotistical, and selfish choices that only serve our selves, our wallets, and our immediate family. In our new world of the Global Village, self-interested choices won't work. If we maintain a shortsighted vision of exclusively personal pleasure, we may make choices that negatively impact others, our community, or nature; and that negative impact will swiftly return to our doorstep, as the karmic boomerang inevitably does. In that way, selfish choices quickly become self-destructive. In letting go of individual *karma* and making choices that derive from the mystical union, from consciousness, we allow that force of love and infinite creativity to work through us. This is how we can act without creating *karma* and in a way that benefits all sentient beings.

OBSTACLES PRESENTED IN THE YOGA SUTRA

Having covered conditioning and *karma* as the general source of obstruction, let's turn now to specific obstacles as described in the *Yoga Sutra*. In sutra I.30 we find the obstacles to yoga listed as sickness, rigidity, doubt, laziness, sense indulgence, false views, failure to attain a state, and failure to retain a state. Yoga discerns three tiers, or layers, of the human being in which these obstacles are located, i.e., the body, the breath (also called the *pranic* sheath), and the mind. In order to remove the obstacles from all three layers, a concerted approach of *asana* (for the body), *pranayama* (for the breath), and meditation (for the mind) is necessary. You will find here a succinct summary of how yogis would tackle individual obstacles, using a combination of these three modes of therapy. Again, this passage is somewhat technical, but its intention is to show how deep yoga intends the complete transformation of human beings to be.

The first obstacle, sickness, is a physical hindrance. Ayurveda describes sickness as caused by an imbalance of the three *dosha*s: *vata, pitta,* and *kapha.* These terms are sometimes translated as wind, bile, and phlegm, but the translations are so ridiculously simplified that it's better to use a foreign term one does not understand at all than to use an English term that loses the meaning. Although superficially the imbalance of the three *doshas* is seen as the cause of sickness, ultimately even this imbalance originates in the mind. The yogi would use a mix of physical therapy (herbs, diet, change of circumstance that caused the disease, and *asana*), *pranayama* to restore the *doshic* balance (for example *Surya Bhedana pranayama* to reduce an aggravated *vata*, *Ujjayi kumbhaka* to alleviate aggravated *kapha*, or *Shitali, Sitkari,* and *Chandra Bhedana* to decrease excess *pitta* (these are all *pranayama* techniques described in my book, *Pranayama: The Breath of Yoga*). Right thought, in yoga what is called *bhavana* (cultivation) and *sankalpa* (resolution), would also be used to target the mental origin of the disease.

The second obstacle, rigidity, is related to excess life force (*prana)* flowing through the solar energy channel, relating to the right nostril (*pingala*). Rigidity again has a physical component, which we would target through *asana*. Although we may feel rigid all over, rigidity at its core expresses itself most often as character armor around the heart, which makes the heart feel as hard and un-pliable as the ribcage. Among other *asanas,* the main therapy here would be backbending postures. Mentally, rigidity expresses itself as seeing only your truth and being unable to accept other truths outside of your understanding. On a *pranic* level, we call this a solar attitude, which is caused by excess breath flowing through the right nostril. Generally speaking *Nadi Shodhana* is the *pranayama* to correct this state, but if solar predominance is strong and persistent, it needs to be tackled with *Chandra Bhedana pranayama*; that is, taking all inhalations through the left nostril and exhaling through the right. This diminishes fundamentalism and increases relativism (being ready to accept the views of others). Additionally, yoga would propose a mental intervention, suggesting thought patterns that lead to accepting the views of others (this being the discipline of *bhavana* and *sankalpa*).

The third obstacle, doubt, is the mirror image of the previous one, rigidity. It means that too much *prana* is flowing through *ida,* the left nostril. This causes a lunar attitude, meaning one sees truth in everything and starts to believe that truth is a relative thing. This ultimately results in paralysis, whereby one is wholly unable to decide what to do. On a *pranic* level, this obstacle is removed through *Surya Bhedana pranayama*, in which course every inhalation is taken through the right nostril and all exhalations are made through the left. This increases fundamentalism, or confidence in one's choices, and decreases relativism. On a physical level, doubt is expressed by lack of strength. This lack of strength is often relegated to the core muscles; the person can still look hard externally, but this superficial strength protects an excessively soft core. On a physical level, yoga targets this obstacle through core strengthening exercises and weight-bearing *asanas*, such as arm balances. These create the impression of someone who "has backbone"; that is, to be un-bowing in the face of adversity, an expression of inner conviction, and an absence of doubt. Yoga would also target the mental component of doubt. Through meditation we come into contact with our inner being and become able to trust our intuition. High-quality choices cannot just be made by weighing reasons against each other (although that may be part of the process). High-quality decisions are made by the voice of the heart. Meditation increases our capacity to hear and listen to that voice.

The fourth obstacle, laziness, indicates an excess of inertia (*tamas*) in the mind and excess *kapha* in the body. Interestingly enough, yoga is not satisfied with labeling somebody as lazy but first admits that lack of drive is a technical obstacle and then constructively inquires into its mechanism. On the physical plane, laziness is caused by a dominance of the *kapha* element. This makes the person appear sluggish and it can be effectively targeted by *pranayama* and *kriya* methods. *Ujjayi pranayama, Surya Bhedana, Nauli, and Kapalabhati* all effectively reduce excess *kapha* and make the person more dynamic and passionate. The excess inertia (*tamas*) in the mind can be targeted through *Kapalabhati* and

Bhastrika. The latter two techniques are used to purify and stoke the inner fire (*agni*), which is the destroyer of inertia (*tamas*). Another technique to reduce sloth (*tamas*) in the mind comprises external breath retentions (*kumbhaka*s), which trigger the sympathetic nervous system. Additionally, the length of the inhalation can be increased, which promotes activity (*rajas*) and reduces inertia (*tamas*). Another way of reducing *kapha* and *tamas* is to perform a passionate daily Ashtanga Vinyasa practice, as I have described in my first two books, *Ashtanga Yoga Practice and Philosophy* and *Ashtanga Yoga The Intermediate Series: Mythology, Anatomy, and Practice*. Additionally, meditating on the dynamic aspect of the divine creative force, which never rests but always creates the world and all beings anew, can reduce the mind's tendency towards inertia. In this context, it is important to not only meditate on stillness. Stillness is a great quality, but from stillness at the center, the Divine creative force expresses itself as endless creativity and an abundance of forms. It is important to integrate this fullness and creativity into meditation; otherwise, if one meditates only on emptiness and stillness, the mind's tendency towards *tamas* (inertia) can increase. It also enables us to realize the active, creative, and dynamic aspect of the Divine. In the end the yogi wants to be free, whether they are sitting and enjoying stillness or being active in the world.

The fifth obstacle is sense indulgence—very popular in today's society. Advertising relies heavily on making you believe your happiness relies on indulgence, on pampering and spoiling yourself; then they can sell you almost anything, and pretty much any amount of it, until your credit card is maxed out and beyond. Capitalism tells us that ecstasy is brought about by sense indulgence, whereas yoga tells us it is our innermost nature and that we need no sensory stimulus to access it—we need only to dive deeply within. And we shouldn't be surprised that we can get it for free and don't have to pay anyone for it! That's why the path to this ecstasy has been kept secret: once you discover this truth, you will become independent of consumption and sensory stimulus and thus will not contribute anymore to increasing gross domestic product (GDP). GDP growth is needed to keep increasing the wealth of the mega rich.

Sense indulgence can be caused by the aggravation of either inertia *(tamas)* or frenzy *(rajas)*. The expression "like a pig in mud," for example, indicates sense indulgence aggravated by *tamas*. The same applies in cases of excess eating caused by depression or the so-called "retail therapy" (that is, combating depression through shopping.) On the other hand, the demon king Ravana in the *Ramayana* (and other dictators and macho men following in his wake) show us great examples of sense indulgence through aggravated frenzy *(rajas)*. To reduce *tamas*, we use the combination of *pranayamas*, *kriyas,* and *asanas* described under the fourth obstacle.

Extending the exhalations combats sense indulgence brought about through frenzy *(rajas)*. *Chandra Bhedana pranayama* is also practiced, in which all inhalations are taken through the left nostril. This *pranayama* makes one docile and introverted, thus reducing frenzy *(rajas)*. If *rajas* is aggravated, a more docile *asana* practice is the better way. It is also beneficial to add meditation, and here one might focus on stillness, peace, emptiness, and the realization that the world is in perfect balance, as it presents itself right now, and does not need to be reinvented. Meditation in this state should also focus on the fact that you are a child of the Divine and good enough as you are. No worldly force can add or detract anything from your total completion, which is divinely willed. The Divine is eternally established in your heart and no amount of indulging can improve on it. Meditate on sayings such as, "Be still and know that I am God" (Psalm 46:10).

The sixth obstacle, false views, results from an imbalance of the right and left brain hemispheres and parasympathetic and sympathetic nervous systems, respectively. This is predominantly a *pranic* imbalance, in yoga called an *ida* (moon) and *pingala* (sun) imbalance. In this case, practice *Nadi Shodhana pranayama* to bring about balance and, in extreme cases, use either *Chandra Bhedana*

63

or *Surya Bhedana* to alleviate your particular imbalance. Apart from this primary approach, the physical and mental planes are also targeted. If a person has a lunar tendency, they will tend toward relativism, meaning they will see so many right ways of doing things that they have difficulty making firm decisions or standing against what's wrong. In this case, a strength-based *asana* practice with many *vinyasas* (sequential movements) and arm balances will supplement *Surya Bhedana pranayama*. Meditation on the Divine as law is also beneficial here. This involves the study of ethics, including the *yamas* and *niyamas* of the *Yoga Sutra* and also texts like the *Mahabharata* or the *Old Testament* of the Bible. These are useful in helping us understand that there are right and wrong ways of doing things and that we must stand up for what is right.

If the person has a solar tendency, their mind will tend towards fundamentalism, which means they give too much importance to having the right view and cannot tolerate views that conflict with their own. In this case *Chandra Bhedana pranayama* would be supplemented with a pacifying *asana* practice and meditation on stanzas such as "Who sees Me in all beings and all beings in Me, loses never sight of Me nor I of him" (*Bhagavad Gita* V.30).

The fundamentalist simplifies the world by applying the same rules to a wide variety of complex situations. In this case we need to meditate on the fact that the world and all beings are inherently complex, and even if we are smart and have studied a lot, we can only understand a small portion of creation's complexity. We need to meditate on the fact that each person we meet is the Divine in yet another disguise, teaching us something new. As long as we are in a human body, we are students of life and never its masters.

Patanjali's last two obstacles are failure to attain and failure to sustain a state. Failure to attain implies a solar attitude that lacks "conquering," which means it's the opposite of fundamentalism. Here we would increase confidence and conviction until we have reached a balanced state. We would add *Surya Bhedana* and *Ujjayi pran-*

ayamas combined with *Nauli* and *Kapalabhati kriyas* and a fiery *asana* practice. Meditation on the Divine in one of its all-conquering manifestations, such as Rama or Narasimha, would also be helpful.

Failure to sustain a state implies a lack of sustenance. Sustenance is a nurturing, lunar quality. If the solar side and fundamentalism are too dominant, we will burn out quickly or charge onwards to the next attainment, forgetting how important it is to sustain the current one. On a physical level, the failure to sustain can be caused by excess *pitta* and lack of *kapha*, in which case pranayama methods such as *Chandra Bhedana, Shitali,* and *Sitkari* are employed. Cautiously extending the time spent in inversions, such as Headstand and Shoulderstand, would be helpful (keeping in mind the safety precautions as spelled out in my earlier books). Sustaining a state is also related to "staying power." Increasing *kumbhaka* (breath retention) length improves staying power, as does holding *asanas* in your practice for a longer time. On the meditation side we would focus on aspects of the Divine as maintaining the world and stanzas such as, "I sustain this entire universe through a small part of myself" (*Bhagavad Gita* X.42).

The *kriya* and *pranayama* techniques mentioned above are described in great detail in my book *Pranayama: The Breath of Yoga*. It is beyond the scope of this text to go into further detail. The message of this passage is that all obstacles to yoga (although they might be predominant in either one of these three tiers) have a physical, a *pranic* (i.e., related to breath), and a mental component. Patanjali says in I.31 that "Suffering and frustration [mental component], unsteadiness of body [physical component], inhalation and exhalation [breath component] result from the obstacles." In other words, the obstacles simultaneously manifest on the mental, *pranic*, and physical level. It is simplistic to believe we could overcome them by working only with the body, only through breathing exercises, or only through meditation. If we use only one of these approaches, we will only purge one of the tiers (*koshas*) in which the obstacles are lodged. But we need to target all three. This realization will form the foundation of the next chapter, which deals with how to prepare the mind for *samadhi*.

Chapter 3
PREPARING THE MIND
FOR SAMADHI

This chapter summarizes yoga's path to *samadhi*. It is of great importance that yogis understand the technical process of *samadhi* early on and not just when they embark on its practice. Otherwise, they may later become aware that much of their practice (for example, if they put exclusive emphasis on the body and *asana*) did not contribute much to yoga's goal. If we endeavor to understand *samadhi* right at the outset of our yogic life, we will not fall into such traps. The yogi must understand how *samadhi* is connected to and rises out of the practice of *asana, kriya, pranayama,* and Kundalini meditation.

These four disciplines constitute the alchemical process of yoga, or transubstantiation (that is, the transformation of a base substance into a higher one). In this chapter, however, I can only describe the effect of right practice of these four disciplines. I describe the techniques themselves in my previous volumes on the subject. Please note that this is exactly the approach the *Yoga Sutra* takes. In just a few sentences, Patanjali lists the effect of right practice of *asana, pranayama,* and etcetera. He doesn't go into detail, which would require enormous space; modern commentators have often misunder-

Correct posture practice is what releases the physical *strata* of conditioning from bodily tissue. It does so by taking the body through a large number of different postures during which one breathes deeply and lets go of the felt tension and associated subconscious programming. When following the *vinyasa* method, additionally an alchemical heating of the body is undertaken, making it strong and healthy and preparing it for sitting in *pranayama* and meditation postures. *Asana* practice thus forms the foundation of *samadhi* practice.

stood this to mean there is no such detail. When Patanjali describes in three brief stanzas the results of correct posture practice, he doesn't mean you should not undertake decades of such practice to obtain those results. He wishes to convey that you should practice until you have permanently integrated what the three sutras talk about.

To do so may, in fact, take decades of practice. In the meantime, you should continue to practice the other limbs of yoga; in fact, in order to reach the goal of yoga, it is imperative that you do.

HOW INSTANT ENLIGHTENMENT FAILED

I would love to say that decades of preparation are not needed. I would love to tell you I found a shortcut that makes everything else unnecessary. But the problem is, not only have I not found such a shortcut, but I don't believe that one exists. In the mid-eighties when I started going to India, instant enlightenment was all I was looking for. If somebody said I would need to practice for decades, I wrote them off. I wasn't ready to invest more than two years into anything. I tried every approach available, including those that said there was nothing left to offer, that I was already "there." While this is true in theory, it doesn't hold up back in the West, at work, picking up the kids, juggling the mortgage, navigating relationships, teetering on the brink of bankruptcy, and so on. Maybe these methods have worked for a greater person than I was. But for me, in these moments of doubt, assurance that "Thou Art That," was not sufficient. I needed something more—something more . . . let me call it, *substantial*. Yes, that's the word. It wasn't enough for me to have some lofty ideas, such as "verily, I am the *Brahman*," while most of me remained tormented by all the things modern people are tormented by. That's nothing against lofty ideals, but I felt I needed to transform the entire substance of my being; in Christian theology this is called *transubstantiation*.

After I had given all of the instant enlightenment approaches my best shot, I was so humiliated that I became ready to take on something that might require decades of commitment, such as yoga. In hindsight, I understand that instant enlightenment only works if you have the suitable *karma* and conditioning to start with; Rishi Vyasa says that one who has the gift of the last birth (i.e., one who did all the legwork in previous embodiments) needs to hear the non-dual teaching only once. His hair will then stand on end, his face will be awash in tears, and he will be liberated without delay. I had heard the non-dual teaching an awful number of times. Though it made me scratch my head, my hair did not stand on end. Though it made me dumbfounded, my face was not awash with tears. Although it made a lot of sense, it did not liberate me.

Just listening to a lofty teaching doesn't change you on the level of *karma* and conditioning. While it may give you that warm fuzzy feeling for a little while, it does not reduce the obstacles. If obstacles are present, there is no point in avoiding the issue. Sure you can look at the lofty teachings and dupe yourself into believing the obstacles will go away, but they won't. They will come back to haunt you. I have seen many meditators who avoid looking at their personal issues for decades, though they may be experts in their particular method of meditation. You might *think* that you have meditated, *asana*-ed, *satsang*-ed, or *shunyata*-ed your issues away, but what's happened is that your method has created a comfortable space, a bubble for yourself, from which the obstacles are hidden from your sight. They aren't necessarily hidden from other people's sights, though, who are fully aware of your personality issues, which boldly surface when it comes to handling conflicts.

TAITTIRIYA UPANISHAD AND PANCHAKOSHA MODEL

Many people who go on a spiritual search wish to find that one guru who simply looks into their eyes, puts their hand (or foot) on their head, takes their *karma* away, and—through an act of grace—bestows *samadhi* on them. But *samadhi* does not have one single cause (such as a guru). It would be easy if I could just tell you to do this or that simple action and you will enter *samadhi*. Although we like to simplify things, this would be a reductionist view of the subject. As with many other things in life, *samadhi* has many contributing factors.

For example, if you were on a quest for physical health, you would soon learn that it depends not on one but a whole list of factors. You would probably take dietary changes into consideration, but exercise is also important. Adequate rest and reduced stress also play a role. Other aspects of health include your relations with other people, your love life, and mental hygiene. Similarly, our spiritual health does not depend on a single factor, but on many.

In sutra II.28 Patanjali says, "From practicing all the limbs of yoga, the impurities are removed, uncovering the light of knowledge and discernment." The key here is that "all the limbs," not just *asana* and not just meditation, should be practiced. It is a modern tendency to reduce yoga to only one of its elements, whether that is *asana* or meditation. Originally there was only one yoga; today we might call it *Mahayoga,* the great or complete yoga. Nowadays many teachers will tell you that only one of the branches of yoga needs to be practiced. According to Patanjali, the yogi should practice them all.

In the previous chapter, I described the nine obstacles to *samadhi*, as listed in sutra I.30. In sutra I.31, Patanjali says these nine obstacles express themselves on three levels: the physical level, the *pranic* level (related to breath and life force), and the mental level. Patanjali then refers to an even older text, the *Taittirya Upanishad.* The *panchakosha* doctrine, the model of the five layers, is described in this Upanishad. Of these five, two categories of *samadhi* take place within the two innermost layers, called the deep knowledge sheath (*vijnanamaya kosha*) and the ecstasy sheath (*anandamaya kosha*). I describe these in more detail in Chapter 6. In this chapter I cover the three outer layers.

The great freedom lies in the two innermost layers of the human being. But in order to access them, the three outer layers must be transparent; we must be able to see through them like a pure crystal or a clear body of water with a calm surface. In the way that we have organized our civilizations, our societies, and our education, we have created conditioning and *karma* that has made the outer layers opaque; thus we cannot look through to our innermost self. Deep in our core we know we are made in the image and likeness of the Divine, but how many people today can see that, feel that, or be that? Most modern people are disconnected from this wellspring of peace and joy that resides within. Although we can never truly be separated from the Divine, our conditioning might have us believe it is gone, that we are alone, or that—as Friedrich Nietzsche said—"God is dead." This is a delusion. We only need to restore the original transparence of the outer three layers to see into our depths clearly.

The three outer layers of the *panchakosha* model are body, breath (the *pranic* sheath), and mind. Their veiling, or opaqueness, is produced by the obstacles that are a manifestation of conditioning. And those obstacles are located within those three layers (sutra I.31). As we learned in Chapter 2, all obstacles have a physical, *pranic,* and mental component; thus to overcome them, all three components must be simultaneously (not sequentially) removed. *Asana* is the technique used to overcome the physical component of the obstacles and conditioning. *Pranayama* is practiced to remove the *pranic* component of conditioning and the obstacles. And their mental component is suspended by Kundalini and *chakra* meditation. These three categories of techniques must be seen and used as a compound, rather than isolated practices.

Because it may seem daunting to simultaneously embark on the study of three complex disciplines, they can be learned in order, typically with *asana* first. But eventually, after one has become somewhat proficient, the techniques must be practiced together and the tendency to remain bogged down exclusively in *asana* or meditation must be overcome. Once the outer three layers are purified and prepared, *samadhi* can consistently be accessed. Prior to that, it will always remain elusive, a fluke, or a

It is important to understand that the body consists entirely of slowed down or crystallized mind; that is, the body is past thought. There is no such thing as an "enlightened body." There is no single part or aspect of the body that is the crystallized past of your mind, versus another part that is not. The body is one hundred percent the evolutionary past of our mind. If you don't have crystallized mind or the history thereof, then you are not embodied. This is not to reduce the importance of the body, though. Crystallized histories are important, and in order to create our future we must acknowledge and transform them.

fantasy. Let's now consider these three core yogic techniques and their importance for *samadhi*. After that, I will go on to discuss the ancillary yoga skills that support the three core techniques.

THREE CORE YOGIC TECHNIQUES

One of the most important ingredients to *samadhi* is posture (*asana*). Some people who meditate completely deny any importance to the body at all. But the body and mind are intricately connected. Some yogis say the breath links the body and mind, but I would suggest the body and mind are one. Consider the body as being the crystallized mind and the mind as the body in a gaseous or vaporous state (of course, this is a metaphorical and not literal comparison). Because gasses and vapor are quick and dynamic, the mind can change quickly. The body, being comprised of solids, takes longer to change. Therefore the body is the crystallized history of the mind. Whatever you have thought, felt, or done in the past has crystallized as your body today.

Consider how incredibly important this makes the body in your spiritual quest! The idea that one does not need to tend to the body when on a spiritual quest is false. Only a few of the most determined practitioners can succeed without attending to the body at all.

GENERAL ASANA PRACTICE

Asana has three aspects, each of which needs to be covered: general practice, inversions, and sitting postures. Let's look at general *asana* practice first. Sometimes students ask me why it isn't enough to just sit upright with the head, neck, and spine in line. Although sitting in this way is essential for meditation practice, it does nothing to improve your health or your *pranic* state, nor does it reduce the physical aspect of conditioning. A wide set of yogic postures should be practiced daily to make each part of your body vibrant and to distribute *prana* to all cells of the body.

Patanjali lists sickness as the first obstacle to yoga. If you are sick, you are unlikely to think and practice with clarity. You must have a strong and healthy body, because your body is your vehicle on the road to freedom. Remember what I said in the last chapter on *sanchita karma*. This is the *karma* that remains in the karmic storehouse. Since we cannot gauge what remains in the karmic storehouse from our present embodiment, we want to intercept it by awakening in this lifetime. However, this quest may take longer than anticipated. Because spiritual evolution accelerates with age, the older years in particular are very fruitful for yoga. Thus it is important to maintain general health and longevity until we are awakened. This is aided by a daily practice of a wide set of *asanas*, including backbends, forward bends, standing postures, twists, inversions, supine postures, and hip rotations, such as leg-behind-head postures and Lotus and Half-Lotus. My research and experience suggest the benefit of the postures is accelerated when they are practiced swiftly, connected with sequential movements called *vinyasas,* and strung onto the common thread of breath and *bandhas.* I have described this method in great detail in my first two books.

Let's return to the idea of the body as the crystallized history of our thoughts, words, and actions. This means that, to change our mind, we also change its memory bank—the body. Conditioning and emotions such as fear, greed, anger, grief, and so on are stored in bodily tissue.

They must be released. The way to do so is by practicing a complete set of *asanas* while focusing on the breath. You may sometimes notice that feelings, emotions, and images surface in the mind during your practice. Simply let them go with the breath through exhalation. That being said, images do not have to surface in order to release stored emotions. Of importance is that the body remains fluid and that all tension is exhaled. For this to happen, we must not be attached to physical performance or how great our *asanas* look. We should never compare ourselves to anybody else, for this ambition and competition would impose yet another layer of conditioning on the body. Letting go of tension is the attitude to take during *asana* practice.

The idea that personality traits, past, and conditioning are held in bodily tissues may sound bizarre, but psychologists have recognized this phenomena for some time now, through the work of Wilhelm Reich, Alexander Lowen, and others. It is, however, important that we do not claim that *asana* practice can fix all mental disorders. It can only alleviate them and remove its physical component. Ultimately *asana* can only succeed when supported by *pranayama* and meditation. In sutra III.46, it is clear Patanjali is interested in much more than just sitting: "Perfection of the body is beauty, strength, grace, and adamantine solidity." Thus the body must partake in the evolution of the whole human being; it must be transubstantiated.

INVERSIONS

Another aspect of *asana* practice to be appreciated on its own merit is the group of inverted postures. This is a subject I have covered in great detail in my book, *Yoga Meditation: Through Mantra, Chakras and Kundalini to Spiritual Freedom*, so I will mention it only briefly here. The fifth limb of yoga is *pratyahara*, which means "independent of external stimuli." Although Patanjali covers it in only one stanza, it is an important aspect of yoga. Our modern world entices us to depend on external stimuli, chiefly the goods that we purchase. Yoga, on the contrary, holds that as long as you believe all the stuff out there will give you satisfaction, happiness, or freedom, you are enslaved to it. That doesn't mean you cannot enjoy these things; it means that for as long as you "need" sensory stimulus, you are its slave. If we are slaves to sensory stimulus, we will have difficulty turning inwards to discover our empire of consciousness and freedom.

Yogis found a few different approaches to foster independence from sensory stimuli. Ideally we would combine them all (and I have described them all in *Yoga Meditation*). Of greatest interest to us here is that our life force (*prana*) reaches out and attaches itself to sense objects. The mind then follows and we desire the object. This may sound strange, but if you are trained in meditation, you learn to notice how *prana* latches on to something before the formation of a desire takes place; you can then intercept it before it is too late, at which point you "need" to obtain the object.

Yogis found that one of the primary ways of stopping *prana* from reaching externally is by arresting it in some of the higher energy centers (*chakras*), particularly the fifth (*Vishuddha*) and sixth (*Ajna*) *chakras*. Shoulderstand (*Sarvangasana*) and Headstand (*Sirsasana*), respectively, will do this work. I admit that when I first heard this claim, it was one of the many yogic tales that sounded like mumbo-jumbo. However, when I realized that *Siddha* Gorakhnath, one of the ancient luminaries of yoga, had devoted an entire 12 stanzas to this subject in a yoga scripture that contained only 100 stanzas in total (*Yoga Gorakshataka*), I gave it a try. My experience with inversions confirmed Goraknath's claims. I am not suggesting you just go ahead and stand on your head and neck for long periods. The postures have intricate details and must be performed properly, so that no detriment is done. Most important is that the support structures (most importantly, the spine, core stabilizers, arms, and shoulders) are strong enough to hold the weight, not the cranium or the cervical vertebrae. A general *asana* and *vinyasa* (sequential movements) practice is needed to gain the strength required to hold inversions without detriment.

SEATED POSTURES

These are the quintessential yoga postures. It is much easier to enter *samadhi* when sitting upright, with the spine in its natural double-s curve. In most cases, lying down makes the mind too *tamasic* (heavy, dull). Slouching on the sofa or even leaning against something usually means the low back is not lordotic enough. If the low back becomes kyphotic, the so-called *apana*, the *pranic* downcurrent, will become dominant. Keeping the spine in the ideal position facilitates the rousing of Kundalini (the divine creative force) and also means the body is effortlessly aligned against gravitation. Thus we can sit for a long time without discomfort or fatigue. In both cases the body would intercept the pursuit of *samadhi*.

Other important parameters are that both palms of the hands and soles of the feet are turned upward in a receptive position. It is also helpful if the perineum (center of the pelvic floor) is either pressing against the floor or is stimulated with the left heel. The first condition is met by *Padmasana*, if the pelvis were tilted far forward. The second condition is met by *Siddhasana*, (Adept's Posture), by placing the left heel in the right position. Finally, sitting on the floor with the perineum being the lowest part of the body facilitates *prana* (life force) entering the central energy channel (*sushumna*). This in itself is a large subject I have covered in detail in *Yoga Meditation*.

The ability to sit in a high-quality meditation position does not come overnight. I would never have learned it from just sitting and meditating. I gained the ability by practicing a full set of postures interlinked by sequential movements, every day, for over a decade. Once I had learned to properly sit in Lotus Pose, it was crucial that I commence *pranayama*. This accelerated my competence in sitting much faster than meditation alone.

Never try to force your legs into what looks like a meditation position. It must be learned. I describe this in detail in my first four books, but most prominently in *Ashtanga Yoga Practice and Philosophy* and *Pranayama: The Breath of Yoga*. You can achieve *samadhi* without a sophisticated meditation posture, even without yogic posture at all. But it increases your probability, or stacks the odds in your favor, if you are sitting in a high-quality position. The same is to be said for all limbs and techniques of yoga. They are not exclusive or causative by themselves but in the accumulative; the more techniques you cover, the greater your likelihood of success. For me it was necessary to tick off all the boxes. Being a practitioner of only average talent, I needed all the help I could get.

PRANAYAMA

The next of the three main yogic techniques is *pranayama*. *Pranayama* consists of a complex set of breathing exercises. The *pranic* sheath connects the physical sheath with the mental sheath. It closely mirrors what happens in both; the *pranic* sheath is an excellent tool to influence the body and mind. *Prana*, life force, is not the same as breath. The breath is the external anatomical manifestation of *prana*. However, by harmonizing the breath (the manifestation of *prana*), we can harmonize the breath's intrinsic cause (*prana*), too. The practice of *pranayama* affects *prana* in several important ways and thereby impacts the body and mind. I describe both the practices

When tissues are chronically depleted of *prana*, they are more likely to harbor and develop chronic disease. The cause of such depletion is the subconscious mind or, in other words, one's personality issues, with the cause of these being our own past actions (*karma*). When one becomes aware of these weaknesses, one can practice *pranic* healing by distributing *prana* to those tissues. Theoretically, the yogic texts state that any disease can be overcome that way if mastery of *pranayama* is achieved. While such degree of mastery appears to have existed in the past, it would seem quackery to me if I claimed you could easily heal yourself that way. Also, do not overestimate your self-diagnostic skills. I recommend to not exclusively practice such modes of healing but rather in conjunction with Western and traditional forms of medicine.

and effects in great detail, along with the methods to achieve them, in *Pranayama: The Breath of Yoga.* What follows is a summary. One of the main effects of *pranayama* practice is that it draws scattered *prana* back into the body. Scattered *prana*, according to the yogic scriptures, has a decreasing effect on lifespan. It also manifests in our lives through a scattered mind, for example, if we are talkative and involved in manifold activities that don't get us anywhere. This leads to restlessness, to "being out there," instead of resting in one's center. It leads to "being all over the place," instead of resting in one's heart. It results in sustaining relationships that are demeaning, instead of relating to others from a desire to give and in developing unwholesome desires for oneself, instead of living our divine purpose *(svadharma). Pranayama* concentrates *prana* in the body in order to halt the projection of one's psyche out into the periphery. To project one's self here means to seek fulfillment in sensory stimulation, a fulfillment that only the rediscovery of ones un-severable relationship with the Divine can bring. If one rediscovers and embodies this eternal unity, the result is a whole and integrated human being.

Another beneficial effect is the capacity to store and increase *prana*. According to yogic authorities, only a small amount of the *prana* that can be absorbed from the air through deep and controlled yogic breathing is extracted through normal, shallow breathing. The actual storage of *prana* in the body is effectively improved through breath retention (*kumbhaka*), which is used to fixate *prana* in the body. Fixating is simply done by focusing the mind on the required area during breath retention. As *prana* will go where the mind goes, conscious concentration will automatically divert *prana* to that area. Distribution of *prana* to various areas of the body takes place predominantly during the exhalation phase. While the retention phase is used to absorb the *prana* in the navel area (*Manipura chakra),* exhalation is used to transport *prana* from the navel to areas where it is needed more urgently.

The next effect is that *pranayama* draws *prana* into the central channel (*sushumna*). This *nadi* suspends the mind, which is powered by the two outer *nadi*s: the *ida* and the *pingala*. These two solar and lunar *nadi*s contain the *prana* when the mind is activated. When the yogi attains the mystical state, the mind is suspended and *prana* is in the *sushumna* (*Hatha Yoga Pradipika* II: 42–43). Some yogic authorities tell us the induction of *prana* into *sushumna* depends on the practice of breath retention *(kumbhaka),* which is used more than anything else. T. Krishnamacharya held a similar view and said that *pranayama* is instrumental for attaining *samadhi*.

Pranayama will also evenly distribute *prana* throughout the body. This occurs in *Kevala Kumbhaka*, the pinnacle of *pranayama*. This suspension occurs spontaneously once the other forms of *pranayama* are mastered. Patanjali calls *Kevala Kumbhaka* the fourth *pranayama* (*Yoga Sutra* II.51), which leads to *samadhi*. Another import-

Q: What does it mean to deepen one's practice?
A: In meditation you extend your breath count by increasing the number of *mantras* pronounced in each *chakra*. You then use the additional time by visualizing the color of the chakra, its *yantra*, the color of the *yantra*, the number of the petals, and so on. This slows your mind and deepens your concentration, which enables you to increase your breath count again. This is an example of "zooming into the lattice of the practice"; the same would happen during breath retention in *pranayama*.

ant text, the *Hatha Tatva Kaumudi*, says that, in *samadhi, prana* will spread evenly throughout the body (*Hatha Tatva Kaumudi* LI.32). This is due to the lack of mental activity. The mind and its conditioning create uneven distribution of *prana* throughout the body. Compare this with the Ayurvedic texts describing the mind (*adhi*) as the root cause of all diseases (*vyadhi*). Not only does the mind in its normal state prevent samadhi, it also causes disease in the body and ultimately brings about its destruction. In sutra II.52, Patanjali says that when pranayama is achieved, the impediments to yoga are removed and the original state of mind (called *sattva*) is restored. Now the yogi can succeed with the higher limbs of yoga, such as meditation.

MEDITATION

The third main category of yogic technique is meditation. It is not to be practiced as an isolated discipline but combined and interlinked with the others. Done individually, the benefits of the techniques are limited to the sphere they deal with, for example *asana* with the body. To link them, meditation needs to be practiced within *asana* and by consciously extending (slowing down) and retaining the breath *(pranayama)*. This means it is not sufficient to just passively watch the breath for meditation; the structure of the meditation itself must contain mechanisms that require the breath slowing down. Yogic meditation must involve the same elements and principles as yogic postures and yogic breathing; the three combined produce a method that will bring powerful results.

I have described yogic meditation in great detail in an earlier book and will give a short summary here. In *Yoga Meditation: Through Mantra, Chakras and Kundalini to Spiritual Freedom* I describe the Mandelbrot metaphor of yogic technique. The Mandelbrot set is a formula named after the late mathematician Benoit Mandelbrot. Its geometrical representation is called a fractal, a complex pattern that looks the same, or nearly the same, however distant or close your view of it is. As you zoom deeper and deeper into the fractal, the same or similar patterns are repeated over and over again. The same structure and architecture of the fractal are repeated in every minute detail. Similarly, the same patterns are repeated on all levels of yogic technique as you zoom deeper and deeper into each one.

Asana, for example, is only effective if exercised in combination with *bandha* (energetic lock), yogic breathing, focal point (*drishti*), concentration (*dharana*), and so on. We find the same pattern repeated when we zoom deeper into *pranayama*. It is to be executed within *asana*, while applying energetic lock, focal point, *mantra* (sound wave), *mudra* (energetic seal), and so on. Once our zoom has reached the next layer, called *pratyahara* (independence from external stimuli), the same pattern holds true. Independence from external stimuli is achieved by applying the yogic ancillaries together. It is performed in *asana* and *pranayama* by applying *bandha*, *mudra*, *mantra*, visualization, etc. When zoom-

Even the so-called monsters of history, people like Hitler and Stalin, were powered by the same *prana*, the same divine creative force (in this context, often called Kundalini), that drove benevolent geniuses like Mozart and Shakespeare. Other than Shakespeare and Mozart (who expressed this force on the level of the fifth *chakra*, as divine art), the evil genius uses it on the lowest *chakra*, the *Muladhara*, for the destruction of their perceived foes. The divine creative force, if experienced in the base *chakra*, will power a reptile-like experience in the animal, or of a psychopath, if experienced in a human. If raised to the lower abdominal *chakra* it will lead to a mammalian type of group consciousness, where we define ourselves through our nation, our family, our football club, and other forms of belonging. The danger here is that, like mammals, belonging to a club, clan, or tribe always creates an 'other'—a group of people we perceive as threatening or, in the form of territory, as waste dumps to which we can externalize toxic waste or domestic refuse that we don't want anymore.

When elevated to the navel *chakra*, the *Manipura*, the same force expresses itself as manipulation, leadership, acquisition, assimilation, and accumulation of goods, etc. This primate consciousness (defining oneself through the power and status one has within the pack) is our current level of evolution. We attempt to raise ourselves above others through wealth or personal power and, in the process, have brought the biosphere to the brink of environmental holocaust and ourselves to the brink of extinction. Only through sequential activation of the four higher *chakras* might these problems be overcome.

ing deeply into independence from external stimuli, the sixth limb of yoga, *dharana* (concentration) is revealed. *Dharana*, too, is a set of techniques that take place within *asana, pranayama,* and *pratyahara*; it includes *mantra*, concentrating on *chakra*s, *bandha, mudra, drishti*, etc. The final two limbs of yoga–*dhyana* (meditation) and *samadhi* (absorption) – are likewise not separate practices but deeper layers of the existing lattice of yogic technique, which reveals the same patterns and details over and over again.

While Buddhist, *Vedantic*, and *Vipassana* meditation methods are noble pursuits in their own right, to harvest the fruit of your *asana, pranayama, kriya,* and *bandha* practice, you must combine them with yogic meditation—meditation that repeats the structural elements and architecture of your posture and breathing techniques. To progress swiftly in meditation, the yogi must use the skills already acquired in *asana* and *pranayama* practice. As with the Mandelbrot fractal, all yogic techniques were designed according to the same structural formulae. Yogic meditation is thus the mental layer of the physical and respiratory disciplines of yoga. Rather than importing unlinked meditation techniques into yoga, it is important to practice meditation using the same building blocks that the other limbs are made of. What does yogic meditation (or Kundalini meditation, as it is sometimes called) actually do? Many modern people believe meditation is just a technique to still the mind. That's a good effect, but you will not evolve quickly from just slowing or stilling the mind. You will just keep thinking the same thoughts, albeit slower and less frequently. To give a crass example, a psychopath will not become a loving person just by slowing down and stilling his mind.

In his commentary on the *Yoga Sutra,* Hariharananda Aranya states that even a so-called out-of-control (*kshipta*) mind can become single pointed by focusing on the undoing of their perceived enemies. I mention this because I want to challenge the notion that meditation exhausts itself in slowing and stilling the mind, in a similar fashion that *asana* is not only for making the body healthy, beautiful, and more youthful. Of course calming the mind can be useful for all sorts of mental disorders and difficulties, but we are aiming higher than stress reduction and anti-depression with yogic meditation. Its first purpose is to activate the *chakras*, which I describe in my book *Yoga Meditation* as evolutionary brain circuitry. Once they are activated, Kundalini (divine creative force) is to be conducted through these *chakras* (more on direct influence of *chakras* on types of *samadhis* in Chapter 6) and, depending on where it is concentrated, it will determine the type of experience you have, all the way from that of a psychopath to that of a Gautama Buddha. This sounds like a bold claim. When I started yoga, I believed those ideas were hocus-pocus, so I can understand anybody who feels the same. However, my study, practice, and experience have taught me otherwise.

I believe my relatively fast progress in some of the *samadhis* would not have been possible without learning to conduct Kundalini and to activate the *chakras*. I also need to mention that I'm not the first person to air these ideas. The Indian yogi Gopi Krishna explains in twelve books that Kundalini is the force behind mystical states and also behind mental disease, genius, and even evil genius. All I have done is broadened his approach and avoided his pitfalls by grounding meditation practice deeply in the other aspects of yoga, including *asana, pranayama, kriya, mudra*, diet, and philosophy. Gopi Krishna's failure to practice *pranayama* explains his decade-long struggle with Kundalini. You will find a complete map of the chakras from an evolutionary perspective in Chapter 13 of *Yoga Meditation*.

THE ANCILLARY YOGIC TECHNIQUES

Yoga uses several ancillary methods to support the big three that purify the outer layers of the human being (*asana, pranayama*, and Kundalini meditation). While they may not on their own be instrumental causes of *samadhi*, they greatly increase your odds of attaining it. I found that rather than trying to focus on one or two of these areas, some application of each supports a more holistic approach that allows yoga to transform your entire life. In this section I have summarized each technique and indicated where I have covered them in more detail. To describe the techniques thoroughly is beyond the scope of this book.

DEVOTION TO THE DIVINE (BHAKTI YOGA)

Bhakti Yoga is so important that I have dedicated an entire chapter of this book to it (Chapter 4) and hope to write a dedicated volume on it, as well. Additionally, the practical aspect of Bhakti Yoga has been covered in *Yoga Meditation* (Part 3). For many people, including myself, this is central to yoga. However, it is pointless to tell someone who is thoroughly disenchanted with religion that they must "totally and unconditionally surrender to God." Nevertheless, the more devotion to the Divine we can muster in our practice and in life, the faster we will succeed.

MANTRA

Mantras are sound waves that create reality. They can do so because the entire cosmos from the black hole to a quark is comprised of vibratory patterns. I have covered the philosophy of *Mantra* Yoga in *Ashtanga Yoga: The Intermediate Series* (Chapter 3, page 21ff.). Its practical application is covered in *Pranayama: The Breath of Yoga* and *Yoga Meditation*. Some teachers see *Mantra* Yoga as a separate discipline, where the *mantra* becomes more or less the only focus. I prefer to treat it as the auditory component of *pranayama* and meditation. It thus becomes an additional layer within *pranayama* and meditation and increases their impact.

BHAVANA (CULTIVATION) AND SANKALPA (RESOLUTION)

This is a vast subject that is so important I intend to address it in a separate volume. This is an introduction. The term *bhavana*, implying cultivation of right thought patterns, is one of the most frequently occurring terms in the *Yoga Sutra*. For example, sutra I.33 states, "Clarity of mind is produced by cultivating friendliness towards the happy, compassion towards the miserable, joy towards the virtuous, and forgiveness towards the wicked." This is a clear case of *bhavana*. This change in attitude would require far too long to happen spontaneously (such as if caused only by meditating on stillness). It is much more efficient to cultivate such attitudes consciously and purposefully. The idea of *bhavana* is also enshrined in the *Bhagavad Gita*, which says in stanza XVII.3, "Whatever is a man's firm conviction, that he becomes." This means our convictions must be consciously cultivated rather than left to the unconscious.

Sankalpa (resolution), on the other hand, implies a resolution we imprint during practice. For example, if we hold a particular *mantra*, stanza, or *koan* in our mind during meditation or breath retention, or even during asana, this would be a *sankalpa*. A question in this context might be whether I can access *samadhi* just by changing my thought patterns. It is unlikely; in most cases, some additional work must be done. If the question were whether we could access *samadhi* without changing our thought patterns at all, then the answer again would be "unlikely." If we do not change our old thought patterns, they will remain an obstacle, even if we practice meditation daily. While *bhavana* and *sankalpa* alone cannot produce *samadhi*, *samadhi* is difficult to attain without them.

Here a few ideas for *bhavana* (cultivation) and *sankalpa* (resolution). The Divine bestowed the *samadhic* states upon all of us at the beginning of time. But we don't claim, own, accept, or receive them. In fact, we actively refuse to do so. This refusal comes primarily in the form of thought patterns such as the following:

- God does not exist. (So how can She teach me and bestow *samadhi* on me.)
- *Samadhi* does not exist. (How can I attain it, then?)
- I do not deserve to experience *samadhi*. (This thought makes it impossible to experience *samadhi*.)

- I care more about food, money, sex, power, real estate, pleasure, fame, and so on. (In which case, you will attain all of these,
  but not *samadhi.*)
- To make the mind ready for *samadhi* these thought patterns must be reversed, as follows:
- The Divine can teach me to the extent that I realize Her.
- *Samadhi* is my innermost nature.
- *Samadhi* is my birthright and my divine duty.
- Seek ye first the Kingdom of Heaven (*samadhi*) and everything else will be given.

To imprint these patterns you would review them daily before or after your meditation or upon waking or going to bed. The principle of *bhavana* and *sankalpa* is to focus the mind on what you want to attain, rather than on your present shortcomings. This principle has been taught in several popular books, often erroneously directed towards getting something you want. The true secret is to focus on what you want to *become* and what you want to *give.* The supreme *bhavana* is: "I am an embodiment of divine love and a conduit through which divine love radiates out to all beings." The general idea of *bhavana* (cultivation) is that you imagine yourself to be a small part of an infinite intelligence (which you *are,* but the mind may not be ready to accept this reality) and then step aside to allow this super-intelligence to direct your life.

MITAHARA (YOGIC DIET)

I have covered this subject in *Pranayama: The Breath of Yoga,* as pranayama is very sensitive to dietary mistakes. As T. Krishnamacharya put it, "It is always through wrong eating habit that they [practitioners] lose their merit." Although most important for *pranayama,* diet impacts all yogic disciplines. *Apana,* the vital downcurrent, is one of the main forces that holds Kundalini down (the other being gravitation). Yogis choose foods that aggravate *apana* as little as possible, although all foods aggravate it to some extent. It is no accident that most prophets and buddhas, etc., fasted through long periods — particularly preceding their peak experiences. Fasting also plays an important role in the spiritual quest of indigenous cultures, such as the Native American and Australian Aboriginal cultures. However, fasting is a fine art and should not be taken lightly. If you are interested, get a book on the subject written by a medical doctor who is specialized in fasting.

Apart from resorting to food that barely aggravates *apana* (fruit and vegetables are ideal), the yogic diet consists of three tenets: eat little, offer your food to the Divine, and only eat *sattvic* food. Apart from the quality of the food itself, the greater the quantity, the greater the *apanic* effect. A lithe body that is not as much under the sway of *apana* (vital downcurrent) presents less of an obstacle. I have noticed this myself, and it has been confirmed by sages, shamans, and yogis.

The next category is to eat mainly *sattvic* food. This is similar to avoiding *apanic* foods, but not the same. *Apanic* foods are those that increase the gravitational force in the body. *Sattvic* foods increase luminosity, intelligence, and wisdom. Opposed to these are *tamasic* foods, which make the mind dull, heavy, and inert (similar to *apanic*) and *rajasic* foods, which make us hot tempered, passionate, sense-indulgent, inflamed, egotistical, and covetous. Lists showing the influence of foods on the mind can be found in any book on yogic or Ayurvedic diet, and also in the *Mitahara* section of my book *Pranayama: The Breath of Yoga.*

The final advice is to offer one's food to the Divine, which means giving up the belief that food nurtures you. In truth, the Divine takes the food and, through millions of complicated processes, breaks it down into its constituents and then miraculously builds this marvelous body that actually works and functions. You could take 10,000 biologists and tell them to manufacture a body that can do everything ours can and give them a cartload of food to fuel that body, but they would fail in their endeavor. It is the Divine that turns so-called inert matter into a living body; it is the Divine that powers that body and lets it think and write symphonies and have experiences that make it spiritually evolve and eventually attain divine consciousness. It is a miracle, and yogis acknowledge that fact by offering each meal to the One that maintains us.

YOGIC PHILOSOPHY

The study of yogic scriptures (*shastras*) consists first and foremost of the *Yoga Sutra*. I have given a complete commentary on this text

Even in the days of the *Bhagavad Gita*, it was understood that self-knowledge (Jnana) was a high goal, unlikely to be achieved by many. It can't be achieved unless time and energy were invested to induct *prana* into *sushumna*, which usually involved a somewhat lengthy course of yogic techniques such as *asana*, *kriya*, *pranayama*, and meditation. With today's tendency toward feelings of entitlement, teachings that involve no effort and no time whatsoever are the most popular.

in *Ashtanga Yoga Practice and Philosophy* (Part 4). Understanding yogic philosophy enables you to integrate your spiritual experiences. Many people have had such experiences, but have not put them to practical use. Why not? Because we can't meaningfully integrate them into our lives. On a side note, in traditional *Advaita Vedanta* it is considered that the self can only be attained through scriptural study and not through personal experience (Shankara's *Brahma Sutra* commentary 2.1.3). Yoga differs on this. Personal experience is paramount but must be integrated through scriptural study. Many other texts are worthy of study, in addition to the *Yoga Sutra*.

In the past religions have placed too much emphasis on ethics by imposing ethical rules from the outside through threat and scare tactics, rather than growing them from the inside through realization. *Samadhi* gives us the ability to embody ethics naturally because we feel the pain of the 'other' in the same way we feel your own pain. This takes place because in objectless *samadhi* there is no more 'other.' The other being, whom in the past you may have harmed, hurt, lied to, stolen from, or fornicated with, is now experienced as your own self. "Love thy neighbor as thy self," will no longer be a philosophy but an experience.

KRIYAS

Kapalabhati and *Nauli* are important *kriyas* for *samadhi*. I have described them in detail in *Pranayama: The Breath of Yoga*. Please note that *Kapalabhati* can be practiced until *Kevala Kumbhaka* is reached, which leads automatically to *samadhi*. If you want to go down this avenue, read *Pranayama: The Breath of Yoga*. Ensure that all safety precautions are in place, and progress slowly. Progress that is too fast is the enemy of yogis. It will dishevel your life because you will see things you cannot yet digest; too intense of a practice is like opening Pandora's box.

Nauli is miraculous, as it ignites and increases inner fire (*agni*) and converts metabolic fire (*pitta*) into fire of intelligence. Again, it is better to progress slowly over a long period than to burn brightly and quickly burn out. Daily practice is more important than progress. Westerners especially are so obsessed with the idea of progression that sometimes they discontinue their practice because they cannot see improvements. Not progress but regularity in practice is what counts. The Hermann Hesse novel, *Siddhartha,* has an amazing and relevant parable. Siddhartha is a young and ambitious man who chases his luck with much effort. Each stage of his life is preceded by a rite of passage that is symbolized by a ferry ride across the same river, driven by the same old ferryman. During the first few passages, Siddhartha barely notices the ferryman, Vasudeva,

89

as he is too engulfed in this idea of progress. Eventually he asks the old man whether he ever had a yearning to go somewhere, do something, find a teacher, or learn something? Vasudeva's answer is critical. He says, "I don't need to go anywhere, do or learn anything. I listen to this river and it tells me everything I need to know. This river is my teacher and the sound of its waves contains everything that needs to be known. What reason would there be to go somewhere else? The same information would be learned anywhere else." The important component in Vasudeva's practice is not so much the river, but his ability to listen to what is already there. Consider how different this concept is from our idea of progress.

MUDRAS (PRANIC SEALS)

I have described some of the mudras in *Yoga Meditation*, where they form the Raja Yoga approach to *pratyahara* (independence from external stimuli). Some of these *mudras,* such as *Shambhavi Mudra* and *Jihva Bandha* (a mild version of *Khechari Mudra*), are extremely potent. In Chapter 6, I describe *Bhramari* and *Shanmukhi Mudras*, which are used to directly access *samadhi*.

JNANA YOGA

Similar to Bhakti Yoga, this is not an ancillary technique, but the pinnacle of yoga, to be practiced when Raja Yoga (*samadhi*) is completed. You will find an introduction to Jnana Yoga in Chapter 8 of this book, but I hope to cover it more thoroughly in a future volume. Today, Jnana Yoga has gained great popularity, with its promise that you don't have to do anything to attain it. This tendency towards instant gratification has always existed, but it appeals greatly to humanity's current modern expectations and entitlements. That's why the 14th-century *Hatha Yoga Pradipika* (IV: 113) ends with the stanza, "As long as the *prana* is not inducted into the central energy channel, all this jabber about Jnana is just the boastful prattle of madmen."

90

ETHICS

Patanjali defines ten ethical guidelines that form the bedrock of the *Yoga Sutras*. Rather than telling you, "thou shalt not," which nobody wants to hear, I will show how ethics naturally grow out of the *samadhic* state and, conversely, how their opposite impinges on attaining *samadhi*.

The first set of five ethical rules are the *yamas*, the restraints. These restraints are needed because, at this point, we are still in the early stages of our evolution and thus under the influence of animal brain circuitry (in yoga, symbolized by the three lower *chakras*). These urges initially need to be curbed to avoid the *karmic* boomerang, which in turn will intercept spiritual states. Once those states are achieved and evolution is propelled forward, ethics will develop from the inside out.

AHIMSA (HARMLESSNESS)

Ahimsa is the first *yama* (restraint). Although it is usually defined as non-violence, it goes much deeper. We need to abstain from any negativity towards others and ourselves in thought, word, and action. Even better is to maintain a positive attitude towards others. If they have slighted us, the yogi's best response is to forgive them immediately and wish them well. This way we can prevent negative conditioning from establishing itself in our minds. Needless to say, this is a slow process. It is common for us to hold grudges against others. If you become aware of them, don't beat yourself up; replace the grudges or resentments with a positive idea. In the *Gita* (X: 20), Lord Krishna says, "I am the self in the heart of all beings." If we can see each person we meet as a temple of the Divine, harmlessness (*ahimsa*) arises from within.

SATYA (TRUTH)

Speaking the truth has many meanings for yogis, not just abstinence from lying. One of these is to stay silent if nothing truthful can be said. The seeds of conflict are often sowed in moments of mindless gossiping. Yoga suggests we remain silent if nothing essential or meaningful can be said. One might ask themselves, "Is it true?" "Is it kind?" "Is it necessary?" If the answer is no, silence may be the best course. That being said, there are times when staying quiet is more harmful, times when we are called on to make a testimony of truth. But the most important aspect of truth is that which is written with a capital "T." To see the Divine manifested as consciousness, as the universe and all beings, is to see the Truth.

ASTEYA (NON-STEALING)

Patanjali states that if we are established in non-stealing, all riches will appear. The idea is that the entire world is our inheritance—not in the sense that we withhold it from others, but that we share it with others. From admitting this, from admitting how incredibly gifted we are, showered in abundance from the mere fact that we are alive in this world, an incredible inner wealth grows. Then non-stealing comes from the inside. Why would I steal if I know nothing can be taken from me? Because we are pure consciousness, the embodied self, we are forever that which enjoys the entire world.

BRAHMACHARYA (TO SEE CONSCIOUSNESS IN EVERYBODY)

A modern interpretation sees this as meaning celibacy. But it originally meant seeing Brahman (infinite consciousness) in everybody, everywhere. Only after centuries of Mogul rule and British Raj, as India became increasingly prudish, did the term take on this new meaning. Casual sex reduces another person to the body and ignores the infinite consciousness within them. Some yogic texts, such as *Vashishta Samhita* define *brahmacharya* as "*chastity*"; that is, to be faithful to one's lawful partner.

APARIGRAHA (NON-GREED)

Greed is essentially a belief in lack and therefore we are trying to appropriate something that is not ours. Higher yoga reveals the infinite abundance and creativity of the Divine. The Divine literally brings all into existence that can exist, fulfilling the law that "everything that can be, will be." This is the infinite potential of the Divine. In seeing this in the mystical state, greed vanishes.

The next five guidelines are the *niyamas* (observances). Whereas the *yamas* are directed outwards, the *niyamas* are directed inwards.

SHAUCHA (CLEANLINESS)

Cleanliness does refer to cleanliness of the body, but more importantly, it means we don't indulge in toxic thoughts or emotions. Through practicing the higher limbs, we recognize that the negative emotions we harbor against others are nothing but our own externalized inner conflicts. We hate others because of their similarity with what we see in ourselves. By accepting our own dark sides and shortcomings, we can forgive ourselves and thus let go of any polluted thoughts or emotions we have towards others. The very concept of "other" implies we can insulate ourselves from the suffering of other individuals. Although we may be able to uphold this delusion for a while, the suffering of others will eventually break through and manifest as our own suffering.

SANTOSHA (CONTENTMENT)

Contentment is realizing the world is a reflection of Divine perfection. Any layer of imperfection has been introduced by humanity, watering down something eternally perfect. The world is in balance, but humanity has introduced imbalance by superimposing its concepts onto it. The deteriorating influence of humanity is the result of our inability to see the eternal perfection at our core, the pure consciousness. Once this is realized, we will see the perfection in the world and within us again.

In our current situation, it is not enough to withdraw into consciousness and say everything is perfect. Due to our long and serious corrupting influence on the world and on Mother Earth, we must

93

SAMADHI : THE GREAT FREEDOM

now embark on a course of action to restore the original balance of divine order. Then happiness and equanimity will be restored.

TAPAS (ABILITY TO ACCEPT DISCOMFORT)

Tapas is the strength to abstain from unnecessary actions. Many of our modern problems would cease to exist if we stopped doing unnecessary things, such as killing time in trivial pursuits or saying things we later regret. *Tapas* is the strength to perform the actions that will provoke and stabilize our spiritual evolution. When we evolve, parts of ourselves surge ahead, while other parts, those that are comfortable with the status quo, hold us back. *Tapas* is the ability to sustain that friction and boldly move forward despite the discomfort.

SVADHYAYA (QUEST FOR THE TRUE SELF)

Self-study means to place the self first. It is the sincerity that yearns for our true essence, rather than the petty pastimes our current society ensnares us with. We worship celebrities instead of realizing the importance of our own life for the Divine. We are watching television and playing computer games instead of having a life of our own making. We are entertained by sports and shows that overcome our boredom, which is a sign that we are not truly alive. We are killing time because we are bored, only to regret our missed life when on our deathbed. We are working ourselves to exhaustion to make a fortune, only to have a nervous breakdown, descend into depression, or discover that we have a terminal disease. Who are we? What is our true identity? What is the purpose of our life? *Svadhyaya* prioritizes the desire to answer these questions and to not give up, even if repeated attempts to unveil our true nature fail. *Svadhyaya* is the commitment to place oneself in the service of this quest.

ISHVARA PRANIDHANA (PLACING YOURSELF IN THE SERVICE OF THE DIVINE)

This is covered in more detail in Chapter 4. To surrender to the Divine

94

in its three aspects—the holy trinity of God Transcendent (or *nirguna* Brahman as the Father), God Immanent (the universe or divine creative force as Shakti or the Mother), and the individual (or *purusha*) as the son—means to see and treat the entire manifest cosmos as the body of the Divine, to treat all beings as children of the Divine, and to experience one's own pure consciousness as God Transcendent, the point where we are intimately connected and one with the Divine.

You can achieve *samadhi* without covering all of these ancillary techniques, but the more you leave out, the less quickly your success will come. None of these limbs and techniques by themselves causes *samadhi*. The more areas you cover, the greater your likelihood of success. Patanjali summarizes the right attitude to all of these practices in sutra I.14: "One becomes firmly established in practice only after attending to it for a long time, without interruption, and with an attitude of devotion." Even if we are established in all aspects of yoga, we should not expect quick success, but should sustain the practices in a joyful mood and in service to the Divine until success is achieved, however long it may take.

Chapter 4
READINESS FOR SAMADHI AND GRACE

This chapter is about consecrating yourself to the Divine and its importance for *samadhi*. Even ten years into yoga, I found this extremely difficult to stomach and can certainly understand if you do so now. Due to my very heavy-handed Catholic upbringing (this is not a general statement against Catholicism at large), I had a negative attitude towards all things religious and have found that many modern people today share this scar of deep distrust. In the early days I felt nauseous when some of my Indian teachers, being of the *bhakta* variety, embarked on devotional talk. If you find material dealing with the love of the Divine difficult, then feel free to go ahead in the text and come back when you are ready.

GOD IS NOT ANTHROPOMORPHIC

The problem with our idea of the Divine is we think we know what God is, but we don't. We have reversed the claim that "the human is made in the image of the Divine" to state that God is made in the image of man. We have made the Divine anthropomorphic. Because we have projected a human ego onto God, our relationship to the Divine has broken down. We think of God as some aloof and irate tyrant, sitting above the clouds not caring about us (maybe striking somebody down with a lightning bolt or sending a flood once in a while), because that's how we interact with each other. However, the statement that man was created in the image of God means we consist of:

- Pure consciousness (sometimes called spirit or the self).
- I-am-ness or sense-of-I, that is the knowledge that we exist as a being.
- Matter (in India called prakrti, or nature), which means

97

we have a body and we have a mind that takes care of
the survival of the body.

The difference between us and the Divine is that the Divine's body, the sum total of all universes, is infinite and eternal and the I-am-ness of the Divine is omnipresent and omnipotent in these universes. We, on the other hand, have a body that is limited in time and space, and we need to mind its survival. This is where we fall into the trap of identifying with the body, which means that our *own* "I-am-ness" is colored by the limitations of the physical body. Knowing the limitations of the body, we believe our consciousness to be limited as well. This is what we typically call "ego" or "mutative ego," or even "egotism." It is the superstitious belief that we are isolated beings living in a hostile or indifferent universe in which we must compete for limited resources with similar robotic beings who are powered by the same selfish genes.

We project this mutated selfishness onto our perception of the Divine. But the Divine, while it has I-am-ness and beingness, does not have a limited and limiting ego, as we do. The implications of this have not been understood. Because the Divine is infinite, eternal, and formless, it does not have an ego from which to withhold grace or from which to favor one person, tribe, or nation over another. We have projected this idea of our own physical limitations onto the Divine; and from this grew the notion of a "God" who is miserly, who withholds grace, and who dislikes us or doesn't care about us. This flawed thinking exposed us to self-loathing and unworthiness.

The Divine cannot know or understand our self-loathing and feeling unworthy, because it is eternally perfect and cannot know anything contrary to its own nature. The Divine knows only our own eternal perfection, as this is consistent with its nature. Because we are free, we are also free to reject this essential unity with the Divine and, with it, the grace that flows from the Divine to all of us at all times. Grace is an eternal act that ever flows to all beings. It is we who, in identifying with the body, limit ourselves to the finite and impermanent and therefore develop judgments about ourselves, such as being powered and determined by selfish genes, which lead to self-loathing. Deep down we can never accept such judgments and concepts, as we remember ourselves as one with the Divine. Inner strife and self-hatred develop from the strife between our intuitive knowing that we are children of the Divine and the belief that we are selfish gene-powered beings.

By re-evaluating ourselves and the Divine, we may come to the understanding that God is infinite beauty, love, intelligence, freedom, and grace. If God had an ego by which to withhold grace, God could not be eternal and infinite, since ego implies limitation. Because God is egoless, it is implied that grace is always showered upon us, but we don't accept it. The belief in our own unworthiness (unfortunately co-constructed through the religious erroneous teaching of sin) is what cuts us off from grace. Because our unity with the Divine is willed by the Divine, and the Divine is omnipotent, there is nothing we can do to interrupt or destroy it. Grace is here right now; all we need to do is be willing to receive.

ASKING FOR GUIDANCE, CONSECRATION

It may seem the previous passages are removed from the practical situations of our lives. But this is entirely of our own making. So, how do we return to the eternal wellspring of divine love? To resume our contact with the Divine, we ask for divine guidance. This

> **Q: What is meant by "belief"?**
> **A:** A hair-raising intimate encounter with God, and then out of this encounter, a visceral embodiment of God-realization.

guidance will come tentatively at first, but as we begin to trust in it, it will become more and more obvious. It is impossible to re-

99

ceive guidance if we already reject the Divine. You can only receive guidance to the extent that you acknowledge and realize Her.
It is necessary to have a personal relationship with the Divine in
order to receive guidance. There is nothing from "God's side" that
prevents such a relationship; our own rejection of the Divine is what
prevents it. Once we start to meditate over these facts, our refusal to let
God enter becomes increasingly untenable, until we finally give it up.

So, the first step is to ask the Divine for guidance. Now that we
know this guidance cannot be withheld, we also know that if we feel
we don't receive such guidance, it is simply our refusal to listen to
it. We then enter into a phase of pronounced listening and stillness.
One of the most powerful *sankalpas* (affirmations) for meditation is,
"I am now so still that I can hear God." Say this sentence to yourself
at the beginning of your meditation session and then *listen*. If the
thought returns, repeat the sentence again. I cannot think of a more
powerful way to end self-limiting thought. This is Bhakti Yoga.

Once you hear the voice of the Divine (this of course metaphorical,
in most cases there is no auditory sensation), the next step is to con-
secrate your life to the Divine. Rather than thinking, "I am a small,
scared individual trying to figure out what to do," think of yourself as
a servant of the Divine. Hand over all decisions, all thoughts, all actions, to the Divine. In the *Gita,* Krishna calls this, "surrendering the
fruits of all actions to Me." A beautiful story in the Bible illustrates
the point further. At some point Jesus told the disciples they should
go out and teach in his name. The disciples said, "But Rabbi, we don't
know what to say." Jesus' answer was, "Leave now and I'll tell you
what to say when you get there!" The message is simple: if you have
consecrated yourself to the Divine, the Divine will speak through you.

TOTAL ACCEPTANCE

Because we realize our limitations (and it is good that we do), it is
difficult to reach *samadhi* without any external aid. The most powerful help for accessing this state is projecting the power to bestow *sa-*

madhi onto an external, omnipotent agent (rather than on yourself). Of course ultimately it is we who remove the obstacles, but the easiest way to get there is to project this power onto an external agent. This agent should always be the Divine itself and never a human guru. This method will fail when the power to bestow realization is projected onto a human teacher, as we humans are limited. If we give this power to human gurus, we take it away from the Divine, who is the only rightful owner. The fifth chapter of this book is dedicated to withdrawing this projection of power from human gurus. Do not place an intermediary between you and God. We have done so in the past and it has made us collaborators in the crimes of religion.

After having asked for guidance and self-consecration, the final step is total acceptance of the state of *samadhi*. When Paramahamsa Ramakrishna was asked how he attained *samadhi* his answer was, "Through total acceptance of the gift of *samadhi* from the Divine." This is the most direct way! I am not saying the other methods suggested in this text should not be practiced, but they should be supplemented and crowned with this effort of Bhakti Yoga. Initially we may struggle to succeed. Then we must ask ourselves, "In what way is my acceptance of the Divine gift and my surrender to the Divine not complete? Where am I holding back?" Asking in such a way will bring about a deep spiritual revolution.

You may wonder, where is this Divine whom you ask me to surrender to and accept *samadhi* from? Regarding God, we are like

Q: Practically speaking, what does it mean to "admit" this?
A: Our philosophies of life, whether we follow a religious or scientific paradigm, are based on the belief that we are limited beings and that "out there" is the "other," whether this be other people, the environment, or the infidels. In most cases, it is an "other" that we have to defend ourselves against. In the Old Testament this belief started with us eating from the tree of knowledge of good and evil. These are loaded terms, but essentially they stand for God and

non-God or anti-God. When we ate from this metaphorical tree, we started to believe there is non-God, and we became aware of our nakedness. We had to cover up and were expelled from the Garden of Eden and the whole multi-millennia warfare of Kain versus Abel started, which is nothing but war against ourselves.

Today we are still naked, still fighting against ourselves and each other because we still believe there is an "other" to fight against. Psychologically, this is nothing but a part of our psyche fighting against another part, whether we call it the communists, the fascists, the capitalists, the jihadis, etc. Religiously, this is exemplified in the belief in a Devil, the anti-Christ. To propose a Devil is to not know that there is and can only be the Divine. We have projected our own split personality onto God by proposing a Devil. We have constructed a Devil and the corresponding evil within us to prove to ourselves that God cannot exist.

These are powerful beliefs, and while some may say they are not religious and have a scientific worldview, this acceptance of our evil and sinful nature, expelled us from paradise, our symbiotic oneness with nature. Because of that, we could no longer live naked within nature and in harmony with its laws but had to overcome, subdue, control, and exploit them. This led to the whole Gallilean-Cartesian-Newtonian trajectory of rising above and controlling nature and now is finally leading us to the abyss of ecocide and our own extinction.

In the symbolic language of the Bible, to eat from that other tree that grew in the Garden of Eden, the tree of eternal life, is admitting that all matter, all beings, and everything that exists is nothing but the crystallized body of the Divine. We ejected ourselves from the Garden by eating from the tree of good and evil, by accepting that there is a force that effectively neutralizes the Divine. Admitting that this was an error, that there is only the Divine, re-admits us to the Garden.

"Admitting there is nothing in consciousness, in the material world, or amongst the trillions of beings that is not God" means radically ending this trajectory, the conflict of Kain against Abel, the war against ourselves, and the belief in our own evil. It means accepting our own nakedness, which means we are not shielded by nature but live in symbiotic exchange with it. It means we admit there is no "other" and no Devil and that we have left the Garden of Eden only in our imagination. It is still around us and we are welcome to take off the blindfold and start to see again.

Because our whole society and civilization for the last 10,000 years has been built on this foundation of the "other," the anti-God, and therefore our own contamination with 'evil,' it is difficult to say what will happen when we make this shift. It will be nothing short of the birth a new civilization based on harmony with each other, nature, and the Divine. While it is difficult to imagine how this could pan out, it is easy to estimate what will happen if we continue to maintain this error in thinking and move along the technological trajectory: we will follow the same destiny as the 50 percent of species we have already made extinct. I am not saying that science is evil; what I am saying is that our alienation from ourselves and nature (embodied in the myth of the tree of knowledge of good and evil) culminated in our modern concept of science and technology, which we use to manipulate, harness, control, subdue, and exploit nature.

certain tribal forest people who have no word for forest in their language, because they have no experience or concept of non-forest. They have never been outside of it. Similarly there is nothing in the world, in our experience or make-up, that is not God. Because we don't have an experience of non-God, we believe we cannot see God, just as a fish has no concept of the ocean. The truth is, there is nothing in our experience that is not Divine; as there *is* *only* the Divine. When we have admitted there is nothing in consciousness, in the material world, or amongst the trillions of beings that is not God, then we are ready to accept the gift of *samadhi*.

THE DIVINE IN THE YOGA SUTRA

The following section will trace Bhakti Yoga in the *Yoga Sutra*. I will delve into stanza II.45 of the *Yoga Sutra*, as it relates to stanzas II.1, II.32, and I.21–I.29 and their manifold repercussions. Sutra II.45 says, "From devotion to the Supreme Being comes the attainment of *samadhi*," thus linking the attainment of *samadhi* directly to the Divine. I have used "devotion to the Supreme Being" to translate the Sanskrit term *ishvara pranidhana*. Another way of translating it would be "surrender to the Divine" or "love of God." The term *Ishvara* in Patanjali's parlance doesn't stand for a particular form of the Divine or a deity; you are expected to find your own path.

Before I go deeper into this line of thought, I should point out that Patanjali uses this term, *ishvara pranidhana*, four times in the *Yoga Sutra*. In sutra I.23 he says, "Or from devotion to *Ishvara.*" The 'or' here links this sutra to sutra I.20, where he says, "The objectless *samadhi* of yogis is preceded by conviction, enthusiasm, remembrance, objectless *samadhi*, and knowledge." One could argue that Patanjali offers an alternative approach here—that of surrender to the Divine, which replaces the set of five different qualities of attainments the yogi needs. From my experience, Patanjali is suggesting we "add love of the Divine to the five attainments." He didn't include "love of the Divine" in the original list because he did not consider it to be equal to each of the five, but as important as all of them put together.

Then Patanjali mentions *ishvara pranidhana* in stanza II.1. This stanza is in response to a student who was confused by the, quite advanced, first chapter of the *Sutra*. The student asks, "What if all this talk so far went right over my head?" So, Patanjali suggests that beginners start with beginner's yoga (Kriya Yoga), which is mainly comprised of the study of sacred texts and love of the Divine. It is important to note that Patanjali didn't think love of the Divine was something that could be added later, but that it should be present from the very start. In my own life, this was one of the last aspects of yoga to develop, and I believe it was because—as

Q: What is the problem with looking at God as anthropomorphic?
A: Anthropomorphic means having human characteristics. Because we cannot imagine a being that is infinite and eternal, we have projected our own limitations onto It, such as a human ego and personality traits. We imagine God to be a giant human projected into the sky and to some extent most religions have fallen for this. Unless we completely give up the idea that we know what or how the Divine is, we can neither learn from It nor develop an authentic spirituality guided by Her. The Divine is the force behind our evolution, but if we imagine God as a human, we limit the Divine to ideas about ourselves. To see God as anthropomorphic thus hampers our own evolution.

many modern Westerners are—I was thoroughly traumatized and repulsed by the role religion has played in our history. However, I learned to separate the essence of religion and spirituality from what millenniums of corruption and power-broking turned it into. In all sacred traditions of humanity, you can still find this divine essence that provided their initial impetus, despite what has happened since their inception as an organized religion.

Patanjali mentions devotion to the Divine (*ishvara pranidhana*) again in stanza II.32, the section where he explains the eight-limbed (Ashtanga) yoga in more detail. Devotion to the Divine is one of the five observances (*niyamas*), the second limb of yoga. Ashtanga Yoga in Patanjali's system is a mid-tier yoga, which the student practices once he has cleared initial hurdles (addressed by Kriya Yoga), but before he is capable of tackling *samadhi* head-on (called *Samadhi Yoga* or, in Sage Vyasa's language, simply 'Yoga'). Patanjali thus advises the yogi to add "love of the Divine" at each level of yoga practice, but in sutra II.45, he finally creates a causal relationship between it and *samadhi*. He says, "from surrender to the Divine comes *samadhi*." Thus Patanjali implies this devotion or surrender is the pinnacle of all yoga and that all steps before are meant to lead you to it.

The Divine is not only undifferentiated unity, but also multiplicity, as otherwise there would be no "real" universe. The Divine being infinite, there cannot be any place or being where it is not. While the Divine AS ME does anything I do, all phenomena together (shopping centers, goods, cars, customers, and the sum total of all parallel universes) are the God immanent; conciousness that observes them is the God transcendent. It is not possible to be bereft of the Divine as there is *only* the Divine.

In order to understand what Patanjali means by the term "Divine," we must let go of our preconceptions about this word and start afresh. When I was young, I quickly understood that the "God" whom I was taught was just an extrapolation of human qualities, a projection of our own limitations. Instead of a human being made in the image of God, I was offered a God made in the image of human beings, in other words, an anthropomorphic God.

This God had all the weaknesses we have. He would get agitated, vengeful, jealous, angry, and—perhaps worst of all—he "changed his mind" and apparently rebranded himself (when the New Testament replaced the Old). This confirmed philosopher Feuerbach's thesis that God is only a representation of the current values of a society. As you can guess from my frequent quoting of both the Old and the New Testaments, I greatly value both scriptures. The problem is how each was interpreted and communicated through theology in the last 2000 years.

In sutra I.24, Patanjali says *Ishvara* is a distinct form of consciousness (*purusha*), which is untouched by the modes of suffering, and untouched by *karma*, its fruit and its residue. Patanjali says the Divine is not just some underlying first cause or formless Absolute (*nirguna* Brahman). *Ishvara* is not just the universe, the unified field, or the cause of all reality. He says the Divine is a distinct being (*purusha vishesha*). The term *purusha* appears already in the *Vedas*, where it means *cosmic being* or *cosmic person*. In fact, the English person is derived from the Sanskrit *purusha*. Patanjali most often uses the term *purusha* instead of the Vedantic *atman* (the self) to imply that you have your *purusha* and I have mine. The term *atman,* rather, implies there is one self that we all share and that has its own beauty. We'll discuss this in detail later. Thus the term *purusha* is a bit closer to the idea of "soul" as used in the Abrahamic religions, and it means embodied consciousness.

Patanjali says the Divine is a distinct being; but he goes on to qualify it further. In sutra I.24, he says the Divine is not subject to the modes of suffering (*kleshas*). This statement has not been sufficiently considered. The modes of suffering are ignorance (*avidya*), egoity (*asmita*), desire (*raga*), aversion (*dvesha*), and fear (*abhiniveshah*)—of which we all experience a fair share. Let's look at egoity and explain the repercussions.

In sutra I.24, Patanjali says that God does not have an ego/egoity. If you think about it for a moment, a being that is all-pervading and all-knowing cannot also have an ego, because ego limits one to a particular point in space and time. For example, if I come out of a shopping center, my ego reminds me which car to pick from the lot. That's a good thing! If I were an egoless Divinity, I would come out of the shopping center and enter all cars in the lot simultaneously. Let's ponder the matter more deeply. Because I wouldn't be limited in space, I would actually enter all cars in all lots of all shopping centers of the world, simultaneously. But the problem doesn't end there. Because I am unlimited by time, I would also simultaneously enter all cars parked on all lots in the past and future. And I wouldn't be limited to cars, either. Having no ego, I wouldn't think it below my dignity to hop on bullock carts nor beyond my expertise to enter jet fighters or spaceships or any other mode of transportation that has ever been invented. In fact I would eternally project myself forth from, enter into, and rest within all phenomena, whether they be the tiniest atom or the hugest celestial body. I would be equally at home enlivening all beings, from the humblest of all amoe-

107

bas to Alexander the Great and all so-called inert matter, from the smallest speck of dust to the largest of black holes. And this is exactly what the Divine does! But this also means the Divine cannot limit itself to a particular universe, a single car park, a certain car, with an individual person in it, a person like you and me. This is where we enter the equation. The Divine manifests itself through us as infinite permutations of beingness, but more on that later.

Now the repercussions of being an egoless entity are endless, but most important for now is that God does not have an ego by which to withhold *samadhi* from you. It is the ego that limits us. It is due to ego that we can "say no." If we say, "you are not good enough, you don't live up to my expectations, you didn't stick to the rules I gave you," our ego is the point of reference. "I" am making this judgment. "I" am using this and that information to make the judgment, and "I" say you are not good enough. Because the Divine is total giving-ness (meaning that it is life-affirming, loving, giving, and cannot withhold) and perfection, infinite and eternal, it cannot pass judgment. This realization is revolutionary, considering our outdated idea of God as an irate man and a wrathful tyrant, who sends floods, locusts, plagues, and more. Please take time to ponder the many repercussions of realizing that God does not have an ego, brings.

One repercussion is that the only person who withholds *samadhi* from us (or the "act of grace," as it is called in some cultures) is ourselves. The mere fact that *samadhi* is called the *"natural state"* implies it is an attainable state, not outside of our reach. It is, as I have previously argued, our birthright and our divine duty. We are the only ones who stand in our own way of reaching *samadhi* and it was us, too, that exited ourselves from the mythical Garden of Eden. We chose to leave the Garden of Eden ourselves, because for God to have exiled us, this God would require ego. No God is required for this; we are our own most merciless judges.

In sutra I.24 Patanjali implies the Divine is not touched by nor feels ignorance (*avidya*). "Ignorance" is the belief that we are our body and our mind, when in fact, we are pure consciousness. It is the belief that we are finite and temporary, when in fact we are infinite and eternal. It is the belief that we are conditioned by our surroundings, whereas consciousness is eternally free and unstained.

Again, here, the repercussions are endless. The significance of this is profound. The Divine exists in a state of unalloyed truth, which we decided to leave due to ignorance (as represented by the myth of the exit of Eden). We are ignorant of the truth that we are consciousness, but the Divine is ever established in this truth and thus cannot feel nor be touched by the artificial world our ignorance has created, a world in which we believe we are not free. This is akin to saying the Divine does not know our present state, as our state is not in harmony with Divine perfection. Because we are consciousness (*purusha*), we are necessarily eternally free—and that is the truth.

This artificial world of ignorance, ego, pain, desire, and fear cannot touch the Divine. The Divine cannot know anything contrary to its nature and thus can only know our perfection, not our perceived shortcomings. We see this in the biblical metaphor of Adam and Eve. Prior to their eating from the tree of good and evil, we only knew what the life-affirmative Divine knew. This is called "the knowledge of creation," or "affirmation of good" and is the knowledge that we cannot be separate from God. After eating from the tree, we became aware of good and evil. "Evil" is metaphorical for life-negating and the belief that we can be separated or estranged from nature and God. It is an ignorant and self-imposed belief. In fact, we are forever one, united with the Divine, and no human will can undo this. However, because we have erroneously revoked the covenant with the Divine, change must come from us. The Divine, being eternal perfection, cannot even conceive that a part of itself (that is, us) could imagine being separate from the whole; this entire thought is contrary to Divine nature. Our realization that we have never been separated from the Divine will open us to receive the constant and eternal bestowing of grace—grace that was never withheld in the first place.

109

In sutra I.25 Patanjali says, "In the One (*Ishvara*), all-knowing is unsurpassed." This means all knowledge (that is lawful or in accordance with Divine law) rests in the Divine. All physical laws, gravitation, how the world is built from the smallest atom to a quasar, the entire evolution of life, the DNA, the table of isotopes, the make-up of mind, what consciousness is, all sacred knowledge of how to live in harmony with life—all of it rests in the Divine. The Divine cannot know psychosis or anything in contrast to divine law. As pointed out in the previous sutra, all states that are the result of conditioning, modes of suffering, *karma*, and so on, are based on the false assumption that we are the body and not infinite consciousness. Being outside of Divine law, none of these states can touch the Divine, nor can the Divine feel or experience them.

I can understand your fear because I have experienced fear. I can understand your pain because I have experienced pain. I am reminded of these through you; I can say, "Yes I have been there. I know how that feels." This is not the case with the Divine. Because these states cannot be felt by the Divine and because they are contrary to its nature, God cannot come to our rescue. There is no point in saying the current state of the world and all suffering are proof that God does not exist. God is not aware of anything but total perfection. We have created our own misery and we must now extract ourselves from it.

In Sutra I.26, Patanjali says, "The Supreme Being is the teacher of the other teachers, since the One is not limited by time." Patanjali is saying that all sacred traditions go back to the one Divine. However long a lineage of true sacred tradition is, at its end you will always find the fountainhead that is the Divine. The sacred traditions of humanity and much of the indigenous knowledge that has enabled us to live in harmony with nature is based on Divine revelation. This sutra implies we must show respect for those ancient teachings. It also means that because the ancient and original teacher is eternal and independent of time, She is here right now. This is confirmed in the *Bhagavad Gita* when Krishna says to Arjuna, "This most ancient knowledge I have previously taught to Vivashvat and Manu. Lost through the long passage of time I am teaching it now to you (*Bhagavad Gita* IV.1–3)." Love of the Divine makes us ready to receive transmissions of knowledge from Her. Those transmissions are always taking place. It is impossible for the Divine to withhold them from us, because She is pure love. It is us who are not listening. Love of the Divine means bringing ourselves to a state where we can listen to what She is saying. Loving the Divine is the frequency that opens us to the message of beauty, love, intelligence, and freedom that She is continuously sending us.

One way this is communicated to us is through our ability to see beauty and harmony, especially in nature. And yet we seem to be trying our best to destroy it. It is easy to see the Divine in a misty sunrise over the rainforest, but harder to see it in the concrete jungles we have created that are full of crime, frustration, violence, anguish, depression, and pollution. We are currently engaged in a game of veiling, of violating, the Divine.

If we practice yoga sincerely, the Divine cannot but turn towards us and teach us. And it will teach us to exactly that extent that we realize Her. She cannot teach us if we deny Her; it cannot be any other way. It has been said that when Columbus and Captain Cook first reached faraway shores, the indigenous people could not see the European ships. We can't verify that claim, but it makes sense. They couldn't see the ships because they had no concept of or experience with such ships. So it is with the Divine. Its voice is there, but we are so distracted by the noise in our heads that we cannot hear it. We listen to everybody and everything but have lost even the concept of a divine teacher instructing us at all times. Vast ships are anchoring right before our shores, yet we cannot see them.

In my own life, this voice of the Divine was very faint at first. In fact, the reason I couldn't hear it was because of all the noise, the thoughts swirling around in my head. I found *ishvara pranidhana*—surrender to the Divine—the most profound way

SAMADHI : THE GREAT FREEDOM

of becoming silent. One of my favorite meditation techniques is to simply listen and become more and more silent, so that everything the Divine teaches can be heard. And this refers not only to the outer ear, but the inner ear, as well. The more silence there is from within, the louder the Divine voice will become.

In sutra I.27, Patanjali says that God's expression is the sacred syllable OM. Some yoga scholars argue that Patanjali does not subscribe to the idea that God created the world. May they be blessed! In fact, he says that and so much more. According to Patanjali, there is nothing *but* God! When we sit down and pronounce the word *OM*, we are basically humming. That's why some commentators who read this sutra simply imagine a person (in this case, *Ishvara*), who is immortal and all-knowing, but still sitting in the corner humming. This is not what OM means. OM means OMnipresent, OMniscient, and OMnipotent. It is the roar of electrons circling around atomic nuclei; it is the thunder of Higgs Boson particles crashing into each other in the Large Hadron Collider; it is the first cry of all babies ever born and the last exhalation released on your deathbed. It is the sound of our sun exploding into a supernova four or five billions years from now, when it will supposedly incinerate our beautiful planet Earth. It is the sound of the paradise bird at sunrise and the Titanic hitting the iceberg. It is the sound of Beethoven's ninth symphony and the gunshot that killed Martin Luther King. It is the sound of the nuclear bomb dropped on Hiroshima and of Luis Armstrong's "What a beautiful world." It's the song of the lover in rapture and the lie of the politician; it is the cracking of tectonic plates shifting, and the rushing of rivers towards the ocean. It is the sound of all moments of guilt, shame, fame, glory, love, and defeat combined with those of all beings who ever existed and ever will exist. It is the sound of wind, fire, water, earth, and space. It is the silence of the Buddha under the Bodhi tree and the voice of Jesus saying, "Lazarus, come forth." It is the sound of a massive intelligence, transforming itself into everything while remaining miraculously unchanged in the process. It is everything. Our rise and our demise as a civilization, everything we know, don't know, and will never know is OM. Knowledge of all civilizations that have been, those that are scattered through space, and all of those to come are OM. All matter and all forms of energy are vibratory patterns of that one presence that is everywhere in everything and which expresses itself through everything as everything. That one presence expresses itself as kinetic energy, as potential energy, as electrical energy, and as magnetism. It is the alpha and the omega, the beginning, middle, and end of all phenomena and beings. It is, "Be still and know that I am God."

Yoga is experiential. OM must be experienced, and it's meaning cannot be inferred from scholars speculating on words. Once OM is experienced, the realization dawns that there never was, never is, and never will be anything real that is not God. "In the beginning was the word and the word was with God and the word was God." That is the true meaning of OM. By means of this primordial vibratory pattern, the Divine transforms itself to become the phenomena, the material universe, and all beings. In this sutra, Patanjali says there is nothing but God. This statement cannot be intellectually understood. It must be experienced so closely that your hair stands, breath stops, and heart wants to jump out of your chest.

Sutra I.28 then states, "Repetition of OM and contemplation of its meaning should be made." When I studied Hindi in India in the 1980s, I learned from a first-grade schoolbook, and one of the first sentences was, "The *rishi* (seer) sits by the river and silently chants OM." It

Q: What is meant by "sacred texts"?
A: The Sanskrit term *shastra* can be translated as "sacred text" or "scripture," but word-by-word it actually means "path to truth." It is used for texts that remind us of our connection with the Divine. Although the term in yoga is usually reserved for Sanskrit, Vedic, or Tantric texts, here it is used for sacred texts of all wisdom traditions of humanity.

SAMADHI : THE GREAT FREEDOM

concerns me that these schoolbooks don't exist anymore and that now India is in a mad scramble to catch up with the West. But why? Did you know that more people in our children's movies get killed than during adult entertainment? It seems we are breeding a new culture of violence, or at least indifference towards violence. How can we rediscover the original love affair with our own hearts that we had as small children? Where is the fresh laughter, the joy of seeing a bird or butterfly, the happiness experienced in the arms of a loved one? This emotion is invoked by the knowledge that we are an integrated part of nature and that we—the planet, the trees, the rivers, the mountains, the animals, and all people—are one family and one creation.

Patanjali suggests we sit by the side of the river and silently chant OM, like that *rishi* in the Indian schoolbook. Sutra I.28 says the sacred syllable should be chanted while its meaning (see previous sutra, I.27) is contemplated and understood. We simply chant the *mantra* until we hear the sacred utterance, emitted by the Divine, returning to us. To hear OM is to hear all sounds and all creation, entering and uniting into this one sound. It is the mother of all wave patterns; it is the sound of the Big Bang.

Sutra I.29 then declares, "From that [chanting of OM] the consciousness turns inward and the obstacles disappear." For centuries our culture has turned consciousness outwards and sneered at spirituality. We have been told that conquering the outer world and nature is our salvation. An increasing number of people admit that this entire agenda has failed, but humanity is still on this track. Freedom is not found in amassing goods or conquering nature. It is found within. In the ancient days of the *Upanishads*, chanting OM was the most popular form of meditation. Part of this practice is to contemplate the fact that OM is the utterance of the Divine. If we can embody that, realize that, then OM leads to intercepting the obstacles and to knowledge of the self (consciousness).

I introduced the obstacles in Chapter Two. There are nine different obstacles (sutra I.30), located in three different tiers or layers: the

114

Q: **In "Seek ye the Kingdom of Heaven," we are told the only thing we must seek is God. So how does this mesh with Her giving us whatever we ask for? Do these include material things?**
A: "Seek ye first the Kingdom of Heaven and everything else will be added on" means we should make God our only goal and we will end up with God *and* everything else we require, including material things.

Q: **What about all people who believe AND ask and yet still do not receive "whatever they ask for?"**
A: It is difficult for me to talk about all people, as we would have to look at them case by case. Many of the ones I talked to hampered their efforts by consciously doing one thing and subconsciously another. The above biblical quote asks for the complete alignment of conscious, subconscious, and super-conscious (divine) mind. To understand this we need to look at the underlying logic of Jesus' quote in Matthew 21.22: "All things ye ask in prayer, believing [that ye have received], ye shall receive." This is a powerful teaching. Jesus affirms there is no separation between us and creation. In my language this would be "admitting that ye have received, ye receive." What he means is that the only entity hindering us from receiving is our own self. We have already received. God cannot withhold because God has no ego through which to withhold; but we can refuse to receive the gift by not being in alignment with the Divine. In other words, asking is one thing but ending the alienation from the gift, nature, and the Divine in everything is another. It is our own "stone-heartedness" (as Jesus would call it) that makes it impossible for us to embrace the gift.

body, breath, and mind (sutra I.31). Apart from purging these three layers from the nine obstacles, the other beneficial effect of chanting and meditating on OM is that consciousness, which is directed outwards in the normal state, now turns in and eventually onto itself, which is called "the natural state." This links to sutra I.3, where Patanjali says that, when the mind is suspended, the seer (consciousness) rests in itself. Most of the time we are not resting deep within, in the natural state, but rather stumbling through the world, ignorant of our unity with the Divine. This has become the new normal.

But how do we find a suitable approach to the Divine? Yoga does not tell you to adopt somebody else's beliefs. There is a wavelength, a frequency on which you can hear the Divine, like listening to your favorite radio station. Listening to a station you don't like can be alienating. That's why you cannot force people down a spiritual path that feels alien to them. You must find your own path, your own approach. How do you do that? Your own frequency, the wavelength upon which you can understand the Divine is called your *ishtadevata* in yoga (i.e., the form of the Divine that you can relate to).

YOUR ISHTADEVATA

Sutra II.44 says you will find your form of the Divine by studying sacred texts. When reading sacred texts, observe whether you have a strong emotional reaction to a particular form of the Divine. If not, go on to a different sacred text that deals with a different form. Once you have found a form of the Divine to which you have a strong and positive reaction, this could qualify as your *ishtadevata*. Although this is a Sanskrit term, under no circumstance are you limited to a Hindu divine form. Whatever you are attracted to (from Christian to Taoist, or indigenous spiritual concepts) is suitable and "allowed." Do not let anybody else tell you what's right or wrong; find out what works for you. It is important that your divine form is life-affirming. If it tells you to destroy something or kill somebody, it is likely the projection of somebody else's ego and not a genuine divine form. Also be sure that your spiritual role model has a traditional background and is genuinely worshipped in one of the sacred traditions.

Then you may start the practice of Bhakti Yoga. This means that each day you focus intensely and meditate on your *ishtadevata*. Generate an intense love and longing for your divine form and a sense of identification with it. Imagine yourself as being its

116

servant. Once this process has been undertaken, ask the *ishtadeva-ta* for *samadhi*. After that comes the state of accepting *samadhi*. *Samadhi* is not something that can be achieved; it must be accepted. If we have a problem with acceptance, the issue is usually associated with not having transubstantiated ourselves into intense love for the Divine. If love is total, *samadhi* will result. But if we feel ourselves unworthy, *samadhi* will remain unrealized.

Given that we are Her children, why would the Divine deem us unworthy of *samadhi*? She will give us whatever we ask for, unless it is dangerous for others or ourselves.

But *samadhi* is the least dangerous of all states. Before *samadhi* we can be a danger to ourselves, but not after this state. The Divine cannot be aware of anything but our perfection and identity with Her, because we are made in its image. Bhakti Yoga is the realization that, although we seem different on the surface, given our limited body and mind, at our core, in our consciousness, we are one with the Divine. Realizing the Divine lives in the heart of each being is the most powerful means of accessing *samadhi*. If the Divine does live in your heart, as all scriptures say, then nothing can stop you from merging into *samadhi*. Thus the eight consecutive *samadhis* are the process of dis-identification with our surface or periphery and abiding in the heart center.

Chapter 5
DO YOU NEED A GURU FOR SAMADHI?

The previous chapter can really only be implemented if this chapter is deeply understood. Do not give the responsibility for your spiritual evolution away to another human. I call *"guruism"* the belief that another human being can intervene with the Divine on your behalf. How would that work and why would it be necessary? Ultimately this suggests a refusal to directly interact and have your own personal relationship with the Divine. No spiritual work can succeed built on the foundation of this refusal. This chapter is dedicated to debunking the myth that one needs a human guru for *samadhi*. Only when we have surrendered this perceived need can we truly open ourselves to receive guidance from the Divine.

In this chapter I attempt to destabilize any dependency on the mythical cult figure of the guru. For various reasons (some of which I explore here), the guru paradigm has failed, and to hold onto it today is nothing but an impediment to *samadhi*. Do not expect another person to do the work for you, because there is always a price to pay. You either walk this path yourself and assume responsibility for your progress (or lack thereof), or you maintain the illusion that somebody else will "take over your *karma*" or give you *"shaktipat"*— and you'll end up empty-handed in cult land.

If awakening were bestowed by the grace of the guru, then the assumption is that the guru can manipulate the law of cause and effect (i.e., the law of *karma*). But the law of cause and effect is God itself, expressed as divine law. The claim that a human can override divine law is as abstruse as saying you can override the law of gravitation by concentrating on flying through thin air. The guru cannot convey or confer a mystical experience onto a student if the student's *karma* does not permit it. The teacher can only demonstrate through their

119

behavior how the mystical experience has changed them, for example, how it has turned them into a more loving or caring person. That's why the behavior, rather than the claims, of spiritual teachers and gurus is so important; and that's where they often fall short.

In the scriptures there have been manifold references to the importance of guru devotion. The misunderstanding is thinking the scriptures refer to a *human* guru. They refer to the guru as God and guru as the true self, your consciousness. Only later have these passages been usurped to dupe people into believing that devotion to a human guru was a short cut, or that it could get them anywhere. The word *guru* means "from darkness to light." Only the Divine, or your true self, the guru within, can lead you to the light. A human posing as the Divine is a *rugu* (somebody who leads you from light to darkness).

The tragedy is that people have understood the guru to be a body, to have a physical representation. If the scriptures say at every turn that you are not the body and that you must renounce identification with the body, then how can the guru be an embodied being? The guru is always the Divine and pure consciousness—not a body. A body cannot teach you. The belief that we need the physical vicinity to a human guru has hampered us in the past and stopped us from taking responsibility for our spiritual evolution and from letting the Divine into our hearts. Nothing can be learned as long as this attitude persists. The grace of the Divine and the self is always here, but we block it out by insisting the guru come to us in physical form, as a body. The truth is omnipresent, available everywhere, at all times. To reduce it to the time and place of the vicinity of one person is to deny the very nature of the Divine! There is no place, no atom, no moment, no being that you encounter that is not the Divine; reducing it to a single body means rejecting its very nature.

WITHDRAWING THE GURU PROJECTION

The Armenian mystic George Gurdjieff wrote, "There is no initiation but self-initiation!" Yet we (or at least I did) run across the globe seeking someone to initiate and enchant us in the process. This is partly because we are reluctant to take responsibility ourselves. Here is an example to illustrate this point. Decades ago I approached a friend of mine (we shared the same guru) about my doubts concerning the guru's teachings. The deeper I immersed myself into the scriptural quotations the guru gave, the more I found he had misquoted or misrepresented their meaning. My friend responded, saying, "To question everything sounds too complicated and strenuous to me. I just want to find somebody that I can totally devote myself to and have them fix all of my problems in return."

There is a multi-billion dollar guru trade (to my knowledge, currently the biggest trade on earth after weapons, oil, sex, and drugs) that feeds on exactly that attitude. Anytime you enter into a relationship, whether with a guru or a lover, if you have this attitude of giving away your responsibility in exchange for the solution to all your problems, you are destined for disappointment. Such a lopsided relationship will never work. Is it possible you create such a relationship because deep down you want to be disillusioned? I certainly did, and eventually, through some painful experiences, I had to assume responsibility for my own re-enchantment with the sacredness of all creation. This required finding the Divine everywhere, not just in a single person.

Nowadays most gurus and lineages seem bogged down in allegations of sexual misconduct, money laundering and hoarding, tax evasion, and power mongering (i.e., seeking to control their followers). Ram Dass, elucidating the difference between a teacher and a guru, once stated that the teacher shows the path and the guru *is* the path. This is a dangerous projection. Although it makes sense to define the spiritual path as surrendering to the Divine, projecting this onto any one person seems to invoke misconduct. Only one human in the world can cause you to have a spiritual awakening, and that is YOU. The question is under what circumstances does your mind allow you to have such an experience? For many of us the answer is "when we are in the presence of somebody who we can bestow this experience upon us." Though it may seem that you have these experiences often in the presence of your guru, the architect of the experience is still 100 percent you; you are only projecting this ability onto the guru.

The only model our postmodern Western society offers us for seeking true love is to go on dates and try the luck of the draw. Following this model, I endured repeated relationship breakdowns. The myth that I hadn't found the right woman yet, the only one who could make me whole, suggested I continue on the same trajectory. Then I came across the work of Jungian psychotherapist Robert A. Johnson. In his 1983 book, *We: The Psychology of Romantic Love,* Johnson argues that Europe lost its own indigenous spirituality around the time of the King Arthur epos. After we lost our direct personal access to spirituality (Johnson goes into great detail about this), we projected the need onto our erotic relationships and started to believe in the notion of one person waiting to make us whole. So, you find yourself in a relationship in which you burden your partner with this enormous load, but they are incapable of living up to your expectations. We know wholeness to be our birthright and believe it to be our partner's duty to supply it. Seeing them fail miserably fills us with resentment towards them. This builds up until we leave the relationship to seek love and happiness elsewhere. Johnson suggests that happiness and wholeness is found in our own spirituality. Once this feeling of being fulfilled is realized, only then can the abundance of the heart be shared in a relationship.

For me that teaching was revolutionary. I resolved to stop thinking about a new partner until I had found myself. I took a lot of time off, sitting in the forest alone, listening to sounds, watching the surface of lakes or oceans, watching sunsets and moonrises. (A quick disclaimer: I have been criticized by some for "being one of the lucky few who could afford a life spent at the feet of gurus and sitting in meditation. Some of us actually have to work." The truth is I made a conscious decision to prioritize my spiritual pursuit and not worry about money. This meant that, until my mid-thirties, I barely owned more than the clothes on my body.) In that period, something grew within me. I learned the entire vast universe and all beings are one within the Divine and that the Divine is within my heart. From that realization, I experienced intense love for myself, for the world, and all beings. I learned that when I experience ecstasy, it is because ecstasy is my innermost nature; it is not contained in the stimulus, but, rather, is contained within me. Ecstasy is the essential nature of my consciousness (the Hindus call this *sat-chit-ananda*, or truth-consciousness-ecstasy).

When I finally came out of seclusion, I firmly believed I would remain alone for the rest of my life. What was the point of having an annoying relationship in which I have to compromise, if by myself I am already pure ecstasy? Little did I know! The very first woman I bumped into after this spiritual awakening became my wife, and I've been happily married ever since. To this day, I believe I met Monica when I did because I didn't "need" her and wasn't looking for a relationship. Interestingly, Monica had also read Robert A. Johnson's book a couple of years before and was at the same stage of having recognized her individual wholeness. Once you realize you do not need another person, that you can be alone and spiritually free, only then can you can also be free in a relationship. The key is that I stopped believing some woman out there could "make me whole" or "complete me." The key was the withdrawal and radical surrender of my projections.

What does all of this have to do with gurus? Similar to the myth of romantic love is the myth of one guru, one spiritual teacher who is waiting to fulfill you. And so we run from guru to guru and from ashram to ashram in search of "the right one." This projection disempowers you. You are handing over your capacity to achieve spiritual completion to another person. Often at the core of this projection is a feeling of unworthiness, perhaps from not being loved and supported enough by a parent (often the parent of the same sex as the guru you are now seeking).

I invite you to completely drop that notion and accept that you are created in the image and likeness of the Divine. No person in this entire world can eject you from the Garden of Eden or from the Secret Chamber of the Most High, or from the mythical Kingdom of Shangri-La—but yourself. And there is no power but you who can open the door to let you back in. In fact, there is no door to be opened, because you have never left. We are born in a state of eternal grace and our oneness with the Divine is so willed by the Divine, which is omnipotent, eternal, and infinite. It is not something that we or any other human being, not even a "guru," can produce, or undo, for that matter. But we *can* live in a state of ignorance of our unity with the Divine. We can find justification for this separation, such as we are unworthy, we have sinned, our mind doesn't stop thinking, we need more money or more love, we must conquer more *asanas*, meditate longer, and so forth. We have built these imaginary walls. On believing we are powerless, we then look for a parent or master figure we can project that missing power onto. The real yearning is for a father or mother figure, and this figure manifests as the guru, just as the partners in our failed relationships manifested. Whenever we are in the presence of the guru, we feel "accepted," "seen," "one with everything," in "no-mind," or "aware of awareness" (insert your own wording). But the power behind any of these is our own. We reach that state in the presence of the guru because we are not ready to allow it in our own presence. Both of these presences are the unalloyed presence of the Divine; there is no difference between the two.

A good spiritual teacher will provide you with tools and practices that replace the presence of the guru. Some will also give you non-doing to undo all that has been done, but that's just semantics. What's important is that the teacher makes herself obsolete by replacing her student's dependency with their own self-reliance. Ramana Maharishi once stated, "The guru and the self are the same." The spiritual path is a road home to yourself, a path leading to that original guru in your own heart, of whom all external gurus are only reflections.

A NEW WAY OF LOOKING AT THE TEACHER

Thirty years ago I walked across Ashok Road in Mysore, India. A magnificent oriental gentleman with a huge turban, long white beard, and long white hair caught my eye. He wore a beautiful brocade silk robe and had one of the most graceful demeanors I have ever seen in a human. He looked me straight in the eyes with a piercing glance and gestured me to come over to him. I was completely spellbound and, as if drawn into his tractor beam, I slowly stumbled towards him, having lost all free will. Summoned into his presence, the man spoke with a gentle and sonorous voice that seemed to bathe me in love and heal me from all the hurt and ridicule I'd ever experienced. "My child, I have been calling you for such a long time and now, finally, you have heeded my call. Even when you were in your country, I spoke to you so often, but you could not yet hear me. Now the time has come, you have finally become ready to find your guru and be initiated into the great mysteries of life." His hypnotic power was dispersed for a brief moment, when a group of pedestrians awkwardly maneuvered around the two of us. I broke away from his gaze and ran back across Ashok Road and onwards as fast as I could. I've never looked back. This gentleman used to hang out in that location every night for many years to recruit new followers. In hindsight, I commend him for his great act. The way he dressed, spoke, and carried himself was perfect. The reason I managed to escape him was not because I was smart. I wasn't. It was simply that somebody else had warned me of that guy and said, "Watch out when you walk down Ashok Road; you could run into so-and-so. He's a charlatan recruiting followers for his evil cult."

The reason why mountebanks such as this fellow are so successful is because we, their followers, make them successful. Every cult that has existed down the ages was created not by the leaders but by the followers. It is us who are looking for somebody to make us whole, to induce us into the mysteries, into The Secret Chamber of the Most High, into the Tabernacle of the Temple. It is we who are looking for somebody to raise our Kundalini, to bestow grace upon us, and to annihilate our *karma*. No wonder we find somebody who exploits our unwillingness to take responsibility for our spirituality. Just as in a romantic relationship, when we hope to meet that single person who will make us whole, also in the spiritual arena we rely on the guru figure for success; we fail to take responsibility for ourselves and project it onto a guru. When the guru cannot deliver and does not live up to our expectations, we become disappointed.

Although the definition of teacher as "one who shows us the path" doesn't seem to contain any traps, the hope that you will meet somebody who "is" the path invites you to hand over your responsibility. It invokes the belief that, by surrendering to this person, your problems will be solved. And this belief is not limited to students. A student's belief that the guru is omnipotent and can bestow spiritual freedom upon them also makes gurus start to believe their own story, or their "fictional" divine position.

In my youth I witnessed several occasions of unassuming elderly Hindu gentlemen who, though initially beautiful spiritual teachers, had come to believe they were the only avatars of God, having been treated in such a manner by Westerners for many years. They started to act as if they were " god-like": their egos grew to gargantuan proportions and the beauty dissolved. If you give somebody that much power, it will corrupt them, too. We have seen this to some extent in the political arena and have formed our states and governments according to the ideas of Voltaire and Montesquieu (i.e., separation of church and state and separation of legislative, executive, and judicative powers); but we have failed to translate that into the spiritual arena, which is thus rife with corruption.

This does not mean we don't need spiritual teachers. We need them more than ever before. To learn yoga or any traditional spiritual path without a teacher would be as difficult as learning music or medicine on your own. For a few great autodidacts that may be possible, but that's not how most people work. The modern teachers who influenced me most are Ramakrishna, Aurobindo, Ramana, and Krishnamurti. None of them had a human guru (although they had a variety of teachers). They simply taught on their own authority. That being said, we now have gurus who manufacture obscure teachers that nobody ever met and invent them as their own guru who gave them authority. This is reminiscent of 18th- and 19th-century European aristocrats who commissioned architects to build ancient-looking castle and palace ruins, on which they based their claim to be scions of ancient dynasties. While not all of these claims in the guru world may be fraud, I recommend looking at them with great suspicion.

This world is in a deep spiritual crisis and spiritual teachers are in greater demand today than ever before. Yet the current trajectory of gurus being debunked, one after the other, for sexual abuse, manipulation, psycho-terror, accumulation of massive wealth, etc., deeply mars the prospects of spirituality to revolutionize our society and propel our evolution. And this is despite the fact that this revolution is urgent and imperative, as it can turn us away from the chasm of ecocide (destruction of our biosphere). Here I propose some ideas that might enable a spiritual practice, such as yoga, to assume this role. These ideas are intended to create an ecology (relationship of organisms towards each other) and hygiene of the student/teacher relationship.

First, we need teachers who will show students the path, without pretending to "be" the path. This is the best precaution I can offer followers of a teacher or guru—beware of the teacher who claims they *are* the path and puts themselves at the forefront of the relationship. A good teacher, on the other hand, will put the work, effort, and practice of the student at the forefront, making the teacher herself superfluous. She will offer techniques that will replace dependence on herself as the teacher.

Although many current gurus place their own personage into the foreground, a sincere teacher will place the teaching, method, and technique in the foreground. They should offer no false pretense to students nor suggest any sort of mystical hocus-pocus transmission.

127

In this way, the teacher does not elevate himself but places the ball back into the court of the students, instead empowering them. A teacher is someone with the humility to admit they are only the catalyst in the relationship and that the student herself performs the crucial work. The teacher may show the path, but it is the student who must walk it. The teacher is someone who readily admits they can also learn from their students. There is no linear relationship, such as that of the all-knowing, old-world guru who towers above the disciples.

SANGHA TO REPLACE THE GURU

Then why is it that so many gurus in the last 40 years have been deconstructed? Have gurus always behaved like this or has something fundamentally changed? There seems to have been quite a bit of bad guru behavior in the first half of the 20th century, but it rapidly worsened once we entered into the second half. Most gurus in the second half of the last century have a file on them, although some of the claims sound insubstantial or just make the guru sound silly. Moving into the 1990s and the 21st century, criminal and court proceedings and serious allegations had become commonplace. One argument suggests this sort of thing has always gone on, but only now have accusations emerged due to widespread communication over the Internet. Of course anyone who feels hard done by can put up a website and attempt to discredit their former guru. Not all of these claims are necessarily true.

Another hypothesis is that the behavior of gurus today has fundamentally changed. Such an explanation would save the honor of ancient authorities and would suggest that not all religion and spirituality is bad; but convincing arguments are needed to determine what exactly has changed, why it has changed, and where we go from here. This is what I intend to discuss now. The rules of the spiritual game have changed completely in the last 50 to 70 years and will continue to change at an accelerating speed. My thoughts resemble those of civilization critic Charles Eisenstein's, in his article, *"Why the Age of the Guru is Over,"* but with a yogic perspective. In *Yoga Meditation* I have shown the evolution of life on Earth from a yogic and *chakric* viewpoint. The *chakras* are expressions of the Divine as stages of evolution of life on Earth. I have shown the base *chakra* (*Muladhara*) to represent reptilian brain circuitry, the lower abdominal *chakra* (*Svadhishthana*) to represent mammalian life, and the power or navel *chakra* (*Manipura*) to represent primate consciousness, our current social paradigm. The threat of ecocide, global warming, terrorism, school shootings, and the rise of such disorders as depression, ADHD, PTSD, and so on are symptoms of humanity's struggle to move up to the heart *chakra* (*Anahata*) and become truly humane. Noted qualities of the heart *chakra* are love, forgiveness, gratitude, compassion, and relatedness. Notice how these qualities have a more feminine flavor to them, while the qualities of the power *chakra* are distinctly male. The power *chakra* is about leadership quality, certainty, coercion, manipulation, and so on. During the era of the power *chakra,* spiritual teachings (like any other teachings) were passed down in a linear fashion from a strong leader to an admiring group of followers who were looking for a leader to save them. How often have we done that, not just in the spiritual arena, but also in the social, political, scientific, sporting, and other arenas?

We are currently witnessing a transition towards the era of the heart *chakra.* This change is necessary; otherwise, our planet Gaia will pull the curtain on humanity. This transition towards the heart *chakra* is not something that leaders will be able to do for us; leaders themselves are still part of the old paradigm. During the era of the heart *chakra,* the Divine will be expressed less by strong leaders who deliver one truth in a linear, top-down fashion and more as what happens between us, how we interact with each other, how we treat each other, what and how we communicate. The Divine revelation during the heart *chakra* phase will come as interrelatedness, as what Charles Eisenstein calls "inter-being." And that's why the old linear gurus are being dismantled. The new guru is not a person but is what emerges as we teach each other, as we take the next step of human evolution together, as we experience an awakening of the heart *chakra*. Newly emerging Christian theology calls this "the second coming of Christ as the whole of humanity receiving the Sonship collectively." Also here we find the concept of the Divine expressing itself through the entirety of humanity. Interestingly, this was already announced when Jesus said, "And have I not said ye all are gods. Ye all are children of the most high" (Psalm 82:6). In Buddhism, too, this same thread was continued when Thich Nhat Hanh said that the Maitreya Buddha (the coming Buddha) would not be a single person but the emerging consciousness of the *sangha* (community of practitioners) as a whole.

The outgoing second- and third-*chakra* paradigm currently still forms our ideas about the guru. Many of us remain dominated by mammalian *chakra* and limbic brain psychology; that is, we are looking for a leader who will safely guide us, like sheep to a fattening meadow. Those who have activated the third *chakra* are desperately looking for just such a flock of sheep to lead. To paraphrase the great Abraham Maslow, we might say, "For a leader to be ultimately at peace with themselves, they have to lead."

Along this line of enquiry, I have to say that much of the time I spent following gurus was ultimately about the drama of the leader, the guru, and not about my own life. Although so much seemed to happen in our lives back then, we followers were really only pawns on the boards of which the gurus acted out their own drama, their own needs. One such need was to be seen and loved by a large quantity of people. If you have that need, you will develop any sort of charisma to obtain it. But charisma is still just second- and third-*chakra* dynamics. Although in our case, the vehicle of spirituality or yoga is used, the structure of a second- and third *chakra* relationship is no different than that of a commander to their private, a boss to their employee, or a warlord to their mercenary—it is one-dimensional and linear.

All of this must change now. As we are reeling from the abyss of

130

ecocide, to which the belief in and exertion of authority has driven us, the heart *chakra* teaches us to relate from an entirely new paradigm. God immanent wants to express Herself as interrelatedness, inter-being, compassion, forgiveness, love, and gratitude. Part of that is realizing that the structure, not just the content, of human relationships must change, must grow. Activation of the heart *chakra* means realizing that together we receive the Divine. Nobody is an exclusive incarnation or avatar of the Divine. We all need each other to take this next step together. The Divine is now expressing itself collectively through all beings, from the greatest genius down to the most insignificant amoeba. There is no single person who can express this; the nature of the game has changed.

Life and modern society have become too complex for a single person to have all of the answers, or for humanity to be divided into a two-caste system of "enlightened ones" and "unenlightened ones." So what can we do to receive the Divine? Listen to it, feel it, and become it. Try to see the Divine in the eyes of every person you meet. See their struggle to embody the Divine. It may even be that they can only see it in themselves and not in others and therefore are trying to revive the old paradigm game of "I'm the guru."

When interacting with another person as a spiritual teacher, I ask myself what my teaching is and how to get the message across. But more importantly, I consider which aspect of the Divine is the person in front of me expressing. Do I give the person the space to express their divinity? Or do I just care about my own personal agenda? In what way can I support this person in expressing their potential, their own share of the Divine, rather than recruiting them for my own movement? When the heart *chakra* collectively activates, there will still be spiritual teachers, but their conduct will be more important than their teaching. How do we interact with each other? How do I convey my experience through my actions? More important than the fact that I have recognized the Divine within me is whether I can now see the Divine in the person

131

across from me. Most important is how I treat this person. Only through my conduct with them can I convey what I see within them. Thus the opening of the heart *chakra* is the demonstration that I recognize God in every person I meet. This also involves reflecting on what the Divine is teaching and communicating to me, through the people I meet. When I meet someone, I must step aside and let the Divine communicate through me, too. In the outgoing power-*chakra* model, the guru produced our evolution. In the incoming heart-*chakra* paradigm, we collectively evolve spiritually, as humanity.

In the old system, I would ask myself, "How can 'I' attract the grace of the Divine? How can 'I' spiritually awaken?" The heart *chakra* has us rephrase these questions: "How can we foster the emergence of the Divine through our collective? How can we co-create our evolution? How can awakening manifest through us?" The shift is away from the individual. What liberates is not personal attainment but service. However much I have personally attained is still relative, if my neighbor wallows in the mire. We either evolve together, or not at all. I cannot isolate myself against the pain and anguish in the world; I can only numb myself. When I experience yogic super-conscious states, I realize at some point that my being does not end at the surface of my skin but transcends all boundaries. At some point, then, literally all pain experienced by any being in past, present, and future (and all glory, too) becomes mine. This is beautifully expressed in the *Bodhisattva* vow. Monks in the Buddhist Mahayana tradition are taught that spiritual liberation of the individual is not possible. Either we have a vehicle large enough (*maha yana* = large vessel) to take everyone across the ocean of conditioned existence yonder to the shore of freedom, or we all remain here in conditioned existence. The *Bodhisattva* takes a vow to be the last to enter nirvana. This is the language of the heart *chakra*.

Also, the yogi of the heart *chakra* realizes the same. Would I enjoy my own shabby, small-scale enlightenment when others are depressed and suffering? That would suggest this so-called enlightenment isn't worth much. Future spiritual evolution is no longer relegated to individual attainment. Through our interrelations and our expressions of gratitude, through forgiveness, love, and compassion towards each other, the Divine will emerge collectively as *us*.

The Divine is currently embodied in all beings, particularly humans, *but only to the extent that we can consciously feel it and be it.* Collectively we are becoming the guru. And now it is time for us to grow up and share this responsibility. We must withdraw our projections on all forms of authority and reclaim our own power. Let's create an equal humanity in which we are united as free and unconditioned individuals under one super-intelligence, who is the one Divine. In collectively realizing the Divine in these manifold forms, we may co-create our destiny. We are invited to stop being part of the problem and start being part of the solution.

Chapter 6
ACCESSING SAMADHI

In this chapter I bring together all of the strands discussed so far and provide practical tips on what to avoid and how to access *samadhi*. This is in preparation for Chapter 7, where I describe the eight *samadhis*.

THE TWO INNERMOST SHEATHS

In Chapter 3 I mentioned the five-sheath-teaching (*panchakosha doctrine*) of the *Taittiriya Upanishad*. I described the obstacles and how they are lodged in the three outer sheaths, called body, breath, and mind. We need to devote some effort to purging those obstacles; otherwise, we become like the proverbial boastful dimwits, prattling on about their *Jnana*, which the *Hatha Yoga Pradipika* scorns in stanza IV.113. Once the three outer layers are purified, we can access the two deeper layers. In the language of the *Taittiriya Upanishad*, these are called deep knowledge sheath (*vijnanamaya kosha*) and ecstasy sheath (*anandamaya kosha*). This is where the great freedom lies. People who seem to have no interest in spirituality are so because the three outer layers are so opaque they cannot see through to the deeper ones. The outer layers must be made transparent, like pure crystal, so that you can see through them and into your essence.

Due to our civilization and history of conditioning this doesn't happen automatically anymore. It takes work. If the preparation has been successful, then *samadhi* can be accessed. If not, we should not be disappointed but can simply put more effort and time into the practices and methods outlined thus far. I believe there was a time when *samadhi*-like states were natural and spontaneous. This is reflected in the biblical tale of the Garden of Eden. At that time we were naked and natural, but when we ate from the Tree of Knowledge of Good and Evil, we suddenly became self-conscious and wanted to cover ourselves up. What does that mean?

Prior to us knowing of good and evil there was only knowledge

135

of good. We saw the entire universe as a manifestation of the Divine Creative Force. We also saw ourselves as a manifestation of that same force, which cannot produce anything unlike itself—thus we knew that we were good. But when we ate from this metaphorical tree, we duped ourselves into believing in evil. The important aspect of the story is that we had a choice of which way to go. We were neither forced to sustain our belief in good nor were we forced to accept a belief in evil. We were free to choose. In hindsight the choice was poor, but the moral underlying this parable is a good one: you and I are free. We are free to choose.

Another highly metaphorical tale in the Indian *Puranas* is related to the four ages and our current age of darkness (Kali Yuga). The story goes like this: In the beginning we lived in abundance and the earth provided freely for all our needs. But then we became careless and no longer acknowledged the earth, the origin of our wealth. At that time, demons (representative of our lower animalistic nature) came up from the netherworlds and stole the earth, symbolized by the cow of abundance. We then lived in poverty and struggled and hollered a lot, asking for divine intervention. Eventually the Divine did intervene in the form of the Lord Vishnu, who went into the netherworld, retrieved the cow, and gave it back to us (this is a much simplified summary, for the purpose of brevity). He even gave us the bull of *dharma* (symbolic for right action) to protect the cow of plenty. However, there was a hitch: Due to our previous decadence, the bull would lose one leg per age in successive world ages, until eventually being overcome by entropy (disorder) and falling down—at which point we would lose everything again.

The important similarity between the tales is that what seems to be the natural order of today is a *seemingly* normal state we have created through our less-than-ideal choices. In the biblical tale, we chose to eat the forbidden fruit that evoked our unlawful beliefs. In the *Puranic* tale, we stopped appreciating and caring for the abundance of nature and thus succumbed to our lower urges. There is an uncanny actuality in this tale. Are we not in a similar situation today, about to lose nature and its abundance because we have become estranged from it? On one hand, our modern humanity reaches for the stars (where there is nothing to find) and into cyberspace (a mirror image of slavery to our own minds), while at the same time, a few indigenous cultures remain that have preserved a lifestyle of peaceful coexistence with nature. Thus *samadhi* is not a high-fangled, complicated state outside of nature. It is a return to the natural state, to living in harmony with the cosmic order of the world. The only reason *samadhi* and yoga may sometimes look complicated is because it is the undoing of a contrived and artificial path that we have taken up to here. Today we are so far removed from what is simple, what is natural, and often also what is right that it takes some work to undo it all.

THE IMPORTANCE OF OBJECTIVE SAMADHI

The *Taittirya Upanishad* talks about two innermost layers, which are directly related to the two main categories of *samadhi* that Patanjali talks about. Objective *samadhi* relates to the fourth layer, called the deep-knowledge sheath. The second class of *samadhis*, objectless *samadhi*, relates to the innermost sheath, called the ecstasy sheath. Most non-dual religions and philosophies such as Buddhism and Advaita Vedanta deal mostly with the innermost sheath; from the perspective of Patanjali's yoga, they place too much emphasis on this innermost layer and try to get there too quickly. Thus objective *samadhi* and the deep knowledge sheath are often underestimated and neglected.

For example, Shankara, the great Advaitin, suggested we look at the world with the same indifference as one would look at the droppings of a crow. In other words, the world does not matter; it isn't important. That very attitude leads to the caste system that is synonymous with modern India and modern Hinduism. If the world is *maya*, a mirage, an illusion, a con, as Shankara holds it, then it matters little what happens to our bodies, or in which circumstances we live. The excessive otherworldly emphasis of some religions leads us to neglect and ignore pressing issues in this world. This use of religion to dupe people into acquiescence lead Lenin,

Q: What is meant by "religion is opium for the people"?
A: Opium (and many other drugs, as well as entertainment, sports, shopping, etc.) acquiesce you to ignore the pressing issues of the world. Religion has often been the handmaid of our suppressors and oppressors (such as pharaohs, emperors, and dictators) to keep us quiet when we should have risen and changed the world. In this regard, Karl Marx was right when he said, "The philosophers have only interpreted the world differently; what matters is that we change it."

the leader of the 1917 October revolution in Russia, to say, "Religion is opium for the people." We might not agree with him on all counts, but religion must take responsibility for this judgment.

Conversely, objective *samadhi* leads us to realizing the reality of the world. Here there is no spiritually motivated escapism. Like the indigenous cultures, objective *samadhi* can take us back to a state of enchantment, where we see that everything is, indeed, sacred and that the entire world, each breath, each moment, is a miracle and a revelation. Do not mistake this for modern materialism, though. Materialism denies the existence of consciousness and mind as an independent category, reducing mind and consciousness to matter and, more precisely, to bioelectrical and biochemical processes in the brain. The yogi does not do that for the second type of *samadhis*. The objectless *samadhis* show us that consciousness, spirit, and the self are eternal, unchangeable, infinite, and without qualities; however, they are as real as the world is, albeit very different from it.

This is why yoga is called a dualistic philosophy: it accepts the existence of two different categories of creation. Most philosophies are not dualistic but monistic, which means they reduce everything to one category. Monistic schools are again subdivided into two main branches of idealistic and materialistic schools. Idealistic philosophies reduce matter to mind/consciousness/self, such as early Buddhism, Advaita Vedanta, or European Idealism. They essentially believe that world and matter are only ideas in the mind, or that they have no independent existence separate from the mind. On the other hand, we have schools that reduce consciousness/mind to matter, such as Scientific Empiricism (Western Science) and Historical Materialism (communism). These philosophies state that consciousness/spirit/mind have no independent existence from matter; for example, they typically reduce consciousness to biochemical and bioelectrical occurrences in the brain. Although both the idealists and the materialists disagree on many points, they are both monistic in that they reduce the world to a single category—whether it be thought or matter.

Note, then, that the division of *samadhis* into two main categories is not arbitrary, but probably the most important feature of the yoga system. It enabled yoga to see the entire world of matter as sacred, crystallized spirit, while at the same time admitting that each individual has an eternal and divine core that is unchanged through whatever manifestation or embodiment it transits.

OBJECTIVE VERSUS OBJECTLESS SAMADHIS

I find it so important to split the *samadhis* into two categories that I'd have preferred if Patanjali called it the "nine-limbed" yoga, with each category of *samadhi* taking an extra limb. Then it would be clear that not all *samadhis* are equal. When we go into objective *samadhi*, the deep knowledge sheath (*vijnanamaya kosha*) is purified and developed. This means we can start to experience the world as it really is. This has vast applications from the perspective of an animistic and shamanic interaction with the world, all the way to scientific research (by scientific, I don't mean the empirical sciences, but the yogic science of *samadhi*: *samyama*.) This will be covered in great detail later.

Let's look now at objectless *samadhi*. The English term "objectless" is used to translate the Sanskrit *nirbija*. Directly translated, *nirbija* means "seedless," with the seed referring to the object. But seedless is also interpreted to mean that no seed of *karma* remains; hence there is no rebirth once this *samadhi* can be sustained for long periods of time. I won't expand on this discussion here, as it implies a

139

finality to spiritual evolution. Do we really know such a thing exists? Can any human being make a final judgment on whether their evolution is complete? Can any human have the final word on a creation that was set in motion by a being vastly more intelligent than we are?

In any case, if we accept *nirbija samadhi* as that in which the seed of rebirth is parched (so that it cannot sprout anymore), then the objective *samadhi* (*sabija samadhi = samadhi* with seed) is that in which the seed of rebirth is not destroyed. This might explain the mad scramble of novices towards *nirbija samadhi*. Other terms yogis use for these exact categories are *samprajnata samadhi* (*samadhi* with cognition of object or cognitive *samadhi*) and *asamprajnata samadhi* (*samadhi* beyond cognition of object, or super-cognitive *samadhi*). Rest assured these mean exactly the same as objective and objectless *samadhi*, respectively. Different terms are simply used because, in Sanskrit it is considered inelegant to use the same word repeatedly; eloquent use of the language would suggest a different word be used to convey the same meaning. Sanskrit and English are similar in that regard.

You might also hear terms such as *sabikalpa* (for objective) and *nirbikalpa* (for objectless) used to describe *samadhis*. These denote that the speaker is likely to be a Vedantin, as the terms are not used in yoga. In the last few centuries, the Vedanta fraternity has taken to *samadhi;* following Shankara they had previously eschewed it. Although they are putting a different spin on it, the essence remains the same. Vedanta, then, also introduced a new term, *sahaja samadhi*. This so-called spontaneous *samadhi* implies we have gone beyond technique and no more effort is required to attain the state. This is more the domain of Jnana than yoga. I will return to this in the last chapter.

WRONG OBJECTLESS SAMADHIS

Without practicing objective *samadhis*, you are likely to end up in wrong objectless *samadhis*, which yogis consider spiritual "cul-de-sacs." Look closely at the following passage from the first chapter of the *Yoga Sutra*, sutra I.17: "Objective *samadhi* is associated with deliberation (*vitarka*), reflection (*vichara*), ecstasy (*ananda*), and I-am-ness (*asmita*)." This means there are four main stages of objective *samadhi* that must be practiced sequentially (two of which are further subdivided). I will discuss them in great detail in Chapter 7. For now, just keep in mind that *samadhi* has quite technical successive levels, similar to *asana*, *pranayama*, Kundalini meditation, and pretty much anything else that carries the name yoga.

Now let's look at the next stanza, sutra I.18: "The other state (objectless *samadhi*) results from the intention of cessation of the fluctuations of the mind and leaves only residual subconscious imprint." The wording is tricky; but what Patanjali means is that, by stilling the mind, our subconscious imprints (i.e., our conditioning) will be moved from the manifest state to the residue state. This means we are free of them, and although a residue of these imprints remains (without which we could not function), we have become free from slavish and robotic adherence to them. In this sutra Patanjali clearly describes what needs to be in place to enter a mystical state or peak experience.

In sutra I.19, things become very interesting. It states that "Among the bodiless ones and the ones absorbed in *prakrti*, there is the intention of becoming." Because Patanjali has not introduced a new subject, we know he is still talking about objectless *samadhi*. In this sutra he lists two states, two types of objectless *samadhi* that he considers traps and spiritual cul-de-sacs. I won't concern you too much about these traps, because the next stanza provides the means of avoiding them. With that in mind, let's have a quick look at the two states. What they have in common is "the intention of becoming." In other words, we still want to get somewhere, to become somebody. This is particularly true if we still use charisma and personal power to impress others. In sutra I.18, the terminology "intention of cessation" means (in devotional language) that we are giving up the illusion of individual will to fulfill the will of the Divine. Intention of cessation means, "not my will, but thy will." To hand oneself over to the Divine plan, to let the Divine work through you, means you have "the intention of cessation of personal egotism or will." To let go of personal ego or will means to fulfill one's duty (*svadharma*), rather than doing whatever one pleases. The two problematic states in sutra I.19, however, indicate that we are deluded by our power and use mystical insight for our own egotistical purposes; that is, the "intention of becoming" somebody or something. This implies we are on the spiritual career ladder. Compare this with sutra I.10: "The deep sleep fluctuation is based on the intention of non-becoming." Again we have this 'non-becoming.' It is 'non-becoming' because we (our innermost essence, the consciousness) is created in the image and likeness of the Divine. It does not need to become; it is already perfect, eternal, and infinite. When you are resting in deep sleep in the embrace of the Divine, you do not need to become somebody, for you are everything already.

Before we move on to the sutra that explains how to avoid these dead-end streets, let's have a quick look at what those two states really are. The first one is called *videha,* which means *bodiless.* This is an entity that does not have a body and, although it shouldn't be "here," it can't help but fiddle around with the minds of embodied beings. I don't intend to say that all channeled entities are crooks, but we should not trust each strange voice that comes to us. As one of my teachers once said, "Just because they are dead, doesn't mean they're smart."

The second state Patanjali talks about is called *prakrtilaya,* which means "absorbed in *prakrti.*" *Prakrti* is the Divine creative force. We could loosely translate *prakrtilaya* as, "being one with everything." Many people who had spontaneous mystical experiences describe them in those words. I don't want to take the fun out of mystic dabbling, but consider the long-term consequences of being "one with everything." That 'everything,' the world, is in constant flux. All objects and manifestations are moving from the seed state to the manifest state and then into the residue state. They are all comprised of compounds and thus all fall apart and disintegrate. Further, there is a lot in this world that you don't want to be "one with," especially the unsavory side of humanity. Patanjali and yogis in general say the path is not to become 'one with everything,' but to abide in consciousness (aware of everything, yet knowing itself to be different). Because this is a huge concern for some advanced students of meditation, I will delve a little more deeply into the implications of *prakrtilaya,* or being-one-with-everything, before showing how the yogi stays out of trouble. Advanced students keep asking me, "Are consciousness (*purusha*) and the world/nature (*prakrti*) not, on a higher level, one and the same? And if so, why is Patanjali so pedantic, taking the fun out of mystic dabbling by not allowing us to be 'one with everything?' On an abstract and theoretical level, consciousness (*purusha*) and the world (*prakrti*) are one—but only on a philosophical plane. Both are one in the Divine, in God. But we are not the Divine. We are children *of* the Divine; therefore, consciousness and the world are not one in us. How is this so? How can we be so different from the Divine? The ancient teacher Ramanuja answers this in formulating his identity-in-difference teaching (*beda-abeda* doctrine). *Beda-abeda* says that, yes, we are identical to the Divine, in that we are pure, infinite, formless, eternal consciousness (*purusha*); but we are different from the Divine in that we are not the universe. Compare the whole universe to your body. See the difference? The body of the Divine is composed of the universe (or, better, is the sum total of all past, present, and future parallel universes), which means the power and intelligence of the Divine is unlimited, eternal, and infinite. Conversely, our power and intelligence are limited, temporary, and finite. Thus yogis meditate on, realize, and then abide in that part of our self that is identical to consciousness (*purusha*).

If you look at consciousness and the world as one and the same, you will sabotage your realization of both, because they are so radically different. It is difficult for us to conceive of something that is simultaneously the same and yet different. Patanjali emphasizes their difference because this will be the focus of most of our spiritual evolution. In an attempt to clarify this simultaneous unity and separation, I will use God transcendent to refer to *purusha* and God immanent in reference to *prakrti.* God immanent is essentially nature, life, Divine Creative Force, divine abundance, *leela, Shakti, prana*, and the law of *karma*. God transcendent is pure awareness and consciousness; in India it is often called Shiva or Brahman. The weakness of systems that hone in on the identity of *purusha/ prakrti* or Shiva/Shakti is they always end up reducing one to the other, usually declaring that *prakrti* and the world are unreal, an illusion, *maya*. They say that once consciousness (*purusha*) is attained, the world (*prakrti*) dissolves into nothingness. The truth is, this non-existent or unmanifest state of *prakrti*, the world, is only a theoretical and theological speculation. There cannot be any awareness, any consciousness, without anything to be conscious of! Shankara, the great Advaitin, admitted that in his commentary on the *Brahma Sutra*.

The Buddhist nihilists, the *shunyavadins,* have furthered this mode of thinking to state that nothing exists; the world, you, God, matter, mind, consciousness, and everything else are all just a momentary notion that arises within nothingness and by nature is emptiness (*shunyata*). From the yogic point of view, that's a fallacy (although admittedly they have thought consequentially and internally consistently). The yogis look at it the other way round. They say consciousness is real and, therefore, the world must be real, too. However, consciousness and the world are different in that the world is in flux while consciousness is permanent. Thus we must have two separate and completely independent categories—and here we arrive at dualism.

The fact that Jahwe, Brahman, and the Father are eternal, means the world and all beings are also eternal, uncreated, and without beginning or end. Sentences like "In the beginning God created the universe," indicate how our mind works. Our mind can only see and understand things in sequence, one after the other. But because the Divine is eternal and uncreated, you (i.e., your consciousness) are, too. Tantrics such as the Shaktas and Kashmiri Shaivas have developed a worthy theory about this. They propose two levels or layers of reality; let's call them the absolute and relative layers. On the relative layer, *purusha* and *prakrti* are entirely separate and will never meet; at this level, we live and go about our daily business. The Tantrics say that, even if you attain the absolute layer, the relative layer continues to exist. Interesting, isn't it? Patanjali says exactly this in sutra II.22: "Although it (*prakrti*) may cease to be manifest for the liberated one, it will continue to do so for those in bondage."

I don't wish to confuse you with this discussion, but you'd be surprised how many people gripe over it. It is important to understand that yoga will always be yoga, meaning that it will remain true to itself and internally consistent. About 20 years ago, this girl attended my Saturday afternoon beginner's course to Ashtanga Yoga. As usual, I was explaining everything in great detail. Her face was growing longer and longer. After an hour or so, she just threw her hands into the air and said, "But I just came to stretch and feel good!" I looked at her with deep compassion and said, "Wrong school!" I mention this because, if you look at the Ashtanga *asana* system, it is very scientific (ancient science, that is). The same goes for the *Yoga Sutra,* onwards to include the practice of *pranayama* and Kundalini meditation. Of course the same intellectual rigor and exactitude has definitely been applied to *samadhi* and higher states of consciousness.

Finally, I arrive at explaining how to stay on the correct path of yoga and avoid non-yogic, objectless cul-de-sacs. Sutra I.20 states, "In the case of the others [the yogis], it [objectless *samadhi*] is preceded by conviction, enthusiasm, remembrance, [objective] *samadhi,* and wisdom (*prajna*)." First Patanjali wishes to express that those wrong objectless *samadhis* lead you away from the path of yoga; second, he suggests five things that, if practiced, will keep you on course for the right objectless *samadhis*. The first one is conviction (*shraddha*). It is often translated as *faith*, but because this translation belies the questioning and inquisitive nature of yoga, I prefer to call it conviction. In order to be convinced, to know what you are doing and where you are going, you must study the *Yoga Sutra* and other yogic texts to understand the operating manual of yoga.

The second quality is enthusiasm (*virya*). *Virya* actually gave rise to the English *virility* and in Sanskrit means "heroic attitude." The idea is there will be obstacles and setbacks; the path won't always be smooth. Are you in this for the long haul? Or will you turn back when the weather turns bad? The next requirement is *smrti*, or remembrance. Don't forget who you are, where you came from, where you are headed, how you will get there, and what you are doing in the process. We must continuously ask ourselves if our current actions are aligned with our commitment to serving the Divine and reaching *samadhi*. This is particularly important for teachers. So much time today is wasted on idle and petty pursuits. Remembrance also means remembering our mortality. I read a survey that placed the people of Bhutan, a small Himalayan kingdom, at the top of the list of the world's happiest people. When asked the secret of their happiness, they stated that every day, five times a day, they perform a ritual that reminds them death is drawing closer with every moment. In remembering this, they realize how precious and beautiful life is and what a unique and unusual gift it is to be alive. This is the type of remembrance we must practice.

The fourth quality Patanjali suggests is *samadhi*. Wait, we need *samadhi* to reach *samadhi*? What he means is we need objective *samadhi* in order to reach objectless *samadhi*. The various objective *samadhis* discussed in Chapter 7 will show you, without doubt, that the entire world and its objects (including your own body, ego, and mind), being comprised of *gunas* (elementary particles of nature), are subject to change, will go from seed state to manifest state to residue state, will fall apart, and—further—are subject to imprint (and thus are always interacting with other objects that leave their mark on them).

The final and fifth of Patanjali's suggestions is knowledge (*prajna*). *Prajna* is not just any knowledge. The technical term is "complete knowledge pertaining to knowables" (i.e., objects) and is the same as the *vijnana* (deep knowledge of the *Tattiriya Upanishad)*. It is the result of objective *samadhi* and results in the experience of the world as it truly is—not as your subconscious and conditioning portray it to you. A large part of that is realizing there is a real world to experience that is not just an illusion, crow dung, or something conjured up. Thus when you graduate to objectless *samadhi,* you suddenly realize that *this,* the pure, eternal, infinite,

146

and quality-free consciousness, is not subject to any of the previous limitations. And that is the true you! So, while you can be aware of objects of the world, you can witness them and even enjoy them, you cannot be one with them. I hope my explanation makes sense, why you cannot be truly one with anything other than the self.

SAMADHI AND THE BREATHLESS STATE

Having now set the stage for correct *samadhi* practice, let's look into how we start. Yoga says it is the power of breath (*prana*) that moves the mind (and vice versa). In stanza II.2, the *Hatha Yoga Pradipika* also says breath and mind move together. For this reason, yogis say *pranayama* is instrumental for *samadhi*. Consider the following metaphor: Imagine the flame of a candle in a room with open windows. Each gust of wind will make the candle flicker. On the other hand, in a sheltered area, the flame of the candle does not move. It is steady. The wind in this metaphor is the breath and the flame is your mind. In the early stages of learning to access *samadhi,* a lot of attention must go towards mastering the breath to steady the flame of the mind. Yogis use the term "breathless state" to denote mastery of breath. It's quite accurate, because mastery will make you breathless in two ways: first, it removes aberrant breathing patterns and, second, it makes you breathless to behold the eternal beauty of the divine manifestation of life.

The Sanskrit name for the breathless state is *Kevala Kumbhaka,* which also means "spontaneous suspension." Please note that a yogic breath retention or suspension (*kumbhaka*) has about as little to do with holding the breath as *asana* has with rugby. It is a fine art that I have described in great detail in *Pranayama: The Breath of Yoga.* The breathless state is brought about through conscious breath retentions that are set within either slow-breathing *pranayamas,* such as *Nadi Shodhana,* or rapid breathing *pranayamas,* such as *Bhastrika.* It is ideal to practice both. Either way, as you improve your practice of breath retentions, you will sometimes access a deep, trance-like state in which time and the world appear to stand still. That's the

147

first glimpse of the outer phases of *samadhi*. Here the candle stops flickering. The flickering of the candle gives the mind the appearance of change and time, whereas the underlying deep consciousness (*purusha*) is outside of time (or, better, "time is within it").

In order to explain what happens in a breath retention/suspension and how it's related to *samadhi,* let's look at another metaphor. Let's say you are on a camping adventure and you want to tidy yourself up but find you don't have a mirror with you. The easiest way of having a look at yourself is through your reflection in a still lake, pond, or even just a puddle of water. You will find that, on a windless day, this is no problem, as no waves are ruffling the surface of the pond. The situation on a gusty day, however, is much different. The waves will distort your image. In yoga we see that as a metaphor of the mind. When the breath is calm, smooth, and controlled (or, even better, suspended), there is little to no fluctuation of thoughts in the mind. Therefore, the mind can clearly perceive any object you direct it towards. The more excited and out of control the mind is, the more waves it makes and the more warped any image becomes. This happens to the extent that, eventually, your reflection has nothing to do with the image outside of you and everything to do with the content of your subconscious. This is why the easiest way to obtain the first glimpse of *samadhi* is during *pranayamic* breath retentions. When we are performing breath retentions, or even just breathing very slowly and consciously, we are to meditate on the underlying stillness of the mind. The mind is still, pure, and ecstatic if it is constantly directed towards the self or consciousness (consciousness is the embodied self). It is through our habit of continuously driving the mind towards external objects that it becomes excitable and unstable. This outward projection of the mind is no accident. It is caused by subconscious imprints and *karma*, which also moves the breath.

Samadhi, then, is initiated in breath retentions during pranayama; here it comes to us first as the always-present underlying stillness and clarity of the mind. From here *samadhi* spreads into the breath retentions practiced during Kundalini meditation, to eventually engulf the entire breathing cycle. I'm not suggesting you cannot access *samadhi* in another way, but I found this way to be the most straightforward, and it may be an interesting option for those who have spent countless lives (at least, so it seemed in my own meditation practice) in Vipassana meditation or just watching the mind. A lama (Tibetan priest) I used to study with told me that any meditation practice that involved just sitting and watching the breath would take 300 lives to bear fruit. On the other hand, *pranayama* breath retentions are preparation for the breathless state. Looking back over my own practice life, there was an air of inevitability to see how *pranayama* and Kundalini meditation would carry me towards *samadhi*. I could try to explain this, why and how it works, but ultimately you must still do the work yourself.

Bhastrika is another notable technique; it is the most powerful *pranayama* and can easily be overdone. If practiced correctly with all safety precautions in place (such as diet, *asana* practice, *kriyas*, etc.), it is one of the most powerful drivers of *samadhi*. You will find more information on this in *Pranayama: the Breath of Yoga*.

SAMADHI AND CHAKRAS

Once *samadhic* glimpses have been experienced in *pranayama* breath suspensions, it is easier to experience them again during *chakra* and Kundalini meditation, simply because a subconscious imprint that allows their arising is now in place. This is one of the many reasons why yogic meditation or, as I call it here, *chakra*- and Kundalini meditation, is composed of exactly the same elements as yogic breathing; that is, slow and controlled breathing, *mantra*, visualization, *mudra* (*pranic* seal), and *bandha* (*pranic* lock). Even yogic *samadhi* is comprised of these same building blocks.

I have described *chakra* meditation in great detail in *Yoga Meditation: Through Chakras, Mantra and Kundalini to Spiritual Freedom*. Once you have gained proficiency in the method described there, place yourself into *samadhi* by holding awareness in the relevant *chakra* during breath retention. As breathing commenc-

149

es, keep awareness at this *chakra* as long as possible. If awareness moves somewhere else, if you cannot hold the focus, simply re-commence Kundalini meditation and breathe up and down through the central energy channel, focusing on the *chakras* in sequence.

In the next chapter I describe the eight *samadhis*. You will notice the first two are on objects that are perceptible to the senses (such as a flower or a sacred object). The next higher two *samadhis* are on objects imperceptible to the senses; here the *chakras* are ideal. The *chakra* upon which you focus will profoundly influence your experience. However, it is important to note that the yogi is not trying to coerce or force *prana* into a particular *chakra*. It moves there of its own accord, simply by focusing one's attention on a particular *chakra*. No will power or force is implied. What follows is a concise map of the *chakras,* as related to the *samadhis.*

SAHASRARA (CROWN CHAKRA)

This is the prime *chakra* to focus on for *samadhi;* if one succeeds with concentration, it exerts the strongest upwards pull on *prana/ Kundalini*. However, we can glean from Gopi Krishna's book, *Kundalini the Evolutionary Energy in Man,* what the effect of any indiscriminate focus on this *chakra* can have. You need to be ready and prepared to focus on this highest *chakra. Samadhis* based on the *Sahasrara* provide experience of the formless absolute. The Hindus call this *nirguna* Brahman, the Buddhists call it Nirvana, and Lao-tzu called it the Dao. The *Bodhi* of the Buddha is a typical *Sahasrara* experience. *Samadhis* here will usually be objectless and are often so intense that those who experience them say the world is an illusion.

Yogis put these experiences off until last so that they can be fully integrated. Paramahansa Ramakrishna essentially rejected this experience as being not very helpful for our day-to-day life. Thousands of years of religion have told us that earthly life is not worth living, that it's inferior, sinful, painful, full of suffering, a valley of sorrows, and so on and that we need to get out of here either to a state of nothingness (the Buddhist nirvana or the Vedantic *nir-*

guna Brahman) or into a heaven far above our current toils (the Abrahamic religions). From a yogic perspective, we would say the *Sahasrara* experience is given too much import and the experiences of the other *chakras* are not sufficiently integrated, which decreases the weight placed on present life and increases the emphasis on the hereafter. While the intentions might have been noble, religion with this imbalance caused the Western scientific revolution, which denied the hereafter (or transcendence) altogether. Right from the start, yoga aims at an integrated balance between immanence (the here) and transcendence (the hereafter). Don't get me wrong: I'm not saying we should not meditate on *Sahasrara* but that we do so in due time, after all prerequisite experiences have been had.

AJNA (THIRD-EYE CHAKRA)

Samadhis supported by and based on concentration of the third-eye *chakra* lead to Patanjali's *asmita samadhi* and to experiences of revelation of the Divine with form. These *samadhis* are much easier to digest and thus should come before *Sahasrara* experiences, because they change your relationship with the world and others. *Sahasrara* experiences ultimately say that there is no world and no Divine with form; there is only you as the self. Ramakrishna importantly observed it is wrong for a person who lives in society to say, "I am God"; but they *should* say, "I am a child of God." This latter phrase is borne of the *Ajna chakra* experience.

Ajna chakra samadhis provide a clear, direct, and irretrievable experience that you are a child of a force and power that is eternal, infinite, omnipotent, omniscient, omnipresent, pure love, intelligence, beauty and freedom—in other words, the Divine. As these *samadhis* prepare you for a life of service to the Divine and all beings, it is preferable that they be had before the *Sahasrara* experience.

VISHUDDHA (THROAT CHAKRA)

If *prana* is arrested here, it tends to give an animistic and shamanic experience of the world, whereby one sees the entire universe,

151

including all matter and all locations, as the intelligent and animated body of the Divine. Without seeing the Divine directly, one
feels that all matter is sacred and alive, that trees, rocks, mountains,
and rivers are all crystallized spirit. Many indigenous and native
civilizations are founded on these Shamanic and animistic experiences caused by focusing prana in *Vishuddha*; it is something our
own civilization misses so sorely that it may push us into ecocide.
Part of the problem is that our religions, both the East Asian religions and the Abrahamic religions, have pretty much bypassed
these states and called them pagan and heathen. Patanjali calls *Vishuddha*-inspired states (in which we see all matter as crystallized
spirit) *"ananda samadhi,"* and until we manage to integrate these
states and rediscover our own indigenous, tribal, native, animistic, and shamanic origins, humanity will cease to exist, leaving the
planet to the cockroaches (there are scenarios of humanity causing
ecocide that will let cockroaches survive as the highest life form).

It is time we modern people remember that the so-called "na-
tives" were not brutes, savages, or barbarians; in many ways
they are more highly developed than we are. A Native American
chief once said, "Only when the last tree has been cut down, the
last river has been poisoned, and the last buffalo has been shot
will you white people realize that you can't eat money." This attitude that sacrifices nature in exchange for fiat currency is proof
of our complete estrangement from the very nature that carries,
nurtures, and supports us by abandoning *Vishuddha* spirituality.

ANAHATA (HEART CHAKRA)
Concentrating *prana* in the heart *chakra* has several important implications. Patanjali says in sutra I.33, "Clarity of mind is produced
by meditating on friendliness towards the happy, compassion towards the miserable, joyfulness towards the virtuous, and indifference towards the wicked." The belief in our separate, individual,
egoic existence fosters the attitude of envy towards those who are
happy (why are they more fortunate than us?), judgment towards

152

the miserable (they deserve it; they brought it upon themselves), skepticism towards the virtuous (they must have some skeletons in the closet; let's find them), and hatred towards the wicked (look what those bastards have done—let's pay them back).

Patanjali not only advises us to let go of those negative sentiments, but to actively propagate their opposite. He calls the effect this has, "clarification of mind." Why is that so? All conflicts we have with other people are externalizations of inner conflicts. It can be painful and even humiliating to admit this. For example, if I am envious of the success of somebody else, deep down I am thinking that I don't deserve to be fortunate; that's why I don't like to see it showered on others. When I am judgmental towards a person who is suffering and refuse to help them because I think they've brought it upon themselves, deep down I believe that I myself don't deserve support and must be judged because I have not done enough to avert my own misfortune. If I am skeptic towards a virtuous and heroic person, it is because I don't trust my own virtue and heroism and believe that I must be brought down. Again my hatred towards so-called "low lifes" is nothing but an externalization of my self-loathing and my belief that, at my core, I am evil and sinful and deserve to be taken down. Any form of spite I project outwards when I talk about others is an outright refusal to accept that I am worthy of God's love.

This process is very confronting and may be met with much resistance. We all like to sit on the moral high horse and judge or look down on others. Now, look at how often the term 'others' occurred in the last two paragraphs. Jungian dream analysis tells us that all figures who appear in our dreams are projections of our own inner conflicts on external actors; similarly, yoga says that conflicts we entertain during the waking state are externalizations of inner conflicts with ourselves. The moment in which I accept all of my own shortcomings and turn my self-loathing into self-love and self-acceptance, the conflict and projection will end.

This doesn't mean we shouldn't stop corporations from ruining the environment, punish murderers, or stop tyrants from invading

Q: If this verse emphasizes that we are all one, then why must we ask forgiveness or offer it to others?
A: Asking God for forgiveness is actually a smoke screen, but it has been put in place so that we realize how powerful and important the process of forgiving is. God is pure love and forgiveness, is completely beyond judging us (pure consciousness cannot judge) and therefore cannot forgive us, either. It is really us who purify our own subconscious through the process of forgiving. This is so important because, in the process of dying, it is we who pass the 'Last Judgment' on ourselves. When we die, a powerful cocktail of neurotransmitters in the brain is emitted. This makes time seemingly stand still and we have an eternity to go through all situations in our life, one frame at a time.

Our own conditioning (or what Freud called the "superego") then passes judgment on how we fared, based on our judgment of others (and it is this last reckoning that, according to the *Bhagavad Gita*, determines our next embodiment). That is why near-death experiences are so life-changing. Those who had them, often from that time on treat others kindly and with humility, realizing that everything we give out comes back to us.

other countries. What it *does* mean is that we are not going after them with the desire for vengeance in our hearts; we are correcting their behavior without passion, blood thirst, vengeance, or righteousness even entering into the equation. *Samadhi* based on the heart *chakra* enables us to see that there really is no "other." Our interconnection as human beings forms a huge symbiotic organism—one humanity, one family of all beings. Thus all judgment I have or adversity I produce will eventually come right back to me. Any notion that your loss is my advantage is based on the belief that I am my body. But my body is the vehicle in which my consciousness is currently embodied. Underneath it, we all share the same *atman*, the same self, because there is only one self. "Do unto others as you would have done unto yourself," implies our one common existence as children of the Divine. Deep down there is no separation. If I believe that I am separate, why should I treat you as I would treat myself? "And forgive us our trespasses, as we forgive those that trespass against us." The notion of there being no "other" is reinforced here, also. You produce forgiveness and thus can be forgiven by others.

You must first forgive yourself before forgiving another. Radical forgiveness comes from practicing *samadhi* on the heart *chakra*. It teaches us to let go of any spite or antagonism we feel towards another. In Patanjali's words, this process clears our mind, and without a clear mind, no spiritual evolution is possible.

But even when pursuing spiritual evolution, as with the *samadhis* on the higher *chakras*, we must always return to the heart. Here in this axial *chakra,* the integrated human must be centered, and from here we can interact with others from a position of service, compassion, and love. If we are centered in the *Sahasrara*, we cannot make much of a contribution. In the heart we develop our trust in the Divine and in the heart—so the scriptures say—the sacred sound of OM is heard. *Chandogya Upanishad* says, "In the human chest there is a small shrine (the heart) in which there is a small flame the size of a thumb (the soul). And in this flame, miraculously, is this entire universe, with its planets, stars, continents, rivers, mountains, and oceans."

THE LOWER THREE CHAKRAS

Generally yogis do not practice *samadhi* on the lower *chakras*. Gaudapadacharya (Shankara's master's master) said that the lower two *chakras* are eschewed because they are *tamasic* (they create mental torpidity). The three lower *chakras* reflect our evolutionary past, meaning our reptilian, mammalian, and primate brain circuitry. Any *samadhi* based on them would tend to move us backwards in evolution.

In exceptional circumstances, a scientifically minded person (or saint) may do a special type of *samadhi* (called *samyama*) on the lower *chakras* to obtain special knowledge. For exam-

155

The Purpose of Yogic Texts

In ancient days, the job of a *sutrakara* (sutra author) was to keep individual sutras and whole texts as short as possible. For example, there are usually no verbs included, which needs to be inferred from context. Similarly, a subject is mentioned only once and then recycled in as many consecutive sutras as possible. It is only when a new subject is mentioned that the reader must infer that all previous sutras up to this point dealt with a prior subject. While the composing of a sutra itself was an art form, the reason behind leaving out as much information as possible is encrypted in the meaning of the term "sutra." "Sutra" means "thread," and sutra texts are teaching aids for accomplished masters, so that they could instruct their students. In other words, a sutra text is not meant to make sense to the outsider, linguist, or scholar. Like a PowerPoint that contains only lecture notes, it is only supposed to trigger the memory of somebody who has practiced, mastered, and experienced the content through decades of application. In millenniums past, the texts never intended to reveal too much as the system had to be learned through personal instruction. Only in recent centuries, when many of these lineages died out, did their adepts sometimes write longer treatises. This does not at all mean this moment was the inception of such knowledge, but is more a statement that the knowledge was then lost; in other words, some of the larger texts are actually a tombstone or final nail in the coffin of yogic schools and not their blossoming. Even if it looks as though a blossoming tree may throw a final lavishing display of flowers to produce seed right before it dies. This point is often entirely overlooked by modern Western scholars.

ple, in stanza III.29 Patanjali sates, "By *samyama* on the navel *chakra* (*Manipura*) medical knowledge is obtained." Those of you familiar with *pranayama* know that the *Manipura* also serves as the battery for solar *prana*; that is, prana for outgoing activities, such as powering efferent nerve currents, motor neurons, extraversion, and generally for *prana* that powers the body. *Samyama,* though, is a very advanced *samadhi* that should only be tackled by those who cannot be seduced by its opportunities. This *samadhi* will also be covered in the next chapter.

In summary, yogic *samadhis* do not only deal with the crown *chakra* (*Sahasrara*). Reducing *samadhis* to *Sahasrara* tends to make us to look down at the world and all beings, as if they are something to be overcome or to be left behind, and that the yogi has to rise above it all. The *samadhis* on the higher *chakras* teach us the importance of relationships, service to others, the entire world, and all nature as being a sacred site, the Divine as a being, and us as Her expressions. Going past these higher *chakras* and straight to *Sahasrara* explains why the history of religion is full of episodes that clearly reduce this world (the here) to the next (the hereafter) (such as, burning witches, the holy wars, killing infidels and heathens, etc.). For one who practices *samadhis* in a systematic fashion, such a reduction cannot exist; this world is as holy as the next.

SAMADHI AND MUDRAS (PRANIC SEALS)

Patanjali's approach to any of the eight limbs, including *samadhi,* is that he describes what they are but not how to get there. This has lead to many misunderstandings. People believe there is no complex system of *asana* or *pranayama* or meditation underlying the *Yoga Sutra* because Patanjali doesn't describe it. But he doesn't describe any methods because it's simply not within the scope of a text comprising just 195 stanzas. A much bigger text would be required.

A completely different approach is shown in the *Gheranda Samhita.* In Chapter 7 of this text, six *samadhis* are listed, but Sage Gheranda does not differentiate them according to level or depth of contemplation but, rather, according to type of access. The six ways of accessing *samadhi* are as follows:

- *Dhyana* Yoga through *Shambhavi Mudra*
- *Nada* Yoga through *Bhramari Mudra*
- *Rasananda* Yoga through *Khechari Mudra*

157

- *Laya* Yoga through *Yoni Mudra*
- *Bhakti* Yoga
- *Kumbhaka* (breath retention)

I have covered most of these methods in earlier texts. *Shambhavi Mudra* (described in *Yoga Meditation*) is a more intensive version of Bhrumadhya Drishti (gazing between the eyebrows). It must be induced slowly, as otherwise it can strain the optical nerve. As the subconscious expresses itself during sleep through rapid eye movement, during the waking state, eye movement is an outlet for the subconscious. Arresting eyeball activity is an important meditaton aid in yoga. Additionally this *mudra* draws *prana* towards the third-eye *chakra*.

Khechari Mudra is based on a similar reasoning. Here the tongue is reverted onto itself and directed back and up along the soft palate towards the nasopharyngeal orifice. The tongue is another outlet of subconscious activity. By arresting it, the activity is arrested, too. I have also described the milder version of this *mudra*, called *Jihva Bandha*, in *Yoga Meditation*. Both the *mudra* and the *bandha* (a *bandha* is a *pranic* lock) arrest *prana* in the throat *chakra* (*Vishuddha*). Similar to *Shambhavi Mudra*, it needs to be introduced slowly. An early symptom of strain would be a headache. An integrated approach would use both of these *mudras* simultaneously when attempting to access *samadhi*. Even any advanced form of Kundalini meditation should be accompanied by both of those *mudras*. The importance of the breathless state and breath retention was pointed out earlier in this chapter, and I describe Bhakti Yoga in Chapter 4 of this book. *Bhramari* and *Yoni mudras* will be covered next. Of all *mudras* it is probably these two that provide the most powerful introversion of the mind.

BHRAMARI MUDRA

Some scriptures list this method as a *mudra* and some as a *pranayama* technique. Often the difference is whether or not breath retention (*kumbhaka*) is included. *Bhramar* means "black bee." The scriptures agree that the *mudra* consists of producing the sound of the male black bee during inhalation and of the female black bee during exhalation. What they usually don't say is how that sound is actually produced. Let's start with the exhalation; it's much easier. Produce a nasalized 'ng' sound, similar to in *ganga* or at the end of the French *garçon* and sustain it throughout your exhalation. This is the sound of the female bee. Once the exhalation is complete, continue the 'ng' sound, but this time by forcefully inhaling. The sound will continue only if you rapidly suck the air in, which means you cannot sustain it for long because your lungs will fill up quickly. When you manage to produce the sound, you will notice it is much higher pitched and more flimsy. This is representative of the sound of the male black bee, verifying that his life is more short-lived and not good for anything apart from mating. He is very similar to a gigolo in that regard.

Close your ears with your thumbs, place your index fingers on your forehead for resonance, and place the remaining fingers on your closed eyes and cheekbones. Now make the sound and on the inhalation and exhalation, keep any external visual and audio impressions shut out. If you want to perform the *mudra* for some time, it may be helpful to sit on the floor and rest your elbows on a chair or low table in front of you so that your arms don't get tired.

Focus your mind completely on this sound and follow the sound inwards, letting go of any concept and memory of the outside world. Following the sound inwards to the core of your being, memories of the world will quickly fall away and you will arrive at a state of primordial, pure being-ness. Of course this is pending on whether the force of introversion and internalization of the mind is already strong. Most yogic practices are preparations for that state and this *mudra* is a good indicator of how far you have come. By itself, *Brahmari Mudra* will only work if there is already a strong karmic or subconscious tendency to go within.

Another way of performing the *mudra* for an extended period is

159

to use earplugs instead of one's thumbs and, instead of using the fingers to close the eyes, one could look at the rising full moon. The moon is the symbol of lunar *prana*—the power that internalizes and introverts the mind. This method also works well for people who find it difficult to progress in yoga due to excessive extroversion.

YONI MUDRA

Shanmukhi Mudra is also called the "six-headed *mudra*," as it lends itself to contemplating the six *chakras*. It is also the prime means of listening to the *nadanusandhana*, the inner sound. Hatha Yogis like Goraknath considered it the prime method for accessing *samadhi*, but the yoga of inner sound was even approved by such diverse characters as Shankara and Kabir.

Close the ears with the thumbs, the eyes with the index fingers, and the nostrils with the middle fingers. Now place the ring fingers on the upper lip and the little fingers on the lower lip. Lift the nostrils using the middle fingers and inhale through the nose. Some texts suggest inhaling through the crow beak *mudra* (lips pointed in the shape of a crow beak). To be honest, I found that a nuisance, as it dries out the mouth quickly. Place the middle fingers back on the nostrils and then perform a breath retention. If you retain the breath longer than 10 seconds, you must be proficient in *Jalandhara Bandha*, which I describe in *Pranayama: The Breath of Yoga*. Now, exhale again by lifting the middle fingers. *Gerandha Samhita* (III.37–42) further suggests one contemplate the six *chakras*, pronounce the *mantra hamsa*, mingle *prana* (vital upcurrent) with *apana* (vital downcurrent), and finally raise the Kundalini to the *Sahasrara* (crown *chakra*). With these words, Gerandha wishes to express that the *mudra* is not performed simply by covering one's face through a funny position of the hands, but that all aspects of higher yoga internally conspire to bring about *samadhi*. I describe all of these in *Yoga Meditation*. If practiced duly, they are all combined here, contemplating the six *chakras*, pronouncing the *mantra hamsa*, mingling *prana* (vital upcurrent)

with *apana* (vital downcurrent), and finally raising the Kundalini to the *Sahasrara*, and *samadhi* is the fruit. These *mudras* are
not tricks or short cuts but the culmination of previous work.
Again, the key is to radically introvert the mind and to seek the
core of our being, the heart (*hrt*). When the outside is cut off and
the mind is prepared it rushes inwards to meet the self. In the
next chapter I describe the inner states of the various *samadhis*.

Chapter 7
THE EIGHT SAMADHIS
OF PATANJALI

I will now describe the eight classical *samadhis* that Patanjali mentions in the *Yoga Sutra*. This is not the only way in which *samadhis* can be categorized or classified, but since it is the most well known and, at the same time, most misunderstood, I'll stick to it.

The eight *samadhis* are ordered similar to a Richter scale, meaning their power and scope increases exponentially, not in a linear fashion. Each consecutive *samadhi* is about 10 times as powerful as the preceding one. The first four *samadhis* are mind refining and mind purifying; they convert mind into intelligence (*manas* to *buddhi*). They bring out the inherent luminosity and wisdom (*sattva*) of the mind. The final four *samadhis* are revelatory. They consecutively reveal the universe as the body of the Divine and as the Divine in all beings, with complete knowledge of the objective world and pure consciousness (*purusha*).

Of those eight *samadhis*, seven are objective; only the last one is objectless. I have already described the essential differences between these two types of *samadhi*, but the fact that the *Yoga Sutra* talks just one objectless *samadhi* but prolific varieties of objective *samadhi* shows there is a higher discipline to be studied when Raja Yoga is completed. This discipline is Jnana Yoga, as outlined in the *Brahma Sutra*. Although I have succinctly touched upon Jnana Yoga in Chapter 8, I hope to address it in more depth in a later text.

Of the seven objective *samadhis* listed by Patanjali, the first four are collectively referred to as *samapattis*. In sutra I.41, he says, "When the mind-waves are reduced, the mind truthfully reflects any object it is directed towards, like a pristine crystal, whether it be the perceived, the process of perceiving, or the perceiver. This

state is called identity (*samapatti*)." This sutra is often wrong-
ly translated as "*Samapatti* is when the perceiver, perceiving, and
the perceived become one." Identity (*samapatti*) does not mean
you become one with the object of your observation; it means the
image of the object recreated in your mind is identical to the object you observe. Consider the repercussions of this for a moment.

Polish mathematician and philosopher Alfred Korzybski coined
the saying, "The map is not the territory." Yoga has always been aware
of the fact that conditioning makes it impossible for us to perceive
the world as it truly is. Our problem is that we do not take enough
time to receive an object in its entirety. Instead we quickly compare
each new object with all the data we have stored about similar objects
to swiftly arrive at a reasonably close estimation of what the current
object could represent. At this point, the inquiry is interrupted and a
light goes on, saying "match." This 'match,' however, is never 100
percent but only what our minds deem to be reasonably close. Thus
we misapprehend our way through life without ever knowing it.

Samapatti, then, means that the object meditated on is authentically replicated in the mind. This is a seemingly incredible attainment, and Patanjali phases it in slowly in four stages, rather than
going there in one step. But before I explain the four steps of *samapatti* (identity), let me say something about an "object." In yoga,
object does not just refer to a "thing"; it is the entity upon which
our meditation or *samadhi* is based. While early stages of *samadhi*
choose simple and physical objects, later *samadhis* may choose
infinity or the entire creation. However the actual process as such
is very much the same. In the first two *samapattis* (identities) the
yogi is asked to choose a simple object. "Simple" means it is not
complex, but rather homogenous, uniform, and easily discernible.
For example, a steam engine would be too complex because it has
too many movable parts hidden from view. Similarly, a work by
Picasso or Dali would be considered complex due to their manifold associations. In *samapatti* the mind will try to penetrate the

surface of the steam engine or collate all of Dali's surrealist intentions and, in the process, would likely become excited and unsteady. One object that fits this description is a translucent crystal with an even shape, such as a pyramid or a sphere-shaped crystal. We can look straight through it and don't have to worry about what's inside and hidden from view. Also, it looks the same or nearly the same from every angle, so we don't have to worry about changing our perspective to learn more about the object. I am using this metaphor with some hesitation, because today the saying "I don't have a crystal ball" is associated with "I can't look into the future." Don't worry; we aren't trying to. In yoga we would say that trying to see the future inside of a crystal ball would be akin to projecting suppressed subconscious content onto or into the crystal. Yogic *samadhi* or *samapatti* is quite the opposite. For the first time, we are trying to see the pure naked crystal, unimpeded by our subconscious projection.

Our meditation must be *sattvic*; our crystal example meets this requirement. According to yoga, *sattva* is one of the three elementary qualities or elementary particles of nature. These are called *tamas* (mass, inertia), *rajas* (energy, frenzy), and *sattva* (information, luminosity, wisdom, intelligence). Yoga considers them important because of their influence on the mind and acknowledges that, in its typical condition, it is impossible for the mind to arrive at knowledge without being slanted or biased by its surroundings.

Going back to our first proposed object of meditation, the steam engine, yogis would reject this as being too *tamasic* (massive, like a heavy lump of steel) on one hand and too *rajasic* (built to convert heat into velocity) on the other. That's not to say there's something wrong with steam engines (the marvelous attainment that they are), but for our current purpose, a same-sided or spherical crystal is better. In sutra I.41, a crystal is likened to the mind in a state of *samapatti*.

Try using a crystal (such as a crystal pyramid) as a mirror; if the crystal is of good quality, it will only reflect the object, so that the crystal is barely visible. Vijnanabhikshu's 14th-century commentary on this sutra says that if you place a crystal on a red rose, only red-rose-ness is depicted in the crystal, nothing else. This is how we want the mind to behave. If I meet another person, only that person is reflected in my mind and not the fears, prejudices, hopes, desires, etcetera that I usually project onto the individual. That's why yogis say you can only truly meet another person in *samapatti*. Otherwise you are only meeting endless permutations and projections of yourself. This has led to the premise of some philosophies that, "There is only me and nobody else." Yoga affirms the reality of a multitude of beings, but we must look for them beneath our conditioning.

Apart from a pyramid-shaped crystal or crystal ball, other suitable objects include a lotus, a rose, or a frangipani flower. These are not as easy because they are not translucent and especially the rose has quite a complex structure; but all of them are *sattvic*. Another possibility is a representation of the OM symbol, or any other sacred symbol. You can also meditate on a Divine image, if there is one that attracts you, or the name of the Divine written in your sacred language. If you take a written word I suggest it is in one of the old sacred languages, such as Sanskrit, Hebrew, Arabic, Old Greek, etcetera, because the representations that modern languages create in our subconscious are often too *rajasic*. Similarly, meditating on a Divine image is a great idea, but be sure the image is not making your mind *rajasic* in the initial stages. This could simply be due to the complexity of the image. Suffice to say, in the early stages of *samapatti*, the simpler the better.

SAMADHI 1: SAVITARKA SAMAPATTI (DELIBERATIVE IDENTITY)

About the first *samadhi*, Patanjali states in sutra I.42, "In deliberative (*savitarka*) *samapatti*, words, objects, and knowledge comingle through conceptualization." First, let's get this odd word *deliberative* out of the way. When Patanjali uses the word *savitarka*, he is conveying that basing our *samadhi* on a gross object that is perceptible to the senses, while our mind authentically represents it in its depth, the mind is still conceptualizing on the surface.

166

So let's say I have been practicing *asana, kriya, pranayama,* and Kundalini meditation to the extent that I can reasonably assume I have sufficiently arrested my conditioning. I am now gazing at my crystal pyramid (or a similar suitable object). The goal is to represent the crystal in my mind exactly as it is in front of me. While you imprint the crystal into your mind, check the quality of your posture; a good meditation posture such as *Padmasana, Siddhasana, Virasana,* or *Svastikasana* is ideal, but in any case, the back, neck, and head must be straight. Also be aware of your breathing; it is suggested to breathe as slowly as possible and ideally the breath is conducted throughout your entire torso. The next step is *pranic* awareness: breathe with a double-up wave (described in detail in *Yoga Meditation*) and drive *prana* to the higher centers.

During *samapatti, prana* is ideally located in the fifth energy center, called *Vishuddha chakra.* Stare at the crystal as if you were trying to suck it into your mind. Stare at it intently but with little or no eyeball movement; do not look around and don't let your eyes wander. You can stare at the object intently until your eyes get tired. Then close them and look at the afterglow of the object in your mind. Check how long the afterglow remains and how clearly it looks like the object. When the object fades away, open your eyes and stare at it again. This method is called *Trataka* and is important in this early stage of *samapatti.*

Eventually your mind becomes laser-like, so concentrated that it produces a digital copy of the object and then represents it in the mind. *Samapatti,* and all of the *samadhis,* are essentially about cultivating this laser-like capacity of the mind. The objects themselves are almost meaningless in the beginning. It is the mind we are trying to fine-tune. An object that is not overloaded with meaning, such as a lotus or a crystal, is preferable in the beginning. If you select an object with too much meaning too soon, you may become frustrated by not being able to represent it. This form of subconscious sabotage is quite common. It is less likely to happen if you initially choose an object that has little meaning for you.

At some point in your *samapatti* practice, you will succeed with imprinting the object in its authentic form. You will know this to be true when the mind completely settles on the object. You will also find that the eyes move very little or not at all. The perception of the object will not change anymore. If the object in the mind is identical with the object being meditated on, this is *samadhi* stage 1. Patanjali provides a very generous definition of this initial *samapatti*. He says that the object is comingled with knowledge and words, forming a conceptualization. Let's consider what this means in practical terms: I sit in front of my crystal and have finally succeeded at digitally duplicating it in the depth of my mind. At the same time, on the surface, my mind may still be discussing or deliberating on general knowledge about crystals, for example, its physical properties, how immaculate it is, or whether it has any flaws. To fulfill the definition of this *samadhi* (stage 1) my mind must successfully duplicate the object, but at the same time is allowed to engage in a dialogue about it. Can the mind really do both at the same time? You'd be surprised at how powerful the computational capacity of the mind is. This is also another reason why we initially choose simple objects. The mind can duplicate the objects, while only partially changing its structure.

Savitarka samapatti, identity with ongoing deliberation, is a humble beginning and introduction to *samadhi*. And it is actually possible. It is not a remote or elusive achievement. We find here in *samadhi* the same principle repeated that is the foundation of learning *asanas*, *kriyas*, *pranayamas*, and meditations: Start with simple and achievable steps. Once we have accepted that our mind is capable of practicing the first *samadhi*, we believe we can tackle the next. If we had to jump straight from our current state of confusion all the way to objectless *samadhi* or spiritual freedom, we might never take that first step.

SAMADHI 2: NIRVITARKA SAMAPATTI (SUPER-DELIBERATIVE IDENTITY)
Patanjali describes the next step in sutra I.43: "When memory is purified, the mind appears to be emptied of its own nature and only

the object shines forth. This is super-deliberative (*nirvitarka*) *samapatti*." In the last *samapatti*, two separate things were occurring. First, the object of meditation (our crystal pyramid) was digitally duplicated in our mind. The way we would typically discuss such an object was there, as well. In this new *samapatti,* the discussion ceases to exist. That's why it's called super-deliberative identity. It means "identity with object beyond discussion." Even the word "crystal pyramid" no longer exists. Nor am I worried about whether the future may or may not appear in the crystal or what its molecular structure is, or for how much I bought it, and so on.

Patanjali refers to this as an instance where "only the object shines forth." Notice the term "only." For *only* the object to shine forth, the mind needs to be emptied of its own apparent nature. The apparent nature of the mind is to project the past onto the future. The mind performs this action so that we can quickly identify objects for the purpose of survival. Imagine how challenging life would be if we had to relearn how to walk or drive a car every day. When quickly identifying objects for the purpose of survival, we don't drop into the heart or essence of the object—that would take too long. We take a short cut and project our past experiences onto the object. Indeed this is faster, but the problem is we are using our existing conditioning to identify new objects, thus prejudice enters the picture. For the duration of this *nirvitarka samapatti* (*samadhi* 2) memory has to be purified. This is an arcane way of saying I short-circuit my memory and do not allow it to be projected onto the present. Thus for the period of time in *samapatti,* we are aware only of the present object independent of any interpretation or modification that usually occurs through our mind.

Another way of saying this is to state that perception and knowledge have become asemiotic. That is, the object is seen for the first time, entirely independent of the meaning that the mind gives it. Modern philosophers, such as structuralists and postmodernists, criticize the yogic belief that perception can be asemiotic. They

169

claim that knowledge and perception are always subject to semiotics. (Semiotics is the theory of how we arrive at meaning, including the relation between verbal signs and what they refer to, or semantics). The theory of semiotics says that our very language contains cultural biases that influence and even determine how we see the world. Let me give you an example: I was sitting in the lecture of an Indian Tantric master who said, "Sigmund Freud is a scientist not a philosopher. What he says has weight. What he says matters." Needless to say, this Indian Tantric was actually a materialistic atheist, but my point concerns to what extent the currently predominant ideology of materialistic reductionism is embedded in our language.

Freud was a psychologist, and around 1875, modern psychology became an adjunct to medicine, rather than one of the humanities. Both modern Western psychology and medicine subscribe to materialistic reductionism, in that they reduce mind and consciousness to biochemical and bioelectrical impulses. In other words, they reduce mind and consciousness to matter. Do you notice how materialism is subtly (or, actually, quite overtly) embedded in the statement, "What a scientist says matters"? This cultural bias equates matter with importance. To communicate the same emphasis to a shaman of the amazon jungle, we would have to reword the statement to say something like, "What a scientist says spirits," as the shaman would not place such import on matter as such.

Consider the statement, "What a scientist says has weight." Again, weight is the prime property of "what matters"; it's mass. So imprinted in our language is the bias that matter matters and that what has the properties of matter, such as weight, is important. We also say "such and such an idea or person had impact," or we ask someone to "weigh- in on" a topic of discussion or controversy, thereby equating matter with importance, because *impact* refers to one material object crashing into another. Thus the opinion that what a scientist says "has weight, has impact, and matters" is already embedded into the semantics of our language.

170

Over the last 300 years we have developed a deep bias toward discounting anything that runs against the reduction of human beings to matter, to bioelectrical and biochemical processes in the brain. I describe this at length to make clear that, in deep *samadhi*, even the word processor in our brain must be suspended. There cannot be deep *samadhi* as long as cultural biases are present. Semiotics prevent us from accessing what yogis call the-object-as-such (i.e., the naked object, free of the affiliations and modifications that the word processor has attached to them). In some Buddhist schools, the same thing is called the *suchness-of-an-object*. It can only be cognized when the mind is steady and still, free of fluctuations— which leads me to what happens when one comes out of *samadhi*.

In *nirvichara samapatti*, any form of mental interpretation is suspended, and I am in a mystical state, during which I can experience the essence (*dharmin*) of an object. Then, at a certain point, I will come out of the *samadhi*. This is signaled by the mind switching on and, usually, interpreting my experience. I will try to cast into words what I have seen, either to explain it to myself or to pass it on to others. It is important to pass it on, but in order to do so, by definition I have to leave the mystical state. Now at this point, my word processor will switch back on–and with it, all semiotics, semantics, and cultural biases. You must understand that there are two distinctly different states. First is the cognition of the essence of the object in *samadhi* and then, when we start to describe the object and what we have seen, there is the exit of *samadhi* and reactivation of the mind.

Yogis and mystics often don't notice this change. They have seen something important in *samadhi* and fail to notice that, when the mind switches back on, it is still the same old mind that they are now using to describe an experience entirely beyond the mind. It is not uncommon for yogis and mystics to give too much importance to what they have seen. Semiotics and biases are suspended in *samadhi*; this is what Patanjali calls "*chitta vrtti nirodha*" (sutra I.2, "yoga is the stilling of the fluctuations

of the mind"). When the yogi leaves *samadhi*, the mind is projected forth once again and the yogi reenters the world of semiotics.

I'll give you a practical example: In the 1980s I spent a fair bit of
time in the Poona ashram of the Indian mystic Osho Rajneesh. At one
point he had over two million followers, so it was almost impossible
to get close to him. On this particular day, there was a change in the
security protocol. His Rolls Royce was stopped in a different location than usual and he was ushered down a laneway, where I bumped
into him. I stood right in front of him and had about 20 seconds to
look him straight in the eyes before his security guards managed to
get rid of me. When I looked into his eyes, I saw that he was in a
deep trance, he was in deep *samadhi*. His eyes did not move at all,
nor did he blink. There was absolutely no change of facial expression, no annoyance or concern at me standing in his way. His eyes
were unusually large, with an oceanic quality, as though the space
contained within them was endless—or so they appeared to me. And
when I looked into his eyes, I immediately entered *samadhi* myself.
I felt as though I was lifted off my feet and got sucked into his eyes
and fell into him. Inside there was this vast expanse of emptiness
and silence. He just stood there, infinite and empty and entirely at
peace. He wasn't worried that I might be an assassin and that security enabled me to drop into and duplicate his mystical state. Eventually his bodyguards sent me packing, but the time was enough.

But the story doesn't end here. I went to the visitors' entrance of
the auditorium, where Osho was going to speak. I was eager to learn
what he would talk about, having seen his state of mind. I was also
sure that anything he would say must be close enough to Divine
authority, because what else but absolute purity could be uttered in
such a state? As it turned out, he was speaking about genetic engineering and how soon enough we will be able to do away with
our ridiculous and random means of procreating. He predicted that
parents could soon go to a genetic engineer and select the genes,
personality, and talents of their child. They would be able to deter-

mine how much of Einstein, Genghis Khan, or Buddha's genes their child would have. It was one of the biggest nonsense lectures I had ever heard anyone give. Halfway through I realized that if Dr. Josef Goebbels, Hitler's Reichs propaganda minister, would have been present, he would have had a great time and agreed with most of what Rajneesh said, particularly the scientific breeding of humans.

The seeming contradiction was unsettling. My mind desperately tried to reduce one experience to the other; that is, either the mystical state was authentic and what he said was divine authority (the logic of the cult follower), or what he lectured on was unethical and dangerous nonsense, so his mystical state must have been fake (the logic of the skeptic). To this day I believe the most important thing I learned from Osho is that the two are not mutually exclusive.

Because a guru can display states like this, followers will take anything their guru says as gospel. Cynics and agnostics, on the other hand, will disclaim the validity of mystical states, because the mystic spoke nonsense afterwards. I then realized that mystics do both. Over the years I discussed this with the followers of many gurus, who became upset that I would challenge the gurus' perfection. And then I discovered Agehananda Bharati's book, *Light at the Center,* in which he says the mystical or peak experience confers absolutely no benefit outside of the experience itself. In other words, just because you can experience *samadhi* does not make you an authority on life. In my opinion, Bharati nailed it, and now I know why: the Austrian native first studied anthropology before going to India, where he lived for many years as a Hindu monk. Later in life Bharati went to the US and held a chair as Professor of Anthropology. He was probably one the first mystics to ever study concepts such as structuralism, postmodernism, and semiotics. Thus he knew that a simple experience of *samadhi* does not make one aware of the cultural biases that can only be observed by externally studying the development of our minds (versus from inside, through *samadhi*).

Yogis and mystics in general have often failed to under-

To research the cultural biases underlying the *Yoga Sutra* itself would be a vast and worthy subject, but beyond the scope of this text. Of course, in a text of such brevity (195 sutras), biases would be less overt than in a much larger text, such as the *Bhagavad Gita* (750 stanzas), the *Mahabharata* (100,000 stanzas), or the *Bible*, for example. Patanjali is certainly concerned with minimizing biases, which might partially explain the brevity of the text. Most notably, the absence of bias comes to the fore when Patanjali makes statements about *Ishvara* (the Divine). Here his language becomes almost clinical and aseptic and absent of any religious and sectarian undertones. Patanjali has been criticized for this for example by Acharya Ramanuja, one of the great theologians of Vaishnavism, who would like to have seen the text much more devotional. The scarcity of biases in the *Yoga Sutra* is also related to the fact that it does not by itself represent a new philosophy but a spiritual technology grafted onto the philosophy of the Samkhya. If we were to search for yogic biases, we would have to first direct our gaze towards the Samkhya teaching.

stand their own biases, such as sexism, racism, nationalism, and so on. And their followers don't understand the gurus are subject to it. This is part of the problem of charlatan gurus and cult leaders. In some cases these people have really entered *samadhi*, but then they start to believe their own story and don't notice their old biases re-assembling when they leave *samadhi*.

This is the most important thing to remember upon leaving *samadhi*: semiotics and conditioning return. Although terms like "semiotics" and "semantics" were not available in olden times, nor was research on the historical development of the mind, I believe some great teachers had an intuitive grasp of them. For example, in India the highest category of sages was called *mounas*, that means "silent ones." It was understood that if you try to put something inexpressible into words, its essence would be lost. Thus those who taught only through silence where highly regarded. One of those teachers was Gautama Buddha. Often the Buddha remained silent in response to many questions;

he intuitively understood that any response would be tainted with the historical biases of his mind. On other occasions he did speak, and on those occasions, it was impossible to speak without bias.

A teacher cannot be silent all the time, because silence lends itself more readily to misinterpretation than words. Both are subject to bias, but sometimes it is best to remain silent than to speak.

Another teacher who intuitively understood historical bias was Jesus Christ. When the Pharisees asked him, "Where is this Kingdom of Heaven you talk about?" He responded, "The Kingdom of Heaven cannot be gained by perception [(because perception is semiotic)]. For the Kingdom of Heaven is within." Another biblical passage describes "within" as "entering the closet of the Secret Chamber of the Most High." This is *samadhi* in yogic language! The *Upanishads* describe this direct experience of our innermost being, "the shrine of the heart." But as soon as this shrine, this most intimate experience, is expressed in words, it will necessarily be limited by the mind's biases and conditioning. In other words, as humanity spiritually evolves, each new generation reinterprets the teachings in a way that reflects our inherent cultural bias.

When practicing the second stage of *samadhi* we must continue to use our simple object until we can retain its duplication in our mind, with the mind (apart from holding the object) being completely silent and unwavering. I have heard Indian yogis say the object must be held for three hours, but I think that's extreme. Half an hour to 45 minutes is enough. After you have become proficient at duplicating a simple object, such as a crystal pyramid or OM symbol, move on to something slightly more complex. A lotus, frangipani, or rose would be an excellent second object. When you start with a new object there is usually a phase where the mind will want to discuss (deliberating) the object. This usually subsides after a while. If it does not, then the laser-like quality of the mind is not yet sufficiently cultivated, in which case, renewed effort must be made at Kundalini meditation, *kriyas*, *pranayamas*, and inversions.

175

Some teachers have suggested practicing *samapatti* on the sun and moon. The sun is a difficult object, as in most climates, one cannot look at it long enough without damaging the retina. The moon, or a particular star or planet, can make excellent objects. They should be low on the horizon, so that you can look at them without having to tilt your head excessively. To look up for half an hour is likely to make your neck extensors spasm. Although it is enjoyable to lie on the floor and watch the sky at night, entering *samadhi* in a reclining position is much more difficult, because Kundalini is a counterforce to gravitation and thus has a vertical direction.

Once you have mastered objects of medium complexity, move on to more elaborate objects, such as divine images. Many modern people have become thoroughly disenchanted with religion, and for that reason, it may not be possible to meditate on a divine image. Do realize that all of the corruption committed in the name of religion is the responsibility of humanity and not the Divine. I once saw a cartoon drawn by Australian artist Michael Leunig. On it was an old and haggard man meant to depict God. He was interviewed by a journalist who said, "We just found out that God joined the protest movement. What are you protesting for, God? Can you please raise your placard so that we can see it?" On the placard it says, "Not in my name." Our ideas of the Divine have developed alongside our evolution. In 1909 Danish nuclear physicist and Nobel Prize laureate Niels Bohr said, "Our physical laws do not describe the world but only our knowledge of the world." As our knowledge increases, our beliefs about the world change, too. Exactly the same must be said about the Divine. If you don't like what you see, remember that what you see simply is your *idea* of the Divine.

In my own practice, meditating on divine images has helped me to progress faster along the path than other methods. What's important is that you find an image or a tradition that *you* respond to positively. It must elicit a response from your subconscious, otherwise it won't work.

SAMADHI 3: SAVICHARA SAMAPATTI (REFLECTIVE IDENTITY).
Once you have become proficient with super-deliberative *sa-mapatti*, we move to the third stage, *savichara samapatti*. Super-deliberative *samapatti* was a significant step up, compared to the first *samadhi*, and this structure again repeats itself. Whereas the first two *samadhis* were practiced on gross objects (that is, objects perceptible to the senses), the next two *samadhis* are practiced on objects that are imperceptible to the senses. In sutra I.44, Patanjali says, "In this way, reflective (*savichara*) and super-reflective (*nirvichara*) *samapatti*, which are based on subtle objects, are also explained." This means the category of objects changes, but the relationship between the two *samadhis* is the same as with the two previous ones (deliberative and super-deliberative *samapatti).*

So, what are subtle objects? For someone who has been raised within the materialistic reductionist paradigm, it may be challenging to comprehend objects that are not perceptible to the senses, as we cannot obtain empirical data on them. The words of British poet and mystic William Blake come to mind: "There are things that we know and things that we don't know. In between there are doors." Some of the most important yogic subtle objects are the *chakras*, energy centers in the subtle body. I describe these in detail in Chapter 13 of *Yoga Meditation: Through Mantra, Chakras and Kundalini to Spiritual Freedom.* There I explain the *chakras* as evolutionary brain circuitry. Following this model, the three lower *chakras* represent reptilian, mammalian, and primate brain circuitry, respectively. We would not perform *samadhi* on any of these lower chakras, as it would not be helpful. (Please note that practicing *samadhi* on a *chakra* is completely different from the Kundalini meditation described in the above-noted book. There the purpose is to increase your ability to quickly switch between *chakras* to activate the one most suitable for the task at hand.)

Here I refer to practicing *samadhi* on a *chakra*, that is, staying focused on one particular *chakra* for the purpose of gaining deep spiritual insight. The ideal *chakra* for practicing *samadhi 3* (*savichara samapatti*) is the heart *chakra* (*Anahata chakra*). The lower three *chakras*, if meditated on for a long time, tend to draw you backwards towards materialism. The first *chakra* deals mainly with survival and fight and flight. The second *chakra* deals mainly with procreation, family, emotions, belonging, and group and mass psychology; these are all typical mammalian tasks and capabilities. The third *chakra* deals predominantly with personal power, manipulation, accumulation of wealth, linguistic skills, charisma, sales talk, leadership, ability to speak in public and captivate an audience, confidence, business management, and money skills. If you wish to develop any additional capacities in those three areas, I suggest using the method I describe in *Yoga Meditation*. To do so is a viable quest; but *samadhi* is too powerful a method and should only be used for spiritual evolution.

Conversely, if you practice *samadhi* on the fifth, sixth, and seventh *chakra* too soon, you could dishevel your life. The heart *chakra* is an ideal object for the introduction of *samadhi 3* (*savichara samapatti*). It increases our capacity to experience love towards all beings, forgiveness to those we perceive as having injured or slighted us, compassion for those in less fortunate situations, and gratitude for all the gifts we have been given. These amazing qualities will be of great help in most of the situations that life throws at you.

Yogis meditate on the heart *chakra* in the shape of a 12-petaled lotus that faces upwards towards the crown of the head. Petals are bright red in color. Visualize the *chakra* in the center of the chest on the height of the heart, strung like a flower or a bead on what is called the central energy channel (*sushumna*)—an incredibly thin line that runs roughly vertically in the space of the spinal cord in the gross body. A practical method of approaching this *samadhi* would be to get an image of the heart *chakra* and meditate on it with open eyes (you can download such an image for free from my website at *chintamaniyoga.com/product/chakras/*). This is an ad-

178

vanced yogic technique that should only be used when the lower *chakras* are opened through Kundalini meditation. If you start practicing *samadhi* on the heart *chakra* without having first activated your power *chakra* (the *manipura*), a victim mentality might ensue.

Once you have imprinted the image of the *chakra* in your memory, remove the physical image. Continue until you can see this subtle object without resorting to effort or willpower. Once the image is clear, permanent, and effortlessly held, you are technically practicing *samadhi 3*. In this *samadhi* the mind may still compartmentalize, that is, digitally duplicate the object and at the same time reflect on qualities of the *chakra*. It might say, "This is the heart *chakra*. It has twelve petals and is red. It bestows the qualities of love, compassion, forgiveness, joy, and gratitude..." and so forth. This is called *savichara samapatti* and means "identity with subtle object, including reflection on it." As in the previous *samapattis,* Patanjali included reflection for didactic purposes. He wants to offer a stepped path of achievement. Each accomplished step increases your confidence in tackling the next.

You may stay with the heart *chakra* until your mind becomes completely still and has ended any reflection (this is already *samadhi 4*). Alternatively, you may wish to choose a different subtle object, and you can do so right from the beginning, skipping the heart *chakra* (though I consider it an excellent subtle object). Other suitable objects are divine images. Again, you may start with a gross representation, a picture, for example, and then discard it once you have imprinted the image in your mind. You might also use a divine image you have seen in a vision or dream. Patanjali actually advises to do so in sutra I.38.

Although the majority of my meditations and *samadhis* have been on Hindu objects, I'm not trying to sell you Hinduism. Some of the most exulted states I have experienced occurred when meditating on mental images of Jesus Christ. There is an essence and underlying truth beyond words that is the same throughout all religions and sacred traditions. This essence is available for all of us, wherever we

179

come from, whatever our past was. It is the power brokers and orthodox authorities in the traditions that lose when we learn how to bypass
them and access the Divine directly. That's why they discourage it.

Another category of subtle objects is the sutras themselves, but also *mantras*, sayings, and formulas in other ancient languages. I have used stanzas in Hebrew and Arabic, and also Japanese Zen Koans, and I have found them
equally suitable. Of course, you need to understand the meaning
or purpose of the stanza or *mantra*, and it must make sense to you.

The *tanmatras* (quantums) are yet another category of subtle
objects I need to discuss; these are the subtle essences of the elements. In India they are some of the most important subtle objects
and some yogis use the *tanmatras* exclusively. I would not consider
them prime objects for students who do not have a very deep affili-
ation with Indian culture. Whatever your choice of object is, move
slowly from simpler to more complex. A divine image, for example,
is considered more complex than a *chakra,* but if the divine representation is very meaningful to you, it may be the better choice.
Some stanzas or sutras contain more complex concepts than others.

SAMADHI 4: NIRVICHARA SAMAPATTI (SUPER-REFLECTIVE IDENTITY)

Once we go deeper into reflective *samapatti,* we can eventually let go of reflection. In this context, reflection refers to what
the mind projects onto the object, apart from its duplicate representation. Once the mind has become absolutely still, apart from
reflecting the object, we are in *samadhi* 4, called super-reflective
identity (*nirvichara samapatti*). This is considered a momentous
achievement, because now the mind will automatically gravitate
towards freedom, although freedom itself might yet be unattained.

Let's recall what Patanjali says about *samadhi* 2, which is similar
in nature to *samadhi* 4. Sutra I.43 states, "When memory is purified, the mind appears to be emptied of its own nature and only the
object shines forth." This means we have, to a large extent, over-

come the nature of the mind, which is to project any form of content onto the present sensation or object, as long as it seemed to give a reasonably close match. This is far more significant in *samadhi 4,* compared to 2, because the latter still relies on empirical objects that are apprehendable by the senses. For example, "Love" is considered a subtle object because it is not perceivable through the senses. Our emotions, our love life, and our relationships often suffer because the mind projects our needs, hopes, fears, and desires onto a suitable screen—that *"screen"* being another human being. Unless we have done some serious work on ourselves or are what's called an "old soul" (a wise person with a lot of experience), we will project our subconscious content onto the people we meet. We will then relate to them in accordance with our projection and not from who they truly are. This results in us being hurt and disappointed over and over again, until we have learned our lesson. And this is a challenging lesson to learn, because it is difficult to recognize our own projections. We believe we see another person as they truly are, when in fact our perception is nothing but a mirror of our own psyche. Thus when the person behaves in the way we had subconsciously feared, our mind will say, "See? I told you so! You can't trust them!" In truth, the mind has set up a situation in such a way that the initial hypothesis (you will get hurt) will be confirmed.

Can you imagine a mind that is free of projection, whereby you would see other people for who they are, without this reflection of your own psyche? In *samadhi* 4, memory is purified, which means you can decide whether you wish to recall past data concerning a current situation, or not, by mechanically and subconsciously cataloguing them according to their significance for survival. If you choose to recall the data, then your second choice concerns whether you let it color the object or not. For example, when you meet a person of a particular background and recall what you have experienced with other people of a similar background, you are free to reject that information and see this person as a unique individual—or not.

181

What does Patanjali say about the effects of this *samadhi*? Sutra I.41 says, "When the mind-waves are reduced, the mind truthfully reflects any object it is directed towards like a pristine crystal, whether it be the perceived, the process of perceiving, or the perceiver. This state is called identity (*samapatti*)." I consider this sutra to be one of the most important stanzas. I grew up in a haze and instinctively knew there was a real world somewhere, but that I couldn't find nor could I see it. This sutra says that, through training (the *samapattis*), you can cultivate your mind in such a way that it will experience whatever you direct it towards. If you direct it towards *the perceived*, you will experience the world for the first time as it truly is, for you will have withdrawn your biases.

If you concentrate on *perceiving* you will understand the mind itself for the first time. Yoga is the science of the mind, the ancient Vedic form of psychology. If you divert the mind towards "the perceiver," you will experience yourself as pure, infinite, and eternal consciousness, a process that eventually culminates in spiritual liberation. More effects of this *samadhi* are revealed in sutra I.47. Here Patanjali says, "Through skill in super-reflective (*nirvichara*) *samapatti*, the mind is made clear and bright." Notice that he talks about developing a skill, becoming an expert in something. Do not expect that, from entering this *samadhi* once for five minutes, your mind will be transformed. Our attitude should be more that, whenever we enter this *samadhi*, it will have a purifying effect on the mind. This step-by-step process is similar to learning an instrument. It won't happen all at once. It is gradual and progressive. The more we work on it, the closer we come to completing the task. If you are on the path of *samadhi*, do not expect all of your problems to suddenly disappear. Be wary of those who tell you otherwise.

But the benefits of this *samadhi* are even greater. Sutra I.48 says, "There the wisdom is truthful (*rtambhara*)." We see subtle phenomena, such as *chakras*, mantras, sacred stanzas, love, beauty, etc., for the first time, completely independent from us.

This means we recognize they have a life of their own, entirely distinct from our projections. Upon this realization, we experience for the first time a sacred order (*rta*) underlying the cosmos. We realize there are divine laws of harmony ruling all beings. These laws are not of our choosing and are beyond our creation and manipulation. The more we can bring ourselves into alignment with these laws, the freer and more joyful our life will be.

Sutra I.49 says, "This knowledge is different from that gained through scripture and inference, because it is of a particular thing." Patanjali is saying that knowledge gained in this *samadhi* is radically different from all we have known so far. For the first time, we can see an object as it truly is, the *thing-as-such*. Prior to this *samadhi*, Patanjali says there are three avenues to apprehending an object (keeping in mind we are talking about subtle objects, such as love). The first of these avenues is direct perception through the senses; another is inference or deduction from things we already know; and the third is valid testimony, such as sacred texts. In all three cases we only get general knowledge referring to the category of our current object but not about the actual object we are apprehending. This basically means, "You cannot be sure of what's in front of you unless you have suspended your conditioning." Let us consider the object "woman," as an example. This is particularly easy for me to explain, given that I currently live in a male body. Patanjali says that, before *Samadhi* Stage 4, it is unlikely I will genuinely meet a particular woman for the first time. Each time I do, I will first meet and confront my own mother, and then my first partner, and finally all the women I have ever met and who collectively form the imprint in my subconscious called "woman." Thus each time I meet a particular woman, I am also confronting my entire history with women. I could take this a step further and admit that I will also confront my own femininity, the woman within me. So there is little space left to meet any woman anew; in fact, I am meeting an entire category. *Samadhi* 4 frees us from our past so that we can see people or things independent of such categories. In sutra I.50 Patanjali completes the subject by stating, "The subconscious imprint produced from such knowing reconditions us." This is a most radical statement! He says there is a real world out there, but we can't see it. The world we see is a model of the world we have manufactured within our own mind. While this model is helpful for the purpose of survival, it is useless if we wish to know the truth. The truth can only be experienced in small increments, step by step, replacing the superficial model of the world you have built. The good news is such a radical reconstruction of our minds is possible. However, it is a gradual process, almost imprint by imprint, and this is why so many of us lose sight of it. Our spiritual success seems too distant for us to notice the interconnection. Each *samadhi* experience will leave imprints of truth, of reality, on the mind, and once enough of these are planted, once a critical mass has been gained, the whole mind will gravitate towards truth.

SAMADHI 5: ECSTASY (ANANDA) SAMADHI

This *samadhi* is called *ananda samadhi*. *Ananda* means "ecstasy," sometimes more piously translated as *bliss*. This and the next (*asmita samadhi*) *samadhi* are mentioned only once in the *Yoga Sutra*. In stanza I.17, Patanjali says that objective *samadhi* goes through four *stratas*, which he calls *gross object, subtle object, ecstasy (ananda)*, and *I-am-ness (asmita)*. Of these four stages, the first two are subdivided into two sub-stratas. There is a lot of confusion about the meaning of this *samadhi* and its technique, due to the fact that historical commentators have not provided many clues and also because Patanjali himself was tight-lipped. But he offers a hint in sutra I.40: "Mastery is achieved when the mind can concentrate on any object from the smallest atom to the entire cosmos."

In *samadhis* 1 through 4, we learn to consecutively contemplate increasingly complex objects. It is smart to progress slowly, as the mind has difficulty wrapping itself around seemingly large and complex objects. When I started to practice on complex objects, I found myself unable to expand my mind enough. There were glimpses of truth but never anything consistent. I managed to focus on a large and complex object for a few minutes, but then my concentration failed and I found myself thinking again. This state of affairs basically went on for years. I continued to practice all limbs of yoga, but could not go beyond *samadhi* 4. Eventually I realized I could not bring about those other states by sheer will power or effort. The higher *samadhis* were simply not within my reach.

At some point I understood that living in a city scattered my mind enough to prevent me from accessing those subtle states. I had created an oasis for myself, but the general restlessness, frustration, and mad scramble of the city came through in meditation. I used to wake before the crack of dawn to sit in our garden to practice. Before me was a lotus pond with water trickling down over a feature. But above the sound of gentle trickling water was the roar of the awakening city, thousands of cars being started and rushing to the freeway, and onwards to the central business district. I could sense the adrenaline-fueled vibration of over a million people gulping down their early morning coffees to fuel themselves for achieving and attaining their daily goals, or even just to survive the daily grind and continue on for another day in what some people perceive as a meaningless, depressing, and materialistic rat race. Of course this isn't the only thing going on in cities, but it is a recurring theme that enters conversations with my students who describe their practice difficulties.

I tried for years to go deeper but couldn't. I had hit a wall in my practice. Eventually I was forced to admit that a greater practitioner than I would have managed despite the obstacles of city life, but that my mind was too fragile and too susceptible to the general undertone of the hustle and bustle of the metropolis to succeed. And then I received an intuition that there was a place in nature where I could go to receive those higher states. My particular subconscious was organized in a way that being secluded in nature

185

The *Gaia* theory was originally put forth by chemist James Lovelock. It shows that organisms shape their environment and collectively maintain factors that support life. For example, oceanic life evolved under certain salinity levels; without life essentially taking control of salinity levels in the oceans, they would have spiked to such extent that all life would have been wiped out long ago. For example, if floods wash out large salt deposits on the continents, ocean salinity will spike. During phases when the planet warms, large ice sheaths will melt and salinity will drop.

Nevertheless it has been found that oceanic salinity during the last two billion years was steady within certain narrow parameters. This is due to the fact that if salinity rises, sea organisms bind salt to their shells, bones, and coral reefs; and if salinity drops, the bio mass releases salt back into the oceans, so that it remains constant. Considering the size of the ocean and the amount of water contained in it, it is a breathtaking feat that sea organisms managed to achieve this. Similarly, the content of the atmosphere, particularly its oxygen/carbon dioxide balance, is subject to ongoing fluctuations that would quickly put an end to life on land; otherwise, life itself would control the content of the atmosphere by a subtle cooperation between plants and animals. If no animals were present on the planet, the atmosphere would become so oxygen-rich that a single lightning bolt would ignite the whole planet. To prevent this, animals use the oxygen and convert it into carbon dioxide. Plants absorb carbon dioxide and convert it back into oxygen to feed the animals (and humans).

The whole mechanism functions only as long as there is a subtle balance between the plants and animals. We could say the atmosphere is co-created by plant and animal life and the oceanic environment is co-created by sea creatures. Similar are the effects of life on global surface temperatures and the balance between acidity and alkalinity (ph). The totality of all organisms on Earth, as if directed by one common intelligence, provide the homeostasis (the maintenance of stable and surprisingly constant conditions) that life needs to flourish. Gaia (Earth) can thus be called a live super-organism, not in the sense that it reproduces, but in the sense that it is comprised of trillions of organisms, each of them fulfilling their own part to keep harmony of the super-system.

would enable it to receive these states. Most of humanity's sacred traditions advise retreating to a secluded spot in nature, but it isn't necessary for everyone. At one point I had a vision of myself, sitting in meditation on a forest-covered mountain, on what looked like the Australian East Coast, overlooking the Pacific Ocean. I knew this was the place I was looking for; I felt the urge to find this place, to go live and practice there. On the other hand, buying such a mountain property was well outside our financial means. Soon enough I began to doubt my vision and then forgot it altogether.

About a year later, my wife and I came across a photo advertising a property that attracted us enough to arrange an inspection. Several kilometers of driveway snaked up steep slopes, cliffs, and ancient rainforests. When we arrived on top of the mountain and set our feet on the soil, that mountain gripped us and took possession of us. We looked at each other and knew. This was the place. After several months of scraping together the funds, and after it appeared for some time that the whole idea would fail, we somehow managed to secure the property. A few days later, a CD arrived containing hundreds of photos of our land taken from a helicopter. Among them was a picture of a jungle-covered mountain overlooking the Pacific Ocean; it was the exact image that appeared in my vision two years before.

After initial problems (we had to get about nine tons of books and hand carved stone statues [admittedly, a few kitchen utensils, too] up a 400-meter-high cliff face), I started going to the mountain top every morning to practice *samadhi* for at least 90 minutes and sometimes for several hours; on occasions when I had no responsibilities, I stayed for up to 10 hours a day. I started before the crack of dawn (called *brahmi muhurta* in India, meaning *the divine time,* or the time during which we are closest to God), facing east, in the direction of the Pacific Ocean. I gained a visceral understanding why solitude and nature make *samadhi* easier to reach.

We are not isolated individuals but a collective psychology. Each nation, group, city, and metropolis forms its own psyche. For ex-

187

ample, if a country is attacked, suddenly everyone is gripped by fear and wants to retaliate. Fear-driven blood thirst develops among the citizens. Similarly, large events, whether terrorist attacks, sporting events, or natural catastrophes, leave marks on our collective psyche. They change us all. When I attempted to practice deep *samadhi* in the city, I was unsuccessful because I could sense our collective anxiety, depression, rage, disappointment, and avarice. The yogi, however, wants to go in a different direction than the collective emotional atmosphere dictated by a frenzied mass media.

Sitting in solitude on the mountaintop, with the last fading starlight over me and the first glimpses of eos on the eastern horizon, everything fell into place. My mind expanded to absorb and duplicate increasingly large systems. I meditated first on the entire mountain and from there felt as though my mind zoomed out to include most of the Australian East Coast. Eventually my mind engulfed the entire Australian continent and from there the whole of the Pacific Ocean. Onwards it was only a small step to concentrate my mind on the whole planet. I saw this incredible beautiful blue object, floating there in black space, and I just held it in my mind. I was suddenly reminded that many of the astronauts who were the first to ever see this image had spiritual experiences when they saw Earth floating in space.

When I saw the planet suspended in space I understood the ultimate power of the infinite intelligence that created it. The planet is such a vast and intricate, complicated system, and yet all its manifold subsystems, including the atmosphere, the oceans, the continents, all life forms, the volcanic core, and so on, work together to keep it in balance. Of themselves these systems may seem limited in, or even bereft of, intelligence, but together they reflect the infinite intelligence that drives them and expresses itself through them. Great ecstasy arose when I saw this. I understood that this magnificent object, our planet, is actually alive and that you and I are part of it.

The system itself contains such a huge number of movable parts and components that even if you put all of the scientists of

188

humanity together to design such a system, they could not replicate even a fraction of it. It is impossible to build such a syn-
chronistic system of perfection. From an artistic perspective,
too, nothing humanity has ever created or might later create,
will ever come close to the awe-inspiring artistic genius of Gaia.

This perfection brings to mind the less-than-perfect integration
of a relatively new add-on, a new component of the super-organism
Gaia: human beings. The interruption that humans pose to the harmony of our planet seems mainly to come from science and technology. Some suggest we need to go back to nature to rectify it.
Our amazing scientific progress has come at the price of spiritual
retardation, with humanity being this technological giant with the
spiritual development of a four-year old. Though we have thrown
everything at conquering the world, nature, and the biosphere, we
have invested little in our spirituality. In the past, humanity seemed
more connected to its spiritual roots than today in our modern
world. The ancient law books, rules, and guidelines—the very foundation of our civilizations—were built on the experiences of mystics. The peak experiences of Confucius, Socrates, Buddha, Jesus
Christ, Muhammad, and others formed our very identities. Science
has become the predominant power over the last 300 years, with
science and religion (which is encrusted mysticism) pitted against
each other. By all means, let's use science and technology to create
solutions, but the choice concerning how to use science must arise
from ethical considerations. And these ethics and insights regarding
how to live harmoniously with nature and the cosmos must derive
from the mystical experiences of people like you and me. This is
why it is so important that we continue to develop our spirituality.

But *ananda samadhi* does not end with *samadhi* on our biosphere.
Patanjali says mastery extends from the smallest to the greatest object. In this *samadhi* we need to expand our mind in order to absorb the object, and we can do so only with finite objects that have
form, as a galaxy does. The mind cannot understand or duplicate

189

consciousness, which is infinite. But it can take in the entire solar system, then the Milky Way galaxy, and eventually all 200 million known galaxies within our own known universe. And it doesn't stop there. The universe we know came out of the Big Bang. In the Vedic teachings, the Big Bang is called *OM*. It is the primordial vibratory pattern that sets all things into motion. And the Big Bang is not a one-off phenomenon. There is an ongoing process of universes being birthed by OM, sustained through billions of years, and then reabsorbed. Astrophysics now tells us there may be almost infinite numbers of parallel universes. They may be of two different types, ones that are adjacent to our own and those that share the same space as our known universe. Scientists are already looking for the former and believe to have spotted the first signs, that is, traces of our universe having bumped into neighboring universes. Those that share the same space as ours may never be found, but either way, try to expand your mind to include even parallel universes, remembering that their number is likely to be close to infinite.

If you can do this, your mind will have achieved the greatest expansion possible for contemporary humans. You will have included the whole cosmos. Sit there and remain in that space, seeing, as the *Chandogya Upanishad* would have it, this entire vast cosmos with all its rivers, mountains, oceans, planets, galaxies, pulsars, quasars, and black holes that reside there in the center of your chest, where there is a small triangular shrine with a small flame inside, the shrine that is your heart.

Upon seeing the vast cosmos comprised of infinite parallel universes, we feel and understand there is no such thing as dead matter. All matter is the vibrant manifestation of divine intelligence, is the body of God, is manifest spirit. It is this view, this *ananda samadhi,* which gave rise to shamanic and animistic culture, the mother culture of our planet. It is the ability to see all matter as crystallized spirit. All places, mountains, rivers, and trees are crystallized spirit; and in recognizing this, we did not rise above the

190

material world, but were enabled to be in it, with it, and through it as an integral part of ourselves. Only later, when we became estranged from nature, did we feel the need to rise above it, felt that we needed to conquer, defeat, and exploit it. We are just a part, a small expression of the vast intelligence that manifests as mountains, trees, and rivers, etcetera—which are all spirit.

To say that rivers and mountains "are" spirit is different from saying they "have" consciousness. Consciousness implies choice; for example, the decision to move to a different place or to act differently. This means consciousness is also linked to creating individual *karma*. Mountains, trees, rivers, and so on do not have choice and don't create individual *karma*. Nevertheless, they are a manifestation of infinite spirit and infinite consciousness and thus are also a sacred expression of the Divine. No matter exists apart from crystallized spirit. There is no place that is not sacred. There is no being that is

The term "consciousness" requires some clarification. In Western psychology it is often used for that which we are conscious of; in other words, it is the content of our mind. In yoga and Indian philosophy, consciousness means "that entity that is conscious." Western scientists would say it is the mind that is conscious and would then reduce the mind to the body (i.e., biochemical and bioelectrical impulses). In deep meditation, usually cultivated over decades, however, we find that consciousness is neither contained nor present within the mind, nor within the body, but you experience that both body and mind are applications that are functioning within the operating system of the "I-thought," in Sanskrit usually called *aham-vrtti* or *ahamkara (i-maker)*. Patanjali uses the term *asmita* for this entity, I-am-ness. If we go even deeper with meditation practice, we find that awareness is not present here either, but that there is an even deeper core to the human being to which body, mind, and even I-am-ness arise to, a core that is aware of all these layers as being superficial or external. It is only in this deepest layer that pure, content-less awareness is contained. This layer is the consciousness, the *purusha*.

not divine. This is common knowledge to indigenous cultures of the world, yet we look down on this belief and consider it primitive and backward. It is not. The indigenous cultures of the planet performed the heroic act of living in harmony with nature for 100,000 years. Native Americans had the technology to make buffalos extinct long ago, but they had the wisdom not to, to take only as much as they needed. We didn't have that wisdom. We shot the buffalo down within decades.

Being able to consciously access and propagate this *samadhi* will help us to reclaim our aboriginal and indigenous ancestry. It is something still alive within us, albeit deeply buried, and it is something we must awaken. The ideology that we are all separate individuals powered by selfish genes competing against each other for limited resources has brought us to the brink of our own extinction. The ecstatic experience of seeing the entire cosmos as a manifestation of divine law and divine love, of which we are a small but integral and responsible part, will encourage us to re-integrate into the larger framework of nature and the cosmos.

None of the existing texts have explained why this *samadhi* is called *ananda*. The ecstasy experienced here has a distinctly raucous character, akin more to the ecstatic dances and drums of shamanic and tribal cultures than the politically correct and upper-class yogic bliss. Psychiatrist Stanislaf Grof divided ecstasies into those with oceanic and those with volcanic characteristics. The one we discuss here is of the volcanic type.

Ecstasy is important. You have a sacred right to ecstasy. It is the birth right of every organism, because our Divine Mother is in a constant state of ecstasy. In fact, it is questionable whether any organism can truly flourish without the sacred sentiment of ecstasy. The bedrock of all yogic teachings, the fertile ground from which all yoga rose, is the *Upanishads*, the mystical doctrines of the *Vedas*. Of the *Upanishads*, foremost, oldest, and largest is the *Brhad Aranyaka Upanishad*. In the *Brhad Aranyaka* the most important sections are those taught by the *rishi* (seer) Yajnavalkya, the same seer who invented the Brahman doctrine, that everything is infinite consciousness. Yajnavalkya was invited to the court of the emperor Janaka and was there challenged by Janaka's court priests. When asked to describe how it felt to experience infinite consciousness, the seer answered, "Imagine the joy of the richest person in the world, combined with the pleasure of the greatest sexual orgasm, combined with exultation of the most powerful person in the world. Now multiply this by three trillion. Then you will have the ecstasy of apprehending Brahman." Nobody could call these old seers prudish, could they? In a similar passage in the *Vijnana Bhairava*, we are advised to look closely at sexual ecstasy. Such ecstasy, according to the *Vijnana Bhairava*, is not due to sensory stimulus but to the ecstatic nature of the consciousness that observes it (Shiva).

In the *Bhagavad Gita*, revelation is also described in stark language. Stanza XI.12 reads, "Even the simultaneous effulgence of thousands of suns in the sky would barely compare to the splendor of the Divine [witnessed by Arjuna]." Again this is a far cry from pious bliss!

After having concentrated upon an incredible large object, we have completed Patanjali's requirement of sutra I.40. In sutra I.41 he recommends focusing on the *seen*, the *seeing,* and the *seer*. Where *ananda samadhi* focuses only on the seen, *samadhi* 6 will focus on seeing (*asmita* and *buddhi*). Seeing is divided into I-am-ness (*asmita*), which is experienced in *samadhi* 6, and intelligence (*buddhi*), which is discussed in *samadhi* 7. The seer, which is consciousness (*purusha*) itself, is covered in *samadhi* 8.

SAMADHI 6: INDIVIDUATION (ASMITA) SAMADHI

This *samadhi* also presented me with a brick wall for half a decade, yet when I began meditating on the mountain, its arrival was almost effortless. *Asmita samadhi* presented me with a great riddle, and the fact that Patanjali only mentions it in one stanza doesn't help! What's strange is there is a mode of suffering (*klesha*) that shares the name of a type of *samadhi*. How can *samadhi* be called

193

the same as a mode of suffering? Patanjali says the following about this mode of suffering in sutra II.6: "I-am-ness (*asmita*) is to perceive the seer and seeing as one." Those hoping for an indiscriminate being-one-with-everything have long struggled with this and a series of other stanzas in the *Yoga Sutra*. The seer is pure consciousness, the embodied self. Pure consciousness is "that what is conscious" (as opposed to the content of such consciousness).

Consciousness can be understood through the metaphor of a movie screen: When you project movie images onto a screen, the images are all changing, with none sticking to the screen. After the movie is finished, the screen looks exactly the same as it did before the images were presented. Such is consciousness—aware of all that occurs, but free of conditioning. Thus yogis say consciousness is pure, eternal, and infinite; consciousness is the self.

Now let's have a look at "seeing." Seeing is another word for the process and instrument of cognition. Without going too much into yogic psychology (which meticulously differentiates between I-thought, mind, and intellect), let's call the instrument of cognition "the mind." Throughout the duration of my life, my mind has certainly changed—hopefully for the better. I might have purged prejudice, sexism, and racism from it. But on the other hand, some negative experiences may have left post-traumatic stress disorder (PTSD) in their wake. As I grow older, a tendency towards obsessive–compulsive disorder (OCD) may surface, whereas my youth showed a greater tendency to oppositional defiant disorder (ODD) (any similarities with living persons are not intended). In this way the mind tumbles from one disorder to the next (this is slightly exaggerated, but you get the point), whereas consciousness silently looks on, in the meantime, unchanged.

Because the mind constantly receives an imprint of what is happening in our lives, it is said to be stainable (impure), whereas consciousness is un-stainable (pure). This is why the two can never meet. But due to their vicinity, because consciousness is always aware of what the mind presents, the two (mind and consciousness) are often erroneously considered to be a single agency. This misunderstanding is one of the main modes of suffering (*klesha*), and Patanjali calls it I-am-ness (*asmita*). For our purposes, I will translate the term as "egotism." Thus egotism is the inability to dis-identify with our thoughts and perceptions; it is the belief that we are just our mind. The truth is that we have thoughts, just as we have a body. Millions of thoughts go through our mind daily. The trouble begins when we identify with them.

VIVEKANANDA AND EGO BASHING

Modern spiritual teachers, including Swami Vivekananda (1863–1902), see the ego and the mind as culprits for pretty much anything that goes wrong. Vivekananda suggested we "tear out the rascal ego by its root" and "annihilate the mind." But this call to action is too simplistic. During the early 1900s, such calls were made because the usage of terms such as "ego" (drawn straight from Freud's first English editions) gave them a scientific air. But even today similar appeals persist among spiritual teachers and gurus. No modern psychologist can endorse such a view because annihilation of either the mind or the ego would leave us in a vegetated or schizophrenic state. Turning parts of your psyche against itself leads to a psychic battlefield, because who will do the tearing and annihilation? It is the same ego that demands to be destroyed. There is no solution in exclusion, only integration.

I-am-ness in a pure sense means "I-maker." In *Samkhya* philosophy (the philosophy on which yoga is based), this "I-maker" is called *ahamkara*. Sometimes this is translated as "cosmic ego," in that it refers to intelligence that is aware of itself as a being. In other words ego is "God-with-form" or "God as being-ness." When explaining his technique of tracing the I-thought back to its origin, Indian sage Ramana Maharishi used the Sanskrit term *aham-vrtti*, which means "I-thought" in English. He rightly pointed out that 'a' and 'ha' are the first and last letter of the Sanskrit alphabet and that the I-thought is the beginning, end, and everything in between. Similar passages occur in the Bible (Revelation 1:8, 11, and 21:6): "I am Alpha and Omega, the beginning and the end, sayeth the Lord." Notice also that I-AM in the Old Testament is the name of the Lord. Similarly, when the Lord commands Moses to tell the pharaoh to let the Israelites go, and Moses asks in whose name he should go, the Lord answers, "My name is I AM THAT I AM." The *aham-vrtti* or I-am-ness is also called the *chit-achit granthi*, the knot that tics the conscious (self and awareness) to the unconscious (matter and body). We could call it the greatest invention of the Divine (if there was such a thing).

So how do we now reconcile the divinity of the "I-thought" or "I-Am" on one hand and the "rascal ego" on the other? Obviously God cannot have an ego, as ego means limitation in space and time. Our challenge is to understand the term *ego*. Freud's original work in German called the ego "Ich," meaning "I." When his work was translated into English, the more scholarly Latin term *"ego"* was chosen (again to sound more scientific). While the term *"I"* awakes connotations reminiscent of the alpha and omega, the term "ego" reminds us more of the pathological state of mutative ego or egotism. But how are the two related? Individuation (*asmita) samadhi* is contemplation on and revelation of the pure and original I-Am, that pristine I-am-ness. However, this pristine I-AM cannot be limited in time or space and thus can only be aware of its creation in a general sense. In order that I-AM can experience its own creation in detail, it has replicated itself in infinite numbers that are limited in space and time, that being *us.*

Each being is made in the image and likeness of the Divine and therefore must have freedom and choice. Robots cannot replicate Divine Freedom. In order to become conduits for I-am-ness, we must be free. But to be free, we must be free of making poor and sub-standard choices. The individual that is limited in time and space inevitably makes poor choices, which lead to suffering (in addition to high-quality choices). From this arises the entire complex that we now call ego or egotism, which is the perceived need to pursue one's own advantage to the detriment of others.

I will now define some terms more precisely, so that we can rigorously describe this grossly misunderstood subject. Let's call the Divine's feel of knowing itself as "being-ness," "I-am," or "I." When it forms the core of an embodied being, limited in time and space, it morphs into ego. The very fact that we have a mortal body creates our identification with and desire to preserve it. At this point, ego is not yet pathological, because the individual is still aware of cosmic I-am expressing itself through that person. Once this awareness is completely lost and we identify exclusively with the body, the *I* becomes pathological egotism, mutative ego, or as Patanjali would have it, the mode of suffering (*klesha*) referred to as *asmita*.

The way back to the pristine I-Am, the cosmic I-maker, is through individuation (*asmita) samadhi. Asmita samadhi* shows us we are not the body but rather pure consciousness, a living and purposeful conduit of a vast being-ness that breathes, lives, experiences, and co-creates the world with and through us. Through *asmita samadhi* we experience what the *Gita* calls, "the self in the heart of all beings." There is no being that is not divine, no infidels, no cretins, no *untermenschen*; there are only those in whom we do not (yet) comprehend the Divine. This *samadhi* tells us to see the Divine in people we don't understand. Each being becomes an expression through which the Divine manifests itself. Jesus Christ expressed this when he said, "You will recognize my disciples by their love for one another."

When we understand and experience this, we can let go of the idea that ego can be completely destroyed. It can be suspended in a mystical state for some time, but it must then resurface because it serves a purpose. To experience ourselves as channels for the Divine leads to a letting go of egotism (the perception that we are limited to our body and mind) and a sublimation of ego, but never to its complete destruction. For ego is necessary in order for the Divine to individuate through an infinite number of beings. As long as we are aware that the

Divine is individuating through us, our behavior will not be egotistic. If there were no ego at all, there would be no individual and therefore no perception of the universe in detail, but only in a general sense.

Tradition has it that Gautama Buddha and Jesus Christ were tempted by the devil. In both cases the devil offered them king-doms, armies, palaces, all of the wealth on earth, concubines, and so on. The Devil and Satan are metaphors for egotism or mutative ego. The Divine expressed itself as great wisdom in both Christ and the Buddha; and in both cases, egotism rose and said, "Take you, the body of Buddha or Christ, the limited being, the cred-it for what is happening. It is you who owns this knowledge. Use it for cementing yourself as a world ruler." Both men refused, and Jesus even said, "Let thy will be done not mine." In this *sa-madhi* we feel it is not us who breathes this body, it is not us who moves us and thinks, but an ancient and infinite being that works through us and as us. This *samadhi* allows us to surrender to this guidance. Although we may still appear to be acting in accordance with the body, we are actually acting according to a higher will.

Individuation *samadhi* brings us to the important concept of *svad-harma*, which means "own duty." The *Bhagavad Gita* (III.35) says, "Better your own duty (*svadharma*) fulfilled in a faulty way than somebody else's duty really well." When we experience that this magnificent and benevolent divine presence breathes through us and experiences itself as us, we feel that it wants to do something through us, it wants to become itself as us. Now, this has nothing to do with fate or determinism, but if you listen to this guidance and follow it, you will feel an absence of all inner dialogue. Usually when we make a decision, we continue talking to ourselves, per-haps saying, "I'm not sure this will work; maybe I should have done something else; is this really what I want to do? Am I meant to do this?" These forms of inner dialogue weaken our resolve. When we start to follow the guidance of the Divine, we will notice an absence of such dialogue. We are still, at peace, happy, resting in ourselves, knowing that we are fulfilling our purpose of giving to the world what we came to give it. To do so is *svadharma* (own duty). Most important is that your duty is your own, not somebody elses. Nobody else can tell you what that duty is; only you can feel it. Each person's *svadharma* must be different, because the world has many different needs. We cannot all be rock stars, master chefs, or real estate tycoons. This differs from fate in that it means the Divine is creating our reality *with* us. It does not imply slavery but true freedom.

Asmita samadhi focuses on one's *I-am-ness* or one's *sense-of-I*. In this state, one dives deeper and deeper into this sense-of-I, and its outer layers begin to fall away. This is an advanced form of contemplation. In order to succeed, one must cease to identify with the body and mind. This identification can be overcome by meditating on the body until one realizes that this body identification (to which the body arises) is not contained in the body itself but is a deeper *strata*. One also realizes that the body changes, though the awareness itself does not. The process is then repeated with meditation on the mind. Thoughts are especially evident when meditating on the mind. One then asks to whom the thought arises, to which the answer is "I," or "me." But when contemplating the "I," one realizes the outer layers comprise identifications such as, "I have this and this title, this is my name, this is my personality, I am this type of person." As one dives deeper into meditation and into deeper layers of our psyche, all concepts of this nature are stripped away and we experience the pure and pristine *I-am*, as we join with the Divine. This is *samadhi* on pure being-ness. Individuation (*asmita*) *samadhi* is to feel how the Divine is becoming aware of itself as life, as you.

SAMADHI 7: SUPER CONCENTRATION (SAMYAMA)

Samyama is a state of extreme concentration. To differentiate it from normal concentration (*dharana*), I will use the somewhat awkward term "super-concentration." When a genius composer like Mozart or Beethoven composes a piece of music, or a Dali or Van Gogh paints, or a Moliere or Shakespeare writes a play, or an engineer like Tesla conceives of a new machine, or a scientist like Newton formulates natural laws, without defining it as such, they are accessing a state that yogis call *samyama*. *Samyama* is the most intense form of concentration the human mind is capable of, and by focusing it on a particular object or theme, the mind can emulate, download, or conceive a given object or theme at its deepest layer. At that level of concentration, the human mind is literally capable of deciphering the code of creation, of listening to the heartbeat of the universe. The yogic *samyama* is about consciously cultivating a skill that the genius for genetic, environmental, or *karmic* reasons (in yoga we look at those three to be *karma*) possesses without being conscious of it.

However, this intense concentration that turns the mind into a laser-like device is not only the phenomena behind genius, but also the driving force behind 'evil.' In his commentary on the *Yoga Sutra*, Hariharananda Aranya says that even the so-called *kshipta* mind (out-of-control, frantic, wild) can attain this state of total concentration by thinking of the destruction of their foes. Thus we must understand it is essentially a spiritual phenomenon that has turned men like Hitler and Stalin into the historical monsters they were, while at the same time giving us people like Gandhi and Martin Luther King. How do we want to use this power? While it is unlikely you or I will become adept at wreaking havoc, we must understand that *samyama* is a state that is essentially free of values. Einstein used it when conceiving the nuclear bomb. *Samyama* and genius itself, are not concerned with whether they are used destructively or constructively, or whether humanity in its currently frail development can be trusted with using it constructively. *Samyama* has therefore received a bad name in many circles.

Yogis, too, have used it to develop powers to manipulate. But so have the non-yogis, from Galileo and Bach to Einstein. By understanding *samyama* we are able to understand the mechanism that powers extraordinary achievements and to only use it constructively. An important aspect of *samyama* is that it must be paired with ethics. This is more likely if it occurs in the proper yogic sequence, or even later. If practiced in the right sequence, we will first experience the entire cosmos as a lawful expression of Divine intelligence (*samadhi* 5) and each being as an avenue of the Divine experiencing and expressing its infinite creativity (*samadhi* 6). Then it is much harder to disregard the ethical rules at the base of all religions, including those of yoga.

In ancient society, *samyama* was used if a *rishi* or *siddha* received a calling to bring new knowledge into the world or to educate and open humanity for an already existing knowledge. Yoga teaches that there is an underlying *strata* of truth and reality that can be accessed through intense concentration, in which the inner limbs (*antarangas*) of concentration (*dharana*), meditation (*dhyana*), and contemplation (objective *samadhi*) are exercised simultaneously and for a long period of time. A *samyama* will last for at least several hours and sometimes several days, depending on the complexity of the object or theme meditated upon. If this concentration is maintained and sustained on the right aspect of the problem, then the solution is revealed or, we could say, downloaded.

By means of *samyama*, Patanjali himself became the founder or co-founder of three ancient sciences, Sanskrit, Yoga, and Ayurveda. He places great emphasis on what the *samyama* is made on. For example, in sutra III.34, he says "Through *samyama* on the heart, understanding of the mind (*chitta*) is gained." Understanding the mind or the science of mind is yoga! Yoga is the ancient Vedic form of psychology. But Patanjali did not simply practice super-concentration on the mind in order to understand it. No, he meditated on the heart. Why? The *Katha* and other *Upanishads* state that the mind is projected forth from the heart. That means the heart is the underlying or substratum of the mind. In Sanskrit, *hrt* refers to the core, not the cardium but the innermost self. It is usually symbolized in yoga as the heart *chakra*, in which the *Chandogya Upanishad* states the entire world is contained.

Similarly, in sutra III.29, Patanjali states that from *samyama* on the navel *chakra* (*Manipura*) medical knowledge is derived. Patanjali articulated this knowledge in the form of the *Charaka Samhita*. This Ayurvedic knowledge was not derived from trial and error but through deep contemplation. Again, what's important is that you don't just super-concentrate on the whole of the body, but on its substratum, the navel *chakra*. The scriptures (*shastras*) say that, like a banana plant grows out of its bulb, so does the body grow out of the navel *chakra*.

Samyama does not lead to significant psychological or mystical states. You may leave *samadhis* 5, 6, or 8 with profound spiritual insights. Compared to these experiences, *samyama* is very different, as information gained about the world of objects is in the foreground, not our experience. By means of *samyama* on the heart, Patanjali "downloaded" the operating manual of the mind—the *Yoga Sutra*. The value of *samyama* is not in the experience but in the information gained.

If a mystic (such as Patanjali) gains information through mystical insight (*samyama*), that information must be taken on its own merit, then checked and confirmed. Patanjali published on three subjects (*Yoga Sutra* on yoga, *Charaka Samhita* on Ayurveda, and *Mahabhashya* on Sanskrit grammar)–and all of his texts remain credible authorities on their subjects, even a few thousand years later. Not all mystics were that prolific, but taking the statements of a mystic at face value does not mean we reject them all outright (as many people do) or accept them all outright (which is equally dangerous). We must consider such knowledge, investigate it more closely, and see whether it works. Just as we do not believe everything a scientist says, nor should we unhesitatingly accept everything a mystic has said.

Samyama-like states have a long history of occurring naturally, and it seems they were more common when we still lived in harmony with nature and creation. The world's indigenous cultures once had—and to some extent, still have—an astonishing knowledge of plant medicine, herbs, etc. Western anthropologists believe shamans of those cultures obtained this knowledge through trial and error over hundreds of generations. Thus we apply our cultural biases to those cultures. Would they really have sacrificed tens of thousands of their kin to experiment with innumerable herbs of the jungle on various diseases? Unlikely, but we moderners can't understand how they could otherwise have collated such knowledge. If you ask the shamans themselves this question, they will answer with a laconic, "the plants told us." They are actually referring to a *samyamic* concentration, by which they could listen to the plants or feel them. Such deep listening can happen after psychological issues are dispersed, which is why this *samyama* arrives at seventh in Patanjali's system and not before. It can also arise through an intense desire to know or learn something, even if the adept is not entirely ready to become the guardian of such knowledge. Thus the phenomenon of evil genius occurs.

The expansive knowledge of the indigenous people is often baffling. For example, on the land I live now, there used to be an Aboriginal reservation, and on it abounds the world's second-most lethal poisonous snake, the Eastern Brown Snake. Nowadays, most people survive its strike if anti-venom is applied within half an hour. One of the local Aboriginal Elders was asked what his people did in the old days if someone was bitten. His answer was, "Then it is too late. Don't cross the path of the snake." When implored what would happen if we crossed its path, he replied, "Don't get bitten; move out of the way before it strikes." When further probed what would be done if all of these safety mechanisms had failed, he finally said, "Lie down for two days and do not move." Amazingly, if you could manage to remain completely still for two days, you would have a good chance at surviving, as the venom moves through the lymph system, and the more you move your arms and legs, the faster you die. If you could remain still and even slow down your heartbeat by going into a trance, there would be a chance the body would break down the slow-moving venom before it would kill you. Would anyone be keen to apply the method of trial and error on that? Unlikely. The Aboriginees say, "The snake told us." They also say, "Wherever there is poison in the jungle and on the land, within 10 meters you will find its antidote." Astonishing! This reveals the extent to which these cultures were part of nature, rather than seeing it as a hostile environment that must be overcome in order to survive.

I use these anecdotes to show that *samyama* is not something foreign or impossible to achieve, but that all humans, from the native shaman to the nuclear physicist, have a propensity for accessing it. *Samyama* is a way of accessing the deep-knowledge sheath (*vijnana-maya kosha*) mentioned in the *Taittiriya Upanishad*. All knowledge about creation is contained in this sheath and is accessible to all who have the humility to ask and the stillness to hear the answer. Yoga is simply a structured way of enhancing a talent we always had. I am not suggesting that scientists, artists, and shamans practiced *samyama* but that the human mind has a *samyamic* capability to intuitively drop into this deepest *strata* of reality. The yogic *samyama* is the systematic and conscious development of this capacity, which otherwise occurs only spontaneously and unconsciously.

While *samyama* has worked insomuch that is has given us the ancient sciences, there are many things mystics and shamans have not seen. There is no point in listing the many achievements of modern science, but to give an example, mystics revealed surprisingly little about the natural evolution of life that is now obvious through archeology. While I think that a lot of breakthroughs in the sciences, for example mathematics, were due to a "flash of insight" (actually a mystical state), rather than tedious groveling (which is more typical for science), also modern mystics (who often abhor quantitative study and groveling) should consider the teachings of science. Currently, both sides maintain a smug divide, to the detriment of the continued evolution of humanity.

If humanity is to flourish and continue to evolve, we must develop a new culture that respects the work of scientists and the insight of mystics equally. Mystics are not aware of how their conditioning and cultural background influence their teachings and statements by way of semiotics. Science, and particularly mathematics, are way ahead in their effort to develop and use language that is as objective as possible.

I will now turn to the technique of *samyama*, which consists mainly of an intense capacity to concentrate the mind, as gained through *asana, pranayama*, Kundalini meditation, *kriya*, and the earlier *samadhis*. During *samyama, prana* must be held in the fifth *chakra* (*Vishuddha*), while at the same time focusing on the chosen object of the *samyama*. Divided awareness or multitasking is required here. Activating the fifth *chakra* means seeing the world as divine law and realizing that the entire cosmos is an expression and crystallization of an underlying higher intelligence. We must ask ourselves, in what way and according to what law does this intelligence express itself? While *samadhi* 6 is a *samadhi* on I-am-ness (*asmita*) and *samadhi* 8 is on consciousness (*purusha*), *samadhi* 7 deals primarily with intelligence (*buddhi*), which explains why it is so impersonal. According to yogic philosophy (or, more precisely, the Samkhya philosophy of which yoga is a continuation of), intelligence existed prior to I-am-ness. This means we are working our way up through the *samadhis*, but in terms of cosmic evolution, we are going back in time towards that initial projector of history, the Divine.

In sutra III.1, Patanjali defines concentration (*dharana*) as fixing the mind to a place. *Dharana* implies a willful effort to keep your mind bound to a particular object. Sutra III.2 now tells us that, if in that place of *dharana*, there is an uninterrupted flow of awareness towards the object, then this is meditation (*dhyana*). Then sutra III.3 states that, if in meditation only the object shines forth without being modified by the mind, that is (objective) *samadhi*. These are three consecutively deeper stages in which the mind of the meditator (not the meditator him/herself) merges with or duplicates the object meditated on. Please note that these two phrases actually mean the same thing: merging with the object means duplicating it. Finally, sutra III.4 says that if the three are practiced together, it is called *samyama*. Initially we perceive that as a contradiction in terms. *Dharana* (concentration) implies willful effort. *Dhyana* (meditation) is the tentative overcoming of effort and the establishment of a fragile permanent contact with the object beyond will. Objective *samadhi* means this contact is now established and the object present in the mind of the meditator is identical to the object outside of the meditator.

But then Patanjali overthrows this nice order by mingling the three states together. How can a state that implies exertion of will (*dharana*) be combined with a state beyond will (objective *samadhi*) and why? The answer is this: They are separate as long as we are performing spiritual training for the purpose of self-realization or spiritual freedom. We need to overcome will or go beyond will on the way to attain what is forever beyond will, the pure consciousness. *Samyama* now is objective knowledge pertaining to the world outside of us (meaning outside of pure consciousness). In order to obtain such deep knowledge pertaining to particular objects, we require discipline to keep the mind focused on that place for a significant time (under certain circumstances, days). And because the purpose is not spiritual insight about ourselves (*samadhi* 6) or our relationship to or our place within the world (*samadhi* 5), the will is no obstacle. That's how *dharana* (willful concentration) enters back into the equation.

In the third chapter of the *Yoga Sutra*, Patanjali gives a long list of powers and how they are to be obtained through *samyama*. But in sutra III.37, he tells us that all these powers for the emerging (*vyutthana*) mind are impediments for (objectless) *samadhi*. This sutra has lead many practitioners to completely abandon *samyama* and even to be suspicious of the third chapter. The primary misconception in this instance is that only objectless *samadhi* and spiritual liberation matter. This discounts life and the world; after all, spiritual liberation (*moksha*) is only one of four human goals (*purusharthas*), the other being acquisition of wealth (*artha*), sexual satisfaction (*kama*), and right action (*dharma*). Even a liberated person is still in the service of others.

In writing texts on a variety of subjects (including medicine), Patanjali shows us that things outside of objectless *samadhi* do matter. After all, if life is only something to overcome, then why attend to the body at all? Why heal it? What Patanjali wants to express with this stanza is that we shouldn't look at those "powers" as personal powers designed to serve egoic interests, but as tools to be used to benefit the greater good. This is the attitude of the suspended mind (*nirodha*). This mind will do whatever is required without attachment and will act out of service to the Divine and all beings rather than for egoic satisfaction. The suspended (*nirodha*) mind knows that, because all beings in and of the world are interconnected, egoic action is based on false perception. Any selfish use of power will end right back on my own doorstep, eventually. Although selfless action may seem more difficult in the beginning, it will benefit us all, myself included, in the end.

In sutra III.23 Patanjali clearly shows how *samyama* can be used beneficially: "By practicing *samyama* on friendliness, compassion, and joy, one acquires their powers." This sutra is closely linked to sutra I.33, where Patanjali says that those three qualities are to be practiced towards the happy, miserable, and virtuous, respectively. Right from the first chapter, Patanjali suggests meditating on these qualities for psychological reasons, that is, to purify our mind. In Chapter 3 he suggests we develop those attitudes in order to positively influence and heal others. Indian myths have many stories of sages who influenced and healed people who were in negative states. Patanjali suggests we become so firmly entrenched in these attitudes that we literally embody them.

It is not necessary to practice *samyama* to go on to objectless *samadhi* (*samadhi* 8). In fact, as Patanjali has pointed out, the knowledge derived from *samyama* due to attachment may prove to be an obstacle for the arising of objectless *samadhi*. For many yogis, then, the most effective route is to leave out *samyama* and go directly to objectless *samadhi*. Whether or not you need to practice *samyama* is often a case of *svadharma* (own duty), which was discussed under *samadhi* 6 (*asmita*).

DISCRIMINATIVE KNOWLEDGE (VIVEKA KHYATEH)
The various objective *samadhis* result in *viveka khyateh* (knowledge of the difference). This is not a *samadhi* but a precursor or bridge to objectless *samadhi*, without which the latter cannot be attained. In sutra II.26 Patanjali states, "The means to liberation is permanent discriminative knowledge." And again in sutra III.54 he says, "Discriminative knowledge enables one to cross over. It is all comprehensive and beyond time. The difference referred to here is between what is temporary, finite, prone to conditioning, stainable, and with qualities, versus that which is eternal, infinite, pure, and without quality. The yogis have us practice objective *samadhis* until we know beyond a doubt that our body, our mind, our intelligence, our ego, and all objects around us are temporary imprints from the world (i.e., are conditioned) and have qualities such as hot, cold, good, bad, beautiful, ugly, etc. This may seem obvious, but the yogis at the level of objective *samadhi* (that is, having knowledge of the world) are not talking about theoretical or academic knowledge but experiential, substantial, and visceral knowledge that has the capacity to transform you from the very fiber of your being.

Second, they want us to realize there is something within us that doesn't fit the category of the phenomenal, which is subject to dualities, such as right or wrong. This new category contains the opposite description: it is eternal, infinite, cannot be conditioned or changed, and does not take on traits or characteristics. It is the pure consciousness (*purusha*), the self (*atman*). Although we may not have direct knowledge of this second category, our experiences in meditation allow us to deduce that it is there. This deduction, glimpse, or trust that consciousness is there affords us dis-identification (*paravairagya*) with everything in the first category. Dis-identification allows us to maintain a certain distance, but without a detached attitude. Detachment leads to substandard choices and lack of involvement in worldly affairs. We are here to fulfill our purpose and role in society

208

in a way that we aspire to our greatest potential. Without attachment, that isn't possible. For example, it would be inappropriate to have a detached attitude towards our partner, children, or the Divine.

In sutra IV.29 Patanjali states, "If, in permanent knowledge-of-the-difference (*viveka khyateh*), one dis-identifies from any gain to be had from meditation, one enters into the cloud-of-characteristics-dispersing *samadhi* (*dharma megha samadhi*)." Patanjali explains how objective *samadhi* comes about. First we need "knowl-

Ordering of Practice of the 8 *Samadhis*

The eight *samadhis* are ideally practiced in the sequential order presented in the *Yoga Sutra*. Their ordering is from gross to subtle, with the first *samadhis* being practiced on objects that are perceptible to the senses and the final *samadhis* being practiced on pure consciousness. The samadhis also increase in difficulty, with the initial *samadhi* being very achievable, whereas the final is quite elusive. The type of *samadhi* also depends on where, for example, in which *chakra*, prana is concentrated during the *samadhi*, whereas the length of the samadhi mainly depends on the practitioner's ability to stay merged with the object of the *samadhi* (if the object is consciousness, i.e. the subject; we don't use the term "merging" but "to abide in").

Each *samadhi* confers a different depth of knowledge or view; previous *samadhis* do not automatically become obsolete or superseded just because the sequentially next *samadhi* has been reached. Similarly, we do not give up asana because we have reached *samadhi*, because asana keeps the body healthy. Without a healthy body, it is difficult to fulfill our *svadharma* (our own duty, our highest potential). For example, mastery of all *samadhis* would give a yogi the ability to consciously experience them sequentially similar to how a musician would play a scale. This gives the yogi a much deeper and multifaceted appreciation of reality than becoming stuck at or overemphasizing a particular *samadhi*. It is especially important to realize that the first seven *samadhis* are not just training to reach the eighth, objectless, *samadhi*. *Samadhis* 4, 5, 6, and 7 in particular show you things that objectless *samadhi* never can.

edge-of-the-difference." Then we must combine this with complete dis-identification (*paravairagya*). In the early stages we tend to identify with and hold on to our achievements in *samadhi*. We must let go of this, too, because our essence, pure consciousness, cannot hold on to anything, cannot achieve, and cannot become. We must dis-identify with the world of objects, attainments, achievements, of doing and becoming. Only then can we enter the final, the objectless, *samadhi*.

SAMADHI 8: OBJECTLESS (NIRBIJA) SAMADHI

There is only one objectless *samadhi*. It is varyingly referred to as *nirbija* (objectless) *samadhi*, *asamprajnata* (super-cognitive) *samadhi*, and *dharma-megha* (cloud-of-characteristics-dispersing) *samadhi*. When Patanjali defines yoga in sutra I.2 as "the suspension of the fluctuations of the mind," he tells us how to access objective *samadhi*. In the next sutra he defines *samadhi* as a state in which "the seer abides in his own nature." It is implied that, when we are firmly established in the underlying stillness of the mind, we stop projecting ourselves outwards onto phenomena and no longer identify with our periphery (such as the body, mind, ego, and intelligence). Then we can passively fall back and abide in our true nature, which is consciousness (*purusha*) or the self (*atman*). Patanjali here calls our true nature the "seer" (*drashta*). In sutra IV.19, he says, "The mind does not possess the light of awareness since it is of the nature of the seen." This means the mind itself is not sentient but more like a computer; it is intelligent and can process amazing amounts of information, but by itself is not conscious. It is the seer (*drashta, atman, purusha*) who is conscious.

About *drashta*, Patanjali says, "The seer only sees. Although pure, it seems to modify sensory data." Here lies the whole drama of human existence. How can it be that we have this enormous infinite being called consciousness within us and yet reduce it to the body, mind, ego, and intelligence? Patanjali answers in sutra IV.22: "In the process of shedding awareness of the intelligence, consciousness appears to take on its form." And what is intelligence's form? It is the modification and analysis of sensory data. Because we are not yet aware of the distinction between our two innermost *strata*, consciousness and intelligence, we are spiritually bound.

In this *samadhi* we experience for the first time that the seer is a distinct entity. It does not modify sensory data as the intelligence does; it does not do anything. It is a passive witness. When happiness occurs to it, it witnesses happiness. If shame arises, it witnesses shame. But for once, we do not identify with or become what occurs to us; instead we remain with the original witness. Our periphery (in this case the intelligence) always modifies what we become aware of. For example, it tries to intensify and prolong happiness and shortcut or rationalize shame. We never take the time to simply remain with pure awareness. And that's why we don't realize that awareness is forever unchanged by whatever occurs to it. It is eternal and infinite. And therein lies the great and limitless freedom.

This *samadhi, dharma-megha samadhi,* means cloud-of-characteristics-dispersing *samadhi.* Characteristics here refer to the particular details we know about objects, and in this case, the subconscious ideas we have about ourselves, our conditioning. Our subconscious identifies with a particular history, our history of painful experiences, rejection we experienced in the past, and our history of separation from the Divine. This *samadhi* disperses those concepts like the sun (of consciousness) would disperse a cloud, so that we can abide in, identify with, and know that we are consciousness. We are bathed in the sun of consciousness. So says Patanjali in sutra I.51, "After those subconscious imprints have ceased, the entire mind is suspended, and that is objectless (*nirbija*) *samadhi.*" This means that active subconscious imprints (other than those that have been scorched or made sterile imprints and thus cannot re-sprout) prevent this *samadhi* from arising.

Another way of understanding *dharma megha samadhi* is to liken it to experiencing the Bardo states while being alive. The Bardo

211

Thodol is the *Tibetan Book of the Dead*. It is authored by the founder of Tibetan Buddhism, Guru Rinpoche, and contains a precise map of states we transit through between death and rebirth. The Bardo Thodol teaches that, in the moment of death, the psyche explodes and its outer, denser layers fly away. For the first three days after death, we abide in our core, the consciousness. After that we slowly start to re-identify with our outer layers, which then promptly return. The *Tibetan Book of the Dead* recommends staying with the pure consciousness, which it calls the primary white light. Rather than rising to the surface and identifying with our returning dense outer layers, we are to go back into the blazing white light of consciousness.

This teaching can also be applied to objectless *samadhi*. When we first access this *samadhi*, we go to our very core, pure consciousness. In deep *samadhi* we remain there and identify with the primary white light. During the normal waking state, pure consciousness is surrounded by the denser layers of our psyche, including anger, fear, avarice, pain, and so on. When we enter *samadhi*, the denser layers seem to fly away and disconnect from us, even while we are abiding in the white light of our core being. Eventually, as abiding in consciousness lapses, the outer layers return, and our awareness and attention rise to the surface to identify again with those layers. These outer layers can be likened to the cloud of characteristics, wherein identification and personality are encrypted and the attachment to who we believe we are causes us to remain outside of the natural state. If we remain in the center of the white light, all external concepts of who we are, our characteristics, will disperse.

What exactly is consciousness and why is it so difficult to abide in it? In yogic parlance, consciousness is "that which is conscious," rather than "that which we are conscious of." So it is not the content of consciousness, but pure awareness. Pure awareness is the function of consciousness and consciousness is the seat of awareness. It is that which is unchangeable, eternal, infinite, and quality-less. Our mind cannot wrap itself around it because mind automatically at-

212

taches itself to form, overlooking that which is without form. Mind has served us very well during the multi-billion-year-long evolution of life (even at first, very tentatively). But at this point of our spiritual liberation, we need to move beyond the mind. Because it cannot grasp consciousness, we must foster a gradual tendency to abide in consciousness. This term "abiding" is important. In truth we are already consciousness, but since we have a mind that rises to the surface, we tend to forget and dis-identify with the being at our depth, which is our true identity. The Buddha said that consciousness is the container that holds all of the world and its beings. Rather than thinking of consciousness as something encased within a body or within a mind, we switch to the perception that the being, the world, the mind, and everything appear or occur within consciousness.

If we follow water through its course down a river, it originates at its source and then may be at the rapids and falls, then at the banks of a wide stream, and eventually at the mouth of the river, where it merges into the ocean. The river, however, is at all of these places simultaneously. Similarly, as we go through life we may think that first we are born, then we are young, then we are old, and then death occurs. But our consciousness is at all of these places simultaneously, eternally unchanged. That's why the mystics say that birth, youth, mature age, and death occur within consciousness.

REDUCING THE WORLD TO THIS SAMADHI

This *samadhi* tends to be so powerful that one wants to reduce the world to this state. But this would lead us to a nirvana of nothingness, where the entire world and all its beings are reduced to emptiness. This is the most important—though not exclusively important—*samadhi*. Some mystics have taught that the only purpose of this *samadhi* is self-annihilation and that our purpose is to overcome and renounce the world. I believe this is an error and that the world itself is divine. Even if this *samadhi* tends to move us into a contemplative direction, we should never look down on the

213

world or on life. Even the overcome-the-world faction admits it is the world that gives beings the opportunity to become liberated. But a perusal of the complete sequence of *samadhis* will teach us that participation in the world is a divine act and an expression of the infinite creativity of the Divine. In many ways, the yogi must not only liberate herself from the modern Western belief that experience is just the outcome of biochemical and bioelectrical occurrences in the brain, but also from the age-old religious belief that the world is bad and a place to be left behind. Religion and mysticism place too much emphasis on this *samadhi* and the attached concept of a God transcendent that is above and beyond this world.

In order to create and conceive of a new humanity, we must emphasize *samadhis* stage 5 and 6; that is, we must realize the world and all matter are the sentient body of the Divine and all beings are avenues through which the Divine expresses and experiences itself. From this understanding, we can build a world based on compassion, love, mutual support, recognition, and forgiveness. From this plateau, then, it is worth venturing into objectless *samadhi* and the realization of the God transcendent— but not before. Otherwise we make the same old mistakes again, where we float aloof in our silence and splendor while the world descends into madness, social injustice, strife, and inequality.

If we do not consider *samyama* as a spiritual or psychological *samadhi*, the last three *samadhis* (*ananda, asmita,* and *nirbija*) reveal the trinity of the Divine. That is, God as the universe, God as all beings (those two comprising God immanent), and finally God transcendent, or pure consciousness. Each aspect is equally as important as the other and cannot be reduced to just one.

MOUNTAINTOP METAPHOR REVISITED

Objectless *samadhi* is like the summit of a mighty mountain. In order to reach the summit you must decide on an angle of approach. Each path leading to the top represents a particular school of thought, a philosophy, a science, a religion, or a school of yoga. On the way up, your view of the mountain is limited. You see only one side. Because you cannot see the other approaches, it might appear as though your path, the particular school that you follow, is the only feasible one. While you are on the path, this is a reasonable belief. You have decided on your angle of approach and there is no point in fantasizing how the other approaches might have been.

Once you are up on the mountain of objectless samadhi (pure consciousness), the scenery changes. Initially you are overwhelmed by the lofty heights, but after a while you grow accustomed to the view and become curious about the paths that were previously hidden, the ones you fantasized about on the way up. You walk around the edge and look down; to your surprise, you see other paths leading up the mountain and realize people have taken these paths for centuries throughout the ages, although many of the paths have now fallen into disuse. Among the ones on top there is great peace and no squabbling. Although they stem from many different cultures, nobody claims their path is the only way up. That would be foolish, because many who have made it to the summit did not take the same path as you. Allegiance is not important here, because all are united in the peak experience, which is beyond mind and words.

You also notice people on the slopes who haven't yet attained this bird's-eye view. They're shouting to the people beneath them that all other paths are wrong, even satanic, and that only theirs is right. Some are so busy deterring others from leaving their particular paths that they lose sight of their goal of reaching the peak. If only they would reach the summit to see a multitude of paths leading to the top, a new era of peace could begin. We'd see that whatever can be expressed in words is of limited value, even of dubious worth. We would understand the limitations of our own words and perspectives and come to a new era of harmony and peaceful coexistence.

What really matters (perhaps the only thing that matters) is not what you believe to be true, but rather a visceral understanding of the divine origin of all beings, the realization that God transcendent expresses itself through all beings, and therefore all beings are sacred. If this experience could be shared among a great number of people, our own inner conflict, and thus conflict with others, would end.

Chapter 8
BEYOND SAMADHI

This chapter is to convey the idea that there is life and a path after *samadhi*. *Samadhi* is an impermanent state. Although most people I meet today consider *samadhi* "too far out there" and an unrealistic attainment, old-school Vedantins, such as Shankara (most Vedantins today are new school), criticized *samadhi* for not aiming high enough. In the technical school of yoga, *samadhi* comes shortly after Kundalini meditation, and its scope is purposely limited so that we don't get overwhelmed when we are starting to integrate it.

The purpose of this book is to show that yoga has a sophisticated system and approach in place to radically transform human beings, an approach that is internally consistent to the very end. Yogis don't just hope that things turn out all right but actively create freedom through a distinct system. On the other side of this excellent set of techniques, modern yoga has lost the goal, instead becoming completely mired in such basic techniques as *asana* (which have their place, but the attention they receive nowadays is completely overdone).

In this chapter I propose a synthesis between Yoga and Vedanta; this is how the two systems were actually practiced in ancient society. Prior to Gaudapada and Shankara, Yoga and Vedanta were practiced sequentially. This is apparent from stanza I.1 of the *Brahma Sutra* (this text is for all schools of Vedanta what the *Yoga Sutra* is for all schools of Yoga), which says, "*Athato brahma jijnasya.*" In English this means, "Then, therefore, the knowledge of the Brahman." "Then, therefore," means two requirements must be fulfilled before one can go on to study or practice this science. The first requirement, "then," the *Brahma Sutra* shares with the *Yoga Sutra*: we need to have realized that the sense objects and the body cannot ultimately give us what we are looking for. There is a thirst that goes deeper. As long as we fulfill this requirement, we are fit to

217

study the *Yoga Sutra*. However, the *Brahma Sutra* has a second requirement: one must be free from wrong cognition (*viparyaya*). Is
anybody out there? How do I get free from error? The entire eight-
limbed yoga of Patanjali culminating in the eight-staged *samadhi* is
nothing but training in the removal of *viparyaya*. In that regard, we
can call Yoga the science of mind; and by studying the science of
mind, we are preparing to practice the science of consciousness (Vedanta). Vedanta is not a beginner's discipline, which is confirmed
by the *Gita* in stanza XII:5: "Attaching yourself to the formless
Absolute (i.e., the pure consciousness) is more troublesome because the embodied self finds it difficult to behold the unmanifest."
However, direct meditation on pure consciousness is achievable
when one is established in all aspects of yoga, including *samadhi*.

Vedanta is the domain of Jnana Yoga and traditionally it is
practiced after Raja Yoga is completed. Jnana is not an alternative path to Raja, but is its culmination, its fruition. Jnana means
that any technique comes to an end and the mystic drops into
consecutively deeper *stratas* of realization, very much as the *ma-
havakyas* (great utterances) suggest. A typical example of that
would be the various night vigils during the *bodhi* of the Buddha.

During such contemplations there is absolutely no activity, but
only a passive acceptance of what has always been there. That
means in a strict technical sense, yoga has come to an end at this
point. Jnana Yoga itself is a contradiction in terms, as yoga means
"activity," "conscious effort," and "concentration" and Jnana means
the absence of all of that. However, over the many thousands of
years that yoga has evolved, it has pretty much integrated and assim-
ilated every possible spiritual discipline and human endeavor. So
says the great yogi Aurobindo, "All life is yoga," and he consciously treats Jnana as only one of the yogic branches to be synthesized
into his greater Integral Yoga. This is the largest possible vision of
yoga, and I believe that Aurobindo is right when he says that each
act, each moment, each part of our being has to be living yoga.

218

Patanjali calls it *kaivalya*, but the *Yoga Sutra* does not actually deal with the subject. He does say that, if you keep applying *samadhi*, you will eventually end up liberated. In sutra IV.30 he says, " From [objective] *samadhi* the modes of suffering (*kleshas*) and *karma* cease. And he closes off with sutra IV.34, "When the *gunas* (elementary particles of nature), having lost their purpose, return to their source (*prakrti*), then liberation takes place, which is pure consciousness established in its own nature." Pure consciousness established in its own nature? This is where Vedanta comes in, with its three steps of reflection as explained by the great *rishi*, Yajnavalkya, in that oldest of *Upanishads*, the *Brhad Aranyaka*. He teaches that the Brahman (infinite consciousness) is reached in three steps. The first is *shravana*, which means "hearing." Hearing the right view means listening to the teaching that our essence is consciousness and the Brahman. The second step is *manana*: reflecting on this truth until there is nothing within us that contradicts it. *Manana* is completed when we enter *nididhysana*, which means completely embodying the truth. For this embodying to occur, it is not enough to just change one's opinion and now profess to be the Brahman. It means complete transubstantiation of the human being. It is to this end that yoga provides what is needed to reach the goal of Vedanta.

Epilogue

The four final *samadhis* of yoga must each be considered on their own merit. There is a tendency to reduce yoga to the eighth *samadhi* because it constitutes the path of spiritual liberation for the individual. The eighth *samadhi* became the abode of religion. Religion has created the perception that spirituality is a realm to be found outside of the world, outside of life, and outside of matter. While this realm does exist and is important to pursue, we cannot reduce life to the realm of consciousness. With religion removing spirituality from material life and placing it on a separate abode, the stage was set for the rise of science and technology, beginning in the 17th century. Science has taken over the space that in ancient society was given to *samadhi 7—samyama*. Because science took the opposite approach to religion, that of materialism, both realms have become disconnected.

Samadhi 8 must be augmented by *samadhi* 6, which shows us that spirituality does not just happen uncoupled from life but through our individuality, which provides an avenue for the Divine to express itself through and as us. *Samadhi* 6 also shows us the sacredness of individuality. While we are all different, the same Divine expresses itself through each one of us, and each different expression is as important as the others. This doesn't mean there should be no civil code of law, as our laws today are based on the teachings of the ancient mystics who saw divine law. In seeing the individuality of others as avenues through which the Divine expresses itself as validly as through ourselves, we can let go of conflict with others. Just because they are different from us, doesn't mean they are wrong. It will also help us to let go of the perceived supremacy of Western civilization that still believes it needs to carry its political, social, and economic values to remote corners of the globe and destroy diversity in the process. *Samadhi* 6 shows us the Divine is expressing itself through animal life, too, and that we do not have the right to make species extinct.

221

Samadhi 7, and what exists today in its place (Western science), must be augmented by *samadhi* 5, the realization that all matter, our biosphere, and the entire universe are nothing but the crystallized body of the Divine. There is no place on Earth that we can use as a nuclear waste dump, just as there is no place that is not sacred. *Samadhi* 5 will re-enchant us with the world as we realize there is nothing that is not crystallized spirit. We will recognize, as we knew in ancient days, that the world is a garden, in which we live in symbiotic harmony with all other organisms and objects. We will also realize that this Gaian garden is created by super-intelligence far beyond our imagination. If we place ourselves in service of this super-intelligence, it can co-create the world with us and the entire organism can continue to flourish. Ultimately all *samadhis* point in the same direction: we are a part of and in service of a being greater than ourselves, a being that shapes this world through love, beauty, intelligence, and freedom.

Bibliography

Adams, G.C., Jr, translator and commentator, *Badarayana's Brahma Sutras*, Motilal Banarsidass, Delhi, 1993.

Agehananda Bharati, Sw., *The Light at the Center*, Ross-Erickson, Santa Barbara, 1976.

Agehananda Bharati, Sw., *The Ochre Robe*, 2nd rev. edn, Ross-Erickson, Santa Barbara, 1980.

Aranya, Sw. H., *Yoga Philosophy of Patanjali with Bhasvati*, 4th enlarged edn, University of Calcutta, Kolkata, 2000.

Ashtavakra Gita, 8th edn, Sri Ramanasramam, Tiruvannamalai, 2001.

Aurobindo, S,. *Synthesis of Yoga*, Lotus Press, Twin Lakes, 2010.

Bhatt, G.P. (ed.), *The Skanda Purana*, part 1, trans. G.V. Tagare, Motilal Banarsidass, Delhi, 1992.

Chandra Vasu, R.B.S., translator, *The Gheranda Samhita*, Sri Satguru Publications, Delhi, 1986.

Cole, C.A., *Asparsa Yoga – A Study of Gaudapada's Mandukya Karika*, Motilal Banarsidass, Delhi, 1982.

Dahlke, P., translator, *Buddha – Die Lehre des Erhabenen*, Wilhelm Goldmann Verlag, Munich, 1920.

Deussen, P., editor, *Sixty Upanisads of the Veda*, translated by V.M. Bedekar & G.B. Palsule, 2 vols, Motilal Banarsidass, Delhi, 1997.

Digambarji, Sw., editor and commentator, *Vasishta Samhita*, Kaivalyadhama, Lonavla, 1984.

Eisenstein, C., *The Ascent of Humanity: Civilization and the Human Sense of Self,* Evolver Editions, Berkeley, 2013.

Eisenstein, C., *The More Beautiful World Our Hearts Know Is Possible,* North Atlantic Books, Berkeley, 2013.

Evans-Wentz, W.Y., editor, *The Tibetan Book of the Dead*, Oxford University Press, London, 1960.

Gambhirananda, Sw., translator, *Brahma Sutra Bhasya of Sri Sankaracarya*, Advaita Ashrama, Kolkata, 1965.

Ganguli, K.M., translator, *The Mahabharata*, 12 vols, Munshiram Manoharlal, New Delhi, 1998.

Gharote, Dr M.L. et al., editors and translators, *Hathapradipika of Svatmarama* (10 chapters), The Lonavla Yoga Institute, Lonavla, 2006.

Gharote, Dr M.L. et al., editors and translators, *Hathatatvakaumudi of Sundaradeva*, The Lonavla Yoga Institute, Lonavla, 2007.

Godman, D. (ed.), *Be As You Are – The Teachings of Ramana Maharshi*, Penguin Books India, New Delhi, 1985.

Goswami, Shyam Sundar, *Laya Yoga*, Inner Traditions, Rochester, 1999.

Grof, S., *Healing our Deepest Wounds: The Holotropic Paradigm Shift*, Stream of Experience Productions, 2012.

Guenther, H.V., translator and commentator, *The Life and Teaching of Naropa*, Shambala, Boston, 1995.

Gurdjieff, G.I., *Beelzebub's Erzaehlungen Fuer Seinen Enkel*, Sphinx Verlag, Basel, 1981.

Gurdjieff, G.I., *Begnungen mit bemerkenswerten Menschen*, Aurum Verlag, Freiburg, 1978.

Gurdjieff, G.I., *Das Leben ist nur dann wirklich wenn ich bin*, Sphinx Verlag, Basel, 1987.

Hamill, S. & Seaton, J.P., translators and editors, *The Essential Chuang Tzu*, Shambala, Boston, 1998.

Hesse, H., *Siddhartha*, Bantam Books, New York, 1982.

Holy Bible, New King James Version, Thomas Nelson Publishers, London, 1982.

Johnson, R.A., *We: Understanding the Psychology of Romantic Love*, HarperCollins Publishers, New York, 2013.

Krishna, G., *The Biological Basis for Religion and Genius*, NC

Press, New York, 1971.

Krishna, G., *The Real Nature of Mystical Experience*, The Kundalini Research and Publications Trust, New Delhi, 1978.

Krishna, G., *The Awakening of Kundalini*, Shambala, Boston, 1989.

Krishna, G., *Kundalini: The Evolutionary Energy in Man*, Shambala, Boston, 1997.

Krishnamurti, J., *Krishnamurti to Himself*, HarperCollins, San Francisco, 1993.

Krishnamurti, J., *Krishnamurti's Journal*, 2nd rev. edn, Krishnamurti Foundation Trust India, Chennai, 2003.

Krishnamurti, J., *The Awakening of Intelligence*, HarperCollins, San Francisco, 1987.

Krishnamurti, J., *The First and Last Freedom*, HarperCollins, San Francisco, 1975.

Kuvalayananda, Sw., *Goraksha Shataka*, Kaivalyadhama, Lonavla, 2006.

Leggett, T., translator, *Sankara on the Yoga Sutras*, 1st Indian edn, Motilal Banarsidass, Delhi, 1992.

Lester, R.C., *Ramanuja on the Yoga*, Adyar Library and Research Centre, Madras, 1976.

Lovelock, J., *Gaia: A New Look at Life on Earth*, Oxford Paperbacks, Oxford, 2000.

Madgula, I.S., *The Acarya*, 2nd rev. edn, Motilal Banarsidass, Delhi, 2001.

Madhavananda, Sw., translator, *The Brhadaranyaka Upanisad*, Advaita Ashrama, Kolkata, 1997.

Maehle, Gregor, *Ashtanga Yoga: Practice and Philosophy*, Kaivalya Publications, 2006.

Maehle, Gregor, *Ashtanga Yoga: The Intermediate Series*, New World Library, Novato, 2009.

Maehle, Gregor, *Pranayama: The Breath of Yoga*, Kaivalya Publications, 2012.

Maehle, Gregor, *Yoga Meditation: Through Mantra, Chakras and Kundalini to Spiritual Freedom*, Kaivalya Publications, 2013.

Mahadevan, T.M.P., *The Hymns of Sankara*, Motilal Banarsidass, Delhi, 1980.

Mueller, Max, editor, *Vedic Hymns*, Motilal Banarsidass, Delhi, 1964.

Muktibodhananda, Sw., *Swara Yoga*, Yoga Publication Trust, Munger, 1984.

Natarajan, A.R., *Ramana Maharshi – The Living Guru*, Ramana Maharshi Centre for Learning, Bangalore, 1996.

Natarajan, A.R., *Timeless in Time – A Biography of Sri Ramana Maharshi*, 2nd edn, Ramana Maharshi Centre for Learning, Bangalore, 2000.

Nikhilananda, Sw., *The Gospel of Sri Ramakrishna*, Sri Ramakrishna Math, Madras, 1942.

Panoli, V., translator and commentator, *Gita in Shankara's Own Words*, Shri Paramasivan, Madras, 1980.

Powell, R., editor, *The Experience of Nothingness – Sri Nisargadatta Maharaj's Talks on Realizing the Infinite,* 1st Indian edn, Motilal Banarsidass, Delhi, 2004.

Powell, R., editor, *The Nectar of Immortality – Sri Nisargadatta Maharaj's Discourses on the Eternal*, 1st Indian edn, Motilal Banarsidass, Delhi, 2004.

Radhakrishnan, S., editor, *The Principal Upanishads*, HarperCollins Publishers India, New Delhi, 1994.

Radhakrishnan, S., translator and commentator, *The Bhagavad Gita*, HarperCollins Publishers India, New Delhi, 2002.

Ram Das, *Miracle of Love,* Munshiram Manoharlal, New Delhi, 1999.

Ramakrishnananda, Sw., *Life of Sri Ramanuja*, Sri Ramakrishna Math, Madras.

Ramanasramam, S., *Sri Ramana Gita*, 8th edn, Sri Ramanasram, Tiruvannamalai, 1998.

Rukmani, T.S., translator, *Yogavarttika of Vijnanabhiksu*, 4 vols,

Munshiram Manoharlal, New Delhi, 1998–2001.

Shastri, J.L. (ed.), *The Siva Purana*, 4 vols, Motilal Banarsidass, Delhi, 1970.

Singh, J., translator and annotator, *Vijnanabhairava*, Motilal Banarsidass, Delhi, 1979.

Sinh, P., translator, *The Hatha Yoga Pradipika*, Sri Satguru Publications, Delhi, 1915.

Subramaniam, K., translator, *Srimad Bhagavatam*, 7th edn, Bharatiya Vidya Bhavan, Mumbai, 1997.

Subramaniam, V.K., translator, *Saundaryalahari of Sankaracarya*, Motilal Banarsidass, Delhi, 1977.

Swahananda, Sw., translator, *Chandogya Upanisad*, Sri Ramakrishna Math, Madras, 1956.

Tapasyananda, Sw., translator and annotator, *Srimad Bhagavad Gita*, Sri Ramakrishna Math, Madras.

Tapasyananda, Sw., translator, *Sankara-Dig-Vijaya*, Sri Ramakrishna Math, Chennai.

Thurman, R., translator, *The Tibetan Book of the Dead*, HarperCollins Publishers India, New Delhi, 1998.

Turiyananda, Sw., translator, *Vivekacudamani of Sri Sankaracarya*, Sri Ramakrishna Math, Madras.

Tyagisananda, Sw., translator and annotator, *Narada Bhakti Sutras*, Sri Ramakrishna Math, Madras.

Venkatesananda, Sw., translator, *The Supreme Yoga [Yoga Vashishta]*, 2 vols, The Divine Life Society, Shivanandanagar, 1995.

Vimuktananda, Sw., *Aparokshanubhuti of Sri Sankaracharya*, Advaita Ashrama, Kolkata, 1938.

Vireswarananda, Sw., translator, *Brahma Sutras According to Sri Sankara*, Advaita Ashrama, Kolkata, 1936.

Whitehead, A.N., *Process and Reality*, Free Press, 1997.

Woodroffe, J., *The Serpent Power*, Ganesh & Co., Madras, 1995.

Glossary

Advaita Vedanta – unqualified monism, an Indian system of philosophy

agni – fire of intelligence, elemental fire

aham-vrtti – the I-thought

ahamkara – *I-maker*, cosmic I

ananda samadhi – *samadhi 5:* ecstasy *samadhi*

anandamaya kosha – ecstasy sheath

Ananta – serpent of infinity

antarangas – inner limbs: concentration (*dharana*), meditation (*dhyana*), and *samadhi*

apana vayu – vital downcurrent

asamprajnata samadhi – *samadhi* 8: super-cognitive *samadhi*, objectless *samadhi*

a*sana* – posture, the third limb of Ashtanga (eight-limbed) Yoga

Ashtanga Yoga – eight-limbed yoga, the yoga of Patanjali

asmita – occurs as a form of suffering (*klesha*) and then means egotism, or as a category of *samadhi* and then means individuation

asmita samadhi – *samadhi* 6, *samadhi* on individuation, *I-am-ness,* pure being-ness.

230

atman – the individual self, pure consciousness

avidya – ignorance, the root of suffering, one of the forms of suffering (*kleshas*)

bandha – energetic lock

Bhagavad Gita – an important text of both yoga and Hinduism

bhakta – a yogi of devotion

Bhakti Yoga – yoga of devotion, an important aspect of Ashtanga (eight-limbed) Yoga

bhavana – cultivation of constructive thought patterns, thinking in alignment with the Divine

Brahman – infinite consciousness, the cosmic self, deep reality, universal spirit, is described as with (*saguna*) or without form (*nirguna*)

buddhi – intelligence, intellect, originates from the Sanskrit root *budh* – to awaken

chakras – energy centers in the subtle body, representations of evolutionary brain circuitry

dharana – concentration, the sixth limb of Ashtanga (eight-limbed) Yoga

dharma megha samadhi – *samadhi* 8: cloud-of-characteristics-dispersing *samadhi,* objectless *samadhi dharmin* – the essence of an object, the *object-as-such*, the *suchness-of-an-object*

dhyana – meditation, the seventh limb of Ashtanga (eight-limbed) Yoga

drashta – seer, the consciousness, alternative term for *purusha* or *atman*

drishti – focal point

ekagra – a stage of mind, the single-pointed mind

God immanent – the Divine creative force, the Divine as crystallized matter, all beings and all creation

God transcendent – pure consciousness, the formless Absolute, the Father, the Dao

guru – teacher, not a body limited in space and time, but the self and the Divine

Hatha Yoga – the first or lowest tier of Ashtanga Yoga, dealing with *asana* and *pranayama*

hrt – core of our being, the heart, often referring to the pure consciousness or the central energy channel

ida – lunar energy channel, the moon

ishtadevata – the form of the Divine you can relate to

Ishvara – the Divine, universal spirit, God

ishvara pranidhana – surrender to the Divine

jnana – knowledge, the final stage of yoga, the domain of the *Brahma Sutra* and the *Upanishads*

kaivalya – spiritual freedom, the term that yoga uses instead of the Hindu "*moksha*" or the Buddhist "enlightenment"

karma – action, law of cause and effect, three types: *sanchita* (in store), *prarabdha* (in fruition), and *kriyamana* (being produced)

Kevala Kumbhaka – spontaneous suspension, the pinnacle of *pranayama,* leads to *samadhi*

kleshas – the five modes of suffering, ignorance, egotism, desire, aversion, and fear of death

koshas – sheaths or layers of the human being

kriya – usually refers to a set of purificatory actions used in Hatha Yoga, such as Nauli and Kapalabhati. In Patanjali's sense the term means introductory yoga

kshipta – a stage of mind, out of control, frantic, wild

kumbhaka – breath retentions, an important technique of *pranayama*

Kundalini – the divine creative force, the force driving evolution, the divine feminine, also *Shakti* or *prakrti*

Kundalini meditation – denotes the yogic meditation technique that awakens evolutionary brain circuitry, differing from Buddhist or Vipassana meditation

Mahayoga – the great or complete yoga, original yoga integrating all of yoga's aspects

manas – mind, thinking agent, thinking principle, presents and modifies sensory data

mantras - bioplasmic sound waves

moksha – spiritual liberation

mudha – a stage of mind, the infatuated and materialistic mind

mudra – *pranic* seal

nadanusandhana – the inner sound, a *samadhi* technique

nadi – energy channel

nirbija samadhi – *samadhi* 8: objectless *samadhi*

nirguna Brahman – the formless Absolute, akin to the Dao

nirodha – a stage of mind, suspended mind, free of conditioning and past

nirvitarka samapatti – *samadhi* 2: super-deliberative identity

panchakosha doctrine – teaching of the five layers of the human being, contained in *Taittiriya Upanishad*

paravairagya – dis-identification

parinama – transformation, yogic deconditioning

Patanjali – author of the *Yoga Sutra*, a sage

pingala – solar energy channel

234

pitta – metabolic fire to be converted into fire of intelligence, one of the three doshas (humors) of the body

prakrti – nature, the divine creative force, the God immanent

prana – life force, the inner breath

pranayama – breath extension, the fourth limb of Ashtanga Yoga

pratyahara – independence from external stimuli, the fifth limb of Ashtanga Yoga

Puranas – a class of scriptures

purusha – embodied consciousness, *atman*, the God transcendent in us

purusharthas – the four human goals: acquisition of wealth (*artha*), sexual satisfaction (*kama*), right action (*dharma*), and spiritual liberation (*moksha*)

Raja Yoga – the top tier of Patanjali's yoga, kingly yoga, *samadhi* yoga

rajas – frenzy, energy particle, one of the three *gunas* of *prakrti*

rishi – a sage, seer

rta – sacred order

sabija samadhi – objective *samadhi*

samadhi – absorption, ecstasy, revelation, a state of heightened awareness, the eighth limb of Ashtanga Yoga, itself subdivided into eight stages *samapatti* – identity, the first four types of *samadhi*

samprajnata samadhi – *samadhi* with cognition of object, objective *samadhi,* the first seven stages *of samadhi*

samskaras – subconscious imprints

samyama – *samadhi* 7, super-concentration, a combination of *dharana, dhyana,* and objective *samadhi*

sandhya – twilight language, method of wording sacred texts ambiguously so that the uninitiated or non-practitioner of the method is led astray

sankalpa – resolution, using the mind creatively and constructively

sattva – information, luminosity, wisdom, intelligence, one of the three gunas of *prakrti,* information particle

savichara samapatti – *samadhi* 3: reflective identity

savitarka samapatti – *samadhi* 1: deliberative identity

semiotics – the theory of how we arrive at meaning, including the relation between verbal signs and what they refer to (semantics)

Shakti – the divine feminine, also Kundalini or *prakrti*

shastras – yogic and sacred scriptures, literally 'path to truth'

Shiva – pure consciousness, the divine masculine

siddha – a perfected being and yogi
nirvichara samapatti – *samadhi* 4: super-reflective identity

sushumna - central energy channel

sutra – thread, a string of aphorisms

svadharma - living our divine purpose, own duty, to be in the zone

tamas – inertia, one of the three *gunas* of *prakrti,* mass particle

tanmatras – quantums, subtle essences of the elements

Tantras – a class of scriptures

trataka – staring, a *samadhi* adjunct

Upanishads – a class of sacred texts, the fertile field from which yoga sprung

vasana – conditioning, the sum total of our past subconscious imprints

Vedas – the oldest sacred texts of humanity

vijnanamaya kosha – deep knowledge sheath

vikshipta – a stage of mind, the oscillating or confused mind

vinyasa – sequential movements

viparyaya – wrong cognition, error, one of the five fluctuations of mind

viveka khyateh – knowledge of the difference, discriminative discernment

Vyasa – a sage, author of the commentary on the *Yoga Sutra,* the *Brahma Sutra,* the *Mahabharata,* and other texts *yamas* and *niyamas* – restraints and observances, the first two limbs of Ashtanga Yoga

yantra – sacred geometry

Yoga Sutra – an ancient treatise outlining the basic tenets of yoga, authored by sage Patanjali

Index

Author Information

Gregor started his yogic practices in the late 1970s. In the mid-80s he commenced yearly travels to India, where he learned from various yogic and tantric masters, traditional Indian *sadhus* and ascetics. He lived many years as a recluse, studying Sanskrit and yogic scripture and practicing yogic techniques.

Gregor's textbook series consisting of *Ashtanga Yoga: Practice and Philosophy, Ashtanga Yoga: The Intermediate Series, Pranayama: The Breath of Yoga,* and *Yoga Meditation: Through Mantra, Chakras and Kundalini to Spiritual Freedom* have sold over 75,000 copies worldwide and so far have been translated into seven languages. His weekly blog articles can be found at **www.chintamaniyoga.com**.

Today Gregor integrates all aspects of yoga into his teaching in the spirit of Patanjali and T. Krishnamacharya. His zany sense of humor, manifold personal experiences, vast and in-depth knowledge of scripture, Indian philosophies, and yogic techniques combine to make Gregor's teachings easily applicable, relevant, and accessible to his students.

Contact Gregor via:
www.chintamaniyoga.com
www.8limbs.com and
https://www.facebook.com/gregor.maehle.

Made in the USA
Middletown, DE
04 July 2017